REINVENTING CYBERSECURITY

Tracy Bannon

Breanne Boland

Amy Devers

Yvie Djieya

Lonye Ford

Alison "Snipe" Gianotto

Lisa Hall

Rachel Harpley

Jasmine Henry

Joyous Huggins

Dr. Meg Layton

Ashleigh Lee

Angela Marafino

Latha Maripuri

Rin Oliver

Carlota Sage

Coleen Shane

Aubrey Stearn

Carla Sun

ISBN:
Imprint: JupiterOne Press

Publisher:
JupiterOne, Inc.
2701 Aerial Center Parkway
Suite 120
Morrisville, NC 27560

Editor-in-Chief: Jasmine Henry
Copy Editors: Scott McFarlane, Melissa Pereira
Design: Valerie Zargarpur, Dave Moy, Lena Semenkova
Formatting and Layout: Scott McFarlane, Valerie Zargarpur

This book is dedicated to the legacy of
Rebecca "Becky" Gurley Bace,
computer security expert and pioneer in intrusion detection.

Contents

SECTION I: Reinventing Our Future

SECTION II: Reinventing What We Do

SECTION III: Reinventing Who We Are

Preface

Amy Devers

Are you here for a riveting collection of stories where change happened by challenging the status quo? You are in the right place. Welcome to *Reinventing Cybersecurity*. Before getting started, let's take a brief journey into the past.

When I think of trailblazers in history, in my mind, I see Ruby Bridges standing bravely on the concrete steps of William Frantz Elementary School in Louisiana. A young girl stands in stark contrast among uniformed policemen, embracing her day as a black student attending an all-white school for the very first time. That was revolutionary.

One might also think of Amelia Earhart flying high with her goggles set and iconic scarf tied neatly at her collar, rebelliously forging a path for future female pilots. Or perhaps we think about Katherine Johnson, Dorothy Vaughan, and Mary Jackson in their pivotal contributions to the Space Race at NASA, proving that women are mathematical wizards. We can only imagine what it must have felt like to be Katharine Graham when she was named the first-ever female CEO of a Fortune 500 company and wonder if she could hear the theoretical glass ceiling breaking. As I cast my ballot, I am grateful to the suffragettes who, amidst ridicule, paved the way for women to vote legally.

We also think of the early women of cybersecurity: Judy Parsons and Mavis Batey, who were instrumental in code-breaking during World War II in their top-secret security posts. Is it possible they knew just how ground-breaking their work would be in inspiring a whole new private industry around code security? Could they imagine the world of cybersecurity today?

These are names and stories we know of women who inspire us. They are the ones who came before us to show the world that their voices, contributions, and leadership matter. We must continue to give a platform to underrepresented groups because, as history shows, great change can come from unexpected places.

From a young age, the rapid immersion of technology's ever-growing and changing capabilities fascinated me. From the moment my hands graced the keyboard of my first computer (an Intel Celeron 400-megahertz processor with 128 megabytes of RAM, to be exact) to the sounds signaling the beginning of the internet — that's right, dial-up; I was captivated. It seemed like magic, the ability to use this awkward and heavy metal box to connect me to a new world from right inside my humble home. Soon I'd find myself amidst endless music, games, chat rooms, and chain emails. I distinctly remember the sound of the keyboard: raised keys click-clacking as I typed up essays, created my first resume, and began to explore the vast World Wide Web. In true tinkerer fashion, I took my computer tower apart, which revealed the fascinating intricacies of the motherboard, where I could upgrade various chips. But beyond the fun, there was the capacity for so much more.

This remarkable machine transported us to new opportunities across the web: exposing new ideas, new businesses, new platforms, and new ways of communicating and storing information. And along with it came the nefarious actors. In the time it took to find and load a new website, a hacker could find an IP address and a way in with a pop-up alert on the screen. As the rapid adoption of business and home computers, use of the internet, and cloud technologies proliferated, so did the vulnerabilities. This revolution in technology led to the explosive growth of the cybersecurity industry.

I vividly recall going into work one day, where we had recently installed four colorful iMacs, only to find that our systems were down from a suspected cyber attack. My manager yelled from across the room, "Don't turn it on!" At a later company, I received a grave email cautioning employees against opening messages from unknown sources or downloading suspicious attachments. It turns out someone inevitably had, and IT spent all night trying to restore backups from the unknowingly affected server.

As early cybersecurity professionals worked tirelessly to develop and install better code protection and monitoring systems, those with ill intentions worked double-time to overcome them. Now, all of our devices are connected to the internet and cloud services, integrating with other devices connected to cloud services and the internet. The attack surface is growing at an alarming rate. It seems not a day goes by where there isn't some new ransomware attack, breach, or data hack in the news. Company data is being held hostage and, by association, its employees and customers too.

In the coming chapters, you will hear from the foremost authorities in cybersecurity through a different perspective than those typically showcased; perhaps you will find a common theme among these trailblazers. Our talented authors will share their expertise, personal experiences of rebellion and revolution, and optimism for the future.

Although my area of expertise is People Operations, I joined JupiterOne because of the intelligent technology. It's exhilarating to grow an organization at the forefront of helping companies better understand their risks and exposure and empowering them to take action on their vulnerabilities. I've been a victim of identity theft; I have suffered the consequences of what happens when a company doesn't mitigate risk or doesn't know it exists until it's too late. Any part of a business can be vulnerable to cyber attack, and having awareness and visibility across all assets and their relationships is fundamental.

Because of people's incredible care and commitment in this industry, I remain hopeful and optimistic for the future. We must reinvent cybersecurity to remain diligent in the fight for protection, authenticity of data, non-malignant use of Artificial Intelligence and Machine Learning, and the ability to keep open-source tools like Starbase safe.

Today, we have an incredible responsibility. The future of cybersecurity is in our collective hands. Our voices have historically been a minor contributing party to shaping this industry, but just as times change, so does the opportunity for our impact. Now more than ever, we can expand our reach into the vast unknown.

My parting advice is to grab a cup of coffee, find a cozy space to settle, and dive right into the incredible stories of these rebels and revolutionaries. Read how they forged ahead on uncharted paths to make significant contributions to the cybersecurity industry. We've come a long way from the dial-up internet era. The ever-changing landscape signals that we need more visionaries, more individuals from unconventional backgrounds, and more cybersecurity talent.

The late Supreme Court Justice Ruth Bader Ginsberg said it best, "Women belong in all places where decisions are being made."[1] And here we are indeed.

1   Biskupic, J. (2009, October 5). Ginsburg: Court needs another woman. USA Today. usatoday30. usatoday.com/news/washington/judicial/2009-05-05-ruthginsburg_N.htm

ABOUT AMY DEVERS

Amy Devers is Chief of Staff and Executive Director of People Operations at JupiterOne. She has over 15 years of experience in business and people operations, specializing in organizational development and maturity, leadership growth, employee attraction and engagement, and total reward strategies. Amy is passionate about creating a more equitable cybersecurity industry and new approaches to talent management, helping top performers from all backgrounds thrive.

Amy has a Bachelor of Science in Human Resources Management from Western Governors University. She is a certified Senior Professional in Human Resources (SPHR®) via HRCI® and certified CompTIA Project+ Manager. Amy volunteers with many community organizations, including the American Red Cross and American Heart Association. She lives in Huntsville, Alabama with her husband, son, and dog.

Introduction

Ashleigh Lee

Cybersecurity has been around since the 1970s and has grown far more complex than computer and network attacks. It's time to unlearn what we thought we knew and learn anew. After all, isn't that what life is about?

> *"We spend most of our lives trying to unlearn much of what we've been taught."* [1]
>
> - Alexandra Stoddard

By unlearning and learning anew, we practice seeing issues in a new light, discovering new information, and exploring innovative solutions. Innovation is all about improvement, whether incremental or disruptive, and requires us to reevaluate the assumptions we make about the problems we encounter every day.

Innovations in technology have substantially expanded the attack surface and risks that security teams have to manage, but there is hope—security awareness is on the rise among business leaders. And while this heightened awareness does not always come with proportional resources to address the problems, constraints are the creative's best friend.

Creative problem solving can be seen in all parts of the business - in engineering, sales, finance, HR, security. The same human ingenuity that is required to pentest an app is the same creativity that others use to build the app, sell the app, manage the business expenses behind the app, and hire talent to grow the organization's success. And just as everyone has a stake to make the company successful, everyone has a part to play in protecting that success.

---

1 Stoddard, A. (2007). Grace Notes: A Book of Daily Meditations. Collins.

Cybersecurity may have started out for technology specialists, but we can no longer outwit the attackers with just these wizards. In fact, that type of security culture is similar to the hero mentality that many engineering organizations fight today. Just as software developers have learned that the collective wisdom of a team often creates better end-products than the lone wolf, security leaders are recognizing the merits of cross-functional collaboration and partnership. Many notable CISOs in the last couple decades rose out of information technology, and the most effective CISOs are the ones who have embraced the rest of the business functions. Security is transforming from being the silo that fights to protect assets into being the team that advises and empowers the business to address risk according to the organization's risk appetite.

As the security profession evolves, we need to rethink how we hire, how we build learning paths, and how we work collaboratively inside and outside the organization - practitioners, vendors, and investors alike.

I've been in the security industry for just shy of 6 years and there are three key things I've learned:

1. You can't feed half-truths to security practitioners.
2. Equipping teams with the framework to evaluate risk and share core security responsibilities is incredibly eye-opening and important to building a culture of security.
3. Creativity can come from anywhere. All security professionals started somewhere. The most common trait is insatiable curiosity.

> "I think there's an aspect of security that marks the evolution of folks who end up in security in that, at some point, you're interested in how things fail."[2]
>
> - Becky Bace (1955-2017)

Failing well seems to be the key to innovation. And if learning about failure continually draws folks into security, then I believe we are on our way to discovering innovative ways to improve security across the board. As

---

2   McGraw, G., &; Bace, R. G. (2007). Silver Bullet Talks with Becky Bace. IEEE Security & Privacy Magazine, 5(3), 6-9. doi.org/10.1109/msp.2007.70

change agents for cybersecurity pave the way, they share their knowledge for more change agents to grow and carve their own paths. Here are the stories of today's change agents as they unlearn, learn, and drive innovation.

Section I: Reinventing Our Future

As the threat landscape continues to evolve, we must be creative with how we drive change in our organizational processes. These authors share strategies for expanding skill sets, partnering across the business, and leading teams.

Five Strategic Priorities for the Modern CISO by *Latha Maripuri*

Over the last decade, many CISOs have struggled with speaking the "business" language. Latha shares her own journey advancing to the CISO role, the pivots she made along the way, and distills her wisdom into five key priorities for any rising modern CISO.

**Revolutionary Leadership, Rebellious Opinions,
and Knowledge Graphs** by *Jasmine Henry*

After scaling a security program at a startup from Series A to Series C, Jasmine has more than a few stories about growing teams and getting in the weeds doing hard security work. Jasmine shares some of her research from JupiterOne, her application of knowledge graphs, and lessons learned from leading a global team at a high-growth company.

Security-as-CTO by *Aubrey Stearn*

As Aubrey likes to say, she's not *in* security. She *does* security. Aubrey shares her experience doing the work of security in her role as fractional, or interim, CTO at organizations ranging from zero technical team members to leading hundreds.

Confronting Inherently Flawed Systems by *Carla Sun*

"To err is to be human." Carla shares her journey to embracing failure and creating order in the midst of chaos as she leads an effort toward predictive failure mitigation with stronger incident response processes.

For the Love of Frameworks: Creating Relevant,
Reusable Patterns for Security by *Lonye Ford*
Frameworks are the foundation for a healthy approach to risk. Rising security leaders - take notes from Lonye as she shares what helped her start on the right foot as started her own company to provide cybersecurity services to the U.S. defense sector.

Section II: Reinventing What We Do

It's clear that the processes and culture that have developed over the last decade are becoming more of a hindrance than an advantage to securing organizations. These authors share how they are actively transforming security cultures across all types of organizations.

Teaching is a Shared Responsibility by *Dr. Meg Layton*
By pulling back the curtain, demystifying security, and adapting to how people learn, we can make security more accessible to everyone. Meg shares learning models and examples of how developers grasp the urgency and importance of secure coding practices.

Tearing Down and Retraining Muscle Memory by *Tracy Bannon*
As organizations build and follow processes in the day-to-day, they often build muscle memory for how things get done. Tracy shares her human-centric approach to transforming corporate cultures that circumvented security into advocates and enforcers of security controls.

Your Greatest Vuln: A Culture of No by *Breanne Boland*
Security teams still often have the reputation of being gatekeepers and naysayers to innovation. Breanne shares her experience working in a culture of "no" and how to cultivate the healthier, more collaborative alternative.

Weaponizing Compliance by *Alison "Snipe" Gianotto*
Alison details her journey developing skills vital to her cybersecurity arsenal - social engineering, evidence gathering, grit to tackle the backbreaking work. By combining these skills with customer demands for better security protocol, Snipe weaponized compliance to build a security program from zero to a trusted vendor in two years.

F*ck Security Maturity;
Let's Talk about Security Health!
by *Carlota Sage*
Security maturity implies that things continuously improve in a security program and teams can reach new heights of sophistication, but that simply isn't reality. Carlota provides a new perspective on security maturity measurement to understand health.

Repositioning Cybersecurity by *Lisa Hall*
Security teams are transforming from roadblocks to revenue generators, where security is an enabler for sales to win business. Lisa shares how building trust with customers and enabling the sales team radically shifted how the rest of the business perceived the security team.

Open Source Lessons
on Smashing Barriers to Contribution by *Rin Oliver*
Open source software (OSS) processes for contributions and documentation have given us strong examples of inclusive execution in a remote, asynchronous, global working environment. Rin presents clear actions companies can take today to create more inclusive documentation to make technology more accessible to all.

Section III: Reinventing Who We Are

Diversity of thought and voice are critical to making better decisions as we modernize cybersecurity practices. It behooves us to revamp the make-up of our teams and who we label 'fit' for cybersecurity. These stories share how authors are challenging the biases that need to be unlearned in cybersecurity.

Project Overhaul: Creating a More Dynamic, Diverse, Credentialed Workforce by *Joyous Huggins*
Joyous shares her journey from tech-interested foster child to military service and how she inspires youth in middle school and high school to grasp basic cybersecurity skills.

Breaking into Cybersecurity by *Yvie Djieya*

Yvie's path to cybersecurity was not linear, like so many of us in this industry. Yvie shares tools and tips from her job search as a budding cybersecurity professional and a special recipe to keep burnout at bay.

A Little Less Yasss Queen, A Lot More Action! by *Angela Marafino*

What if imposter syndrome wasn't just an internal affliction to commiserate but a byproduct of the biases present in the workplace? Angela shares her journey into cybersecurity and how a few tweaks to the managerial and team dynamics can go a long way to actively address imposter syndrome.

Do I Fit? by *Coleen Shane*

For Coleen, community has played a vital role through her major life milestones - divorce, job search, and transition. She shares her learnings from navigating digital and physical communities in InfoSec over the past few years and provides tips on how to get the most out of networking and conferences.

Ageism is Your Achilles Heel by *Rachel Harpley*

Why must "entry level" equate to "young professionals"? Rachel challenges the ageism bias common in hiring and provides a new perspective to bringing more skilled personnel into cybersecurity.

To those who came before us, thank you for paving the way.

To those who are in the thick of it, keep going. Your grit and brilliance inspire those around you.

To those who are just beginning, bet on yourself and stay curious.

We hope you enjoy these stories and share your own as you pave your own path.

Ashleigh Lee

Senior Marketing Manager at JupiterOne

ABOUT ASHLEIGH LEE

Ashleigh is Senior Marketing Manager at JupiterOne, where she co-hosts a bi-weekly streaming talk show *Cyber Therapy*. Previously, she worked at NowSecure, MapR, Sentilla, Ericsson, and other organizations. Ashleigh lives in Colorado with her husband and their cats. In the winter, you can find her skiing the slopes, and when the weather warms up, she walks her cats around the neighborhood. Ashleigh has a Bachelor of Science in Business Administration from California Polytechnic State University. You can find Ashleigh's *Cyber Therapy* episodes on the JupiterOne channel on YouTube.

CHAPTER 1

Five Strategic Priorities for the Modern CISO

by Latha Maripuri

Five Strategic Priorities for the Modern CISO

Latha Maripuri

The modern Chief Information Security Executive (CISO) is a vast, strategic, and expanding role. In a world where every organization competes on technology, the CISO must balance security with risk management, productivity, and product innovation. The new CISO is much more than just a technical and tactical specialist. Instead, the CISO is a strategic business driver, responsible for solving a complex array of cross-functional challenges.

The CISO is a big and critically-strategic role. Today's and tomorrow's CISOs have a huge responsibility to become experts and 360-degree collaborators across an incredible number of business functions, while also elevating and expanding the role. CISOs must create partnerships, be intentional about talent, and embed security into business processes. Security executives must be dynamic risk managers and evolve continuously alongside the changing threat and technology landscape.

The CISO role is challenging but incredibly rewarding. I hope that my experience and perspective will empower rising CISOs to become strategic executives who transform the security of entire organizations and industries.

My Path to CISO

As is the case with many of my peers in the industry, I did not plan to become a CISO. While there have been a number of diverse leadership roles in tech such as Chief Information Officer (CIO) or Chief Technology

Officer (CTO), the CISO role is still relatively new in many industries and continues to evolve significantly. My early career moves were motivated by curiosity and impact more than anything else. I always wanted to avoid being too comfortable in any role which continuously pushed me into new and emerging areas.

My career began as a software engineer at IBM Global Financing, where I architected and built front-end and back-end components for customer-facing financial applications. I enjoyed creating mission-critical financial apps and all that goes into it - user experience, feature development, testing rigor, service management, and oh, security.

I became curious about how to operate applications reliably, and at a global scale, which took me to the IBM CIO organization. How do you support over 400,000 employees operating in over 150 countries? I naturally progressed into roles in infrastructure engineering, enterprise applications, and data platforms where I gained first-hand exposure to performance, availability, incident management, and most importantly these days, employee productivity. I expanded into more strategic roles around technology transformation, innovation, and partnerships. These roles involved presenting to senior leaders on a frequent basis and building a skill that would become critical down the line.

Leveraging Engineering to Drive Business Growth

The roles in software and infrastructure engineering during the first phase of my career made me curious about how technical skills and functions can be applied to customer-facing roles, and ultimately, how to drive growth and revenue for the business. I wanted to learn how to launch products, how to price, how to market, how to sell, how to get customer feedback, and ultimately, how to measure success for the business.

I took a significant risk in moving away from an area where I excelled and had worked hard to build credibility; many peers and mentors thought I was crazy to start over again. But I've always felt that if a role makes you slightly uncomfortable, it's a good thing. From challenge and discomfort comes growth and skills expansion.

I moved into an organization that was being formed to look at growth opportunities in cloud, data, mobile, and security. I became fascinated with all four areas which were fundamentally changing the daily lives of consumers and the dynamics for enterprises. I ended up specializing in cybersecurity because I felt this field actually touched all the other areas!

So much investment and innovation was happening and I was glad to be a part of this 'start-up' space and get experience in helping shape a profit and loss strategy. It opened up my eyes in so many ways and helped me look at engineering through a different, business-oriented lens. I learned the ropes of market research, strategy, product management, product marketing, sales operations, financial management, and mergers & acquisitions as a means to make quick market impact. Ultimately, I became the Global Head of Strategy & Product Management for IBM's security services division, where we created new security solutions across consulting, managed and cloud-delivered services.

I spent a lot of time having conversations with Fortune 500 customers to understand their security needs in order to build better products and services for the market. One of the companies I spoke to was News Corp, who asked me to join them as CISO.

My pathway to the CISO role was not straightforward. It made little sense to others around me. There was no well-defined pathway to becoming a security executive during my early career, especially compared to well-established paths to roles such as Chief Operating Officer (COO) or Chief Financial Officer (CFO). But, I'm proud that I took risks to challenge myself and that taking calculated risks created a path to CISO.

When members of my team tell me that they want to pursue a CISO career path, I help them gain exposure to more areas of the business and create a more well-rounded skill set. Future CISOs need to be proactive about receiving cross-training in as many business and tech functions as possible. CISOs must develop 360-degree expertise across engineering, product, revenue, customer success, and countless other domains to succeed in a highly-collaborative, strategic role.

My Path to CISO

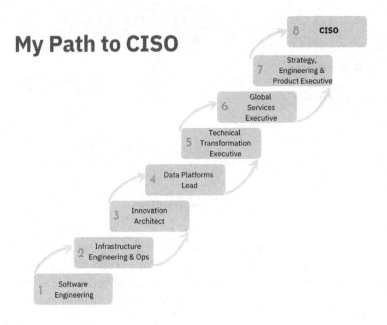

8 CISO

7 Strategy, Engineering & Product Executive

6 Global Services Executive

5 Technical Transformation Executive

4 Data Platforms Lead

3 Innovation Architect

2 Infrastructure Engineering & Ops

1 Software Engineering

Overview: Five Strategic Priorities for the Modern CISO

The CISO is still responsible for overseeing the success of core security functions, such as cyber defense, cloud security or compliance. At the same time, they must focus on creating new security capabilities to drive new value streams.

Redefining the strategic priorities for a modern CISO means focusing on several emerging responsibilities: partnerships, collaboration, innovation, and preparing for the future.

1. Build 360-Degree Partnerships

2. Be Intentional About Talent

3. Embed Security into Business Workflows

4. Create a Dynamic Approach to Risk

5. Continuously Adapt and Evolve

The role of the CISO barely existed 20 years ago, and it was very rare outside of global financial institutions. A decade ago, the CISO was a more common hire, but early CISOs were often highly-tactical technologists. Today, the CISO role is critical to almost every organization, and it's also emerging and evolving each day.

I hope the following lessons I have learned about being a strategic security executive are valuable for today's and tomorrow's security leaders. The CISO's path is incredibly challenging, but also incredibly rewarding and fast-paced.

Responsibility 1:
Build 360-Degree Partnerships

The success of a CISO depends almost entirely on the strength of their partnerships with the entire organization, from engineering to infrastructure, legal, privacy, compliance, communications, and HR. The CISO must have the ability to enlist, educate, and align executive stakeholders on key security objectives. Security is an all-encompassing business function, which requires the security chief to be an expert in both business and technology functions, and someone who can seamlessly collaborate with countless stakeholders in a single day!

1. Build 360-Degree Partnerships

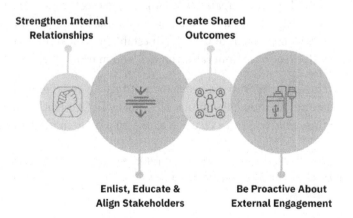

Strengthen Internal Relationships

Create Shared Outcomes

Enlist, Educate & Align Stakeholders

Be Proactive About External Engagement

What is an Effective Strategic Partnership?

A strategic partnership is a business relationship based on mutual trust and shared interests (or, shared risk). A CISO depends on strategic partnerships to achieve results that would be impossible to pull off solo.

The most effective CISOs are proactive about creating a broad set of strategic partnerships. They invest early and often into nurturing these relationships. Research shows that cooperative partnerships are most effective when they are formed proactively since partnerships built in crisis don't drive satisfactory results.[1]

Strengthen Internal Relationships

More than ever before, the CISO is required to have a 360-degree set of business partnerships across the business to achieve security goals. In a single day, the CISO may rely on partnerships with half a dozen teams in order to achieve objectives. In recent weeks, my security team collaborated cross-functionally with cloud teams on a resource optimization project which drove dual outcomes of smaller attack surface and significant cost reduction. I continuously collaborate with experts in the people function, including learning and development, to improve continuous learning offerings for security personnel.

Research shows that the most effective CISOs meet three times as often with non-IT leaders compared to their peers, to create new patterns of collaboration with functions such as sales and marketing. Gartner predicts that by 2024, 60 percent of CISOs will establish critical internal relationships with executives from sales, finance, and marketing teams.[2]

Many core security initiatives depend entirely on collaboration between security and other business units. The CISO will frequently partner with marketing, product, and executive teams on a go-to-market strategy and

---

1 Dubrovski, D. (2020). Characteristics of Strategic Partnerships Between Differently Successful Companies. Journal of Financial Risk Management, 09(02), 82–98. doi.org/10.4236/jfrm.2020.92005
2 (see footnote 1)

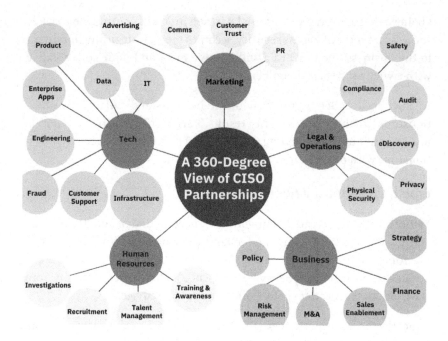

A 360-Degree View of CISO Partnerships

timelines for secure product launches. The CISO will collaborate with HR on security awareness training, and team up on regulatory requirements with risk, policy, and legal teams.

Common Cross-Functional Security Relationships				
Business	Legal & Operations	Human Resources	Tech	Marketing
• Strategy • Risk Management • Finance • M&A • Policy • Sales Enablement	• Compliance • eDiscovery • Audit • Privacy • Physical Security • Safety	• Recruitment • Talent Management • Training & Awareness • Investigations	• Product • Engineering • Infrastructure • Data • IT • Enterprise Apps • Fraud • Customer Support	• Advertising • Communications • Public Relations • Customer Trust

I believe that a broad set of internal partnerships will continue to be a key success factor for CISOs. As security becomes more strategically important to the business, the CISO role will become more and more collaborative with a wide range of stakeholders.

A CISO needs a 360-degree view of the business and collaborative relationships to achieve key security results. This is only possible if a CISO is proactive about strengthening, creating, and nurturing a broad set of relationships with other teams in their organization.

Enlist, Educate, and Align Stakeholders

Before a CISO can create alignment, they need to understand technology and business. A CISO must understand their organization's technology portfolio and innovation roadmap, as well as which cyber assets are most critical to operations. I believe a CISO needs 360-degree visibility into stakeholder perspectives before offering strategic advice.

Education is an important part of the CISO's role, and leaders will find themselves doing a lot of work to educate business stakeholders on security and risk. It is equally important that a CISO is willing to receive an education in their colleagues' key objectives and needs, so they can become well-versed in business leader perspectives.

> "Perhaps the most critical role of leadership in managing security is to understand what has transpired in the past, enforcing a movement toward better security over time," said the late security luminary Becky Bace.
>
> The second role of leadership, Bace said, is to understand that security must fit extremely well when it is applied to any operational context." This is key to optimizing the balance of protection versus pain."[3]

A CISO will often be asked for advice on how the business can safeguard critical assets without impacting the product roadmap or cost targets. The

---

3 Robinson, T. (2021, June 26). Becky Bace's passing hits Cybersecurity Community Hard. SC Media. www.scmagazine.com/news/security-news/network-security/becky-baces-passing-hits-cybersecurity-community-hard

CISO must suggest a course of action with the fewest possible tradeoffs for stakeholders. A CISO needs mutual education and a healthy dose of empathy before they can enlist and align stakeholders.

Create Shared Outcomes

Alignment can be built by quantifying shared objectives. Effective partnerships with both internal and external stakeholders should involve agreed-upon metrics to measure progress towards goals. One way to accomplish this is by creating shared objectives and key results (OKRs) with internal partners.

For example, a CISO may establish the following cross-functional OKRs to drive shared outcomes:

- Security and cloud teams may create objectives on security controls applied at the time of account creation, ongoing scanning and SLAs for issues found.
- Security and data teams might have targets for data discovery and classification to better identify sensitive data across a company.
- Security and facilities operation staff may establish shared physical security objectives to reduce tailgating incidents or deactivate former employee access more quickly.
- Security and HR might set objectives for employee cybersecurity awareness by expanding role-based training requirements for new hires.

Measurement creates transparency in internal partnerships. Quantifying progress toward shared objectives can be a valuable way for a CISO to create meaningful, productive relationships with internal stakeholders.

Be Proactive About External Engagement

The CISO must also have strong relationships with external parties. The CISO drives value in engagements with technology partners, services firms, gov't entities and peer groups. A CISO must maintain appropriate, proactive relationships with regulatory bodies so they are prepared for emerging requirements or incident disclosures.

Strong partnerships between the CISO and other CISOs is also essential - I firmly believe it is an incredibly valuable source of support and insight. The best way for a CISO to succeed in an incredibly complex role is to create a strong circle of support and learn from peers since there is often no playbook for the work that we do.

Responsibility 2:
Be Intentional About Talent

I became a people leader early in my career, and it prepared me for the talent aspects of the CISO role. I was experienced in building diverse, global and high performing teams, and continuously thinking about talent management. This prepared me for the opportunities and challenges of management at a global scale, as well as the complexities of creating a security function that is distributed across internal teams, service providers, and outsourced resources such as contractors.

Talent is an incredibly big part of the CISO role. The war for talent is real. I believe it's essential for a CISO to be very intentional about their approach to talent and people leadership in order to overcome skills shortages and protect their team from burnout.

Talent oversight really stretches your thinking and creativity as a CISO. It's an incredibly rewarding part of the role which energizes me.

Create an Actionable Succession Plan

Today's CISOs must think about their current talent as well as the talent they will need in two or three years. Finding someone with significant security experience can be a bit of a unicorn hunt, especially when it comes to senior-level talent or skilled engineers.

Leaders have a responsibility to create well-defined security career paths for their teams and growth progression. It's also important to be realistic about succession planning for key roles since exceptional team members can leave to pursue their own opportunities. If you cannot afford to have a longstanding gap in a role, you need to have an actionable succession plan. A six-month vacancy in critical functions can have real business implications.

Be Creative About Recruiting Talent

It is hardly a secret there is an active war for cybersecurity talent. Even though I've worked at global organizations where we have an advantage in attracting people, I am strategic about planning. The best security professionals have no shortage of opportunities.

Security is becoming engineering-led, which means an increased need for security engineers who can automate, build tooling, analyze, hunt, or visualize very large data sets. There is still a need for individuals with skills that we traditionally think of as core security capabilities, including security operations, compliance, testing, and scanning. But, there are simply too many security problems for teams to solve and not enough people. As a result, there's an emerging need for security talent who can help programs scale.

I was an early advocate for starting left and embedding more security engineering talent into the teams that build and maintain critical business technologies. I hire many people for security who come from an engineering background, including individuals who come from roles in software, data, or infrastructure engineering. I find these hires have 90 percent of the skills they need to contribute and the security domain can be learned.

It is immensely important for the CISO to be creative in how they think about talent, which also includes considering individuals from non-traditional backgrounds. Vendor companies, government entities, audit and compliance teams as an example can be a great source of talent as well. Being creative about talent can also mean a conscious effort to optimize your balance of in-sourcing, co-sourcing and outsourcing. Managed services are a valuable way to augment key security capabilities, as are well-managed engagements with independent researchers such as bug bounty programs.

Create Diverse, Global Teams

CISOs need to be intentional about considering talent through a lens of diversity, equity, and inclusion. I focus on fostering strong security teams by intentionally working to include a broad array of contributor perspectives. My years of leadership at IBM, News Corp, and now Uber provided me with extensive global management experience, and I have witnessed firsthand that deliberately fostering diverse team culture has an undeniably positive impact on team morale, growth and innovation.

Building diverse teams creates space for healthy, productive debate. In order to create curious organizations that can tackle today's greatest security problems, we must foster diversity. I believe that diversity is the product of intentional efforts toward equity and inclusion and that improving the diversity of talent and skill is another area where CISOs must think creatively.

Recognize, Reward, and Rest Your Talent

Any discussion of security talent should acknowledge that security teams often work in incredibly tough roles. As leaders, we need to acknowledge that our talent is required to operate with intense amounts of focus in high-pressure, high speed environments.

As a CISO, I have made a very conscious effort to recognize and reward my talent, and to make sure my teams have adequate time for rest. It is essential to give security practitioners flexibility in when and where they work. I am intentional about making sure my teams can access recovery periods after an intense rotation especially in cyber defense and incident management.

Competitive compensation is an essential part of recognition and reward, and CISOs should consider a holistic package of salary, bonuses, and non-cash compensation where possible. These are all essential to recognize the incredible efforts of our security teams. Compensation is also a key part of remaining competitive in recruiting and retaining talent. Growth is another essential part of any conversation about recognizing and rewarding security talent. There is no shortage of outside opportunities for security practitioners to grow in their careers, so a CISO must foster the greatest possible number of internal opportunities.

Continuous learning is a particularly effective way to reward security teams, especially since so many people in security are endlessly curious and motivated by learning. Ideally, you can use learning as both a reward and a future strategy for emerging skill requirements such as cloud and analytics. I am currently running bootcamps to help my security teams develop skills in securing cloud services from several major infrastructure-as-a-service (IaaS) providers.

Contribute to a Stronger Talent Pipeline

I believe that CISOs have a responsibility to create a richer and more diverse pool of talent for tomorrow by investing in community outreach programs. Community outreach to students and individuals from underrepresented backgrounds can foster greater interest in security careers and contribute to a more highly-skilled, diverse talent pipeline for the future.

Security leaders are responsible for looking at their internal talent resources to develop a talent pipeline, also. Rising CISOs should be identified and given exposure to a diverse set of rotations in technology and business roles as early as possible.

The amount of interest in security careers among emerging talent gives me hope for the future of the industry. There's more opportunity than ever for students to gain a strong grounding in cybersecurity in high school, college, and graduate school. I am encouraged by the growing interest in security careers among students. Perhaps more than anything else, I am inspired by the growing number of talented, emerging women security leaders.

A CISO is only as great as their team and their successors, including the CISOs they helped to develop and elevate.

Over the years as a technology executive in various companies, I am proud to say I played a role in supporting the careers of 20 rising security leaders who are now CISOs!

Responsibility 3:
Embed Security into Business Workflows

Every business, regardless of industry or age, is now competing on technology. Technological innovation is necessary for organizations to achieve better productivity, lower costs, or happier customers. Digital transformation has made security increasingly important to business strategy and dramatically expanded the CISO's role. Delaying a product launch in order to meet security requirements such as threat modeling or testing can have a real impact on profitability.

The innovation climate has also created a new imperative for CISOs to help streamline their organization's roadmap. There is more pressure than ever for businesses across industries to create "scale-out" architectures that can rapidly expand to new customers, markets, or use cases virtually overnight. I often draw from my experience in transformation strategy to provide strategic recommendations on build versus buy, or evaluations of emerging technology categories.

Enabling the business requires CISOs to be very strategic and creative about how they embed security into every single business process. Security executives must have a deep understanding of business workflows in order to make secure decisions as simple as possible for all teams and users.

Enable Innovation at Speed and Scale

A CISO should have a complete understanding of how the business is evolving across an incredibly broad range of factors - including industry trends, consumer behavior, market pressures, and competitive positioning. I often draw from my background in transformation strategy and services development to create security recommendations that are in

3. Embed Security into Business Workflows

Enable Innovation at Speed and Scale

Start Left

Create Seamless Security Experiences

alignment with business objectives. Knowledge of business strategy is incredibly valuable for a CISO.

Start Left

Expertise in product development is a critical skill for modern CISOs, especially in a business ecosystem where every organization competes on product. I believe that it's important to proactively work with product teams and engineering organizations to create a security culture that starts to the left, or introduces security as early as possible in the product life cycle. Bolting on security requirements after the fact leads to delayed product launches and technical debt.

People will do the right thing, or secure thing, if a CISO makes the right thing easy for them to do. Understand your engineers' go-live environments and make security decisions highly-accessible to make sure they have support.

Product is an increasingly vital part of the business strategy, which is why it's crucial for CISOs to be innovative about how they shift security left. I hope all CISOs can eventually create sufficient alignment between security and product teams, achieving security CEO Erkang Zheng's vision of a world where breaches are improbable, not inevitable.

> "I envision a world where decisions are made based on facts, not fear; teams are fulfilled, not frustrated; breaches are improbable, not inevitable. Security is a basic right." [4] - Erkang Zheng

Shifting left requires the CISO to partner with engineering teams and external vendors to create seamless experiences for product teams, including engineering and DevOps. The CISO must strive to deliver self-serve platform experiences to the teams who build, operate, and optimize proprietary technologies.

Create Seamless Security Experiences

Security should feel seamless to employees, regardless of whether they work in marketing or site reliability engineering. Embedding security controls into existing business processes and tools is only possible for a CISO who understands how other teams work and the day-to-day challenges of different business units.

The CISOs greatest challenge on a daily basis is how to make security at scale and speed the easiest possible option for any team, under almost any circumstance.

Responsibility 4:
Create a Dynamic Approach to Risk

A CISO has a responsibility to measure security objectively, and perhaps most importantly, tell a story about risk that resonates with the board of directors. The first step is to shift your mindset since risk is not an inherently negative concept to the business leaders. A common language is necessary for a CISO to become an effective strategic advisor on risk tradeoffs and emerging opportunities.

---

4   Zheng, E. (2021, March 2). Security is a basic right. JupiterOne. try.jupiterone.com/blog/
    security-is-a-basic-right

4. Create a Dynamic Approach to Risk

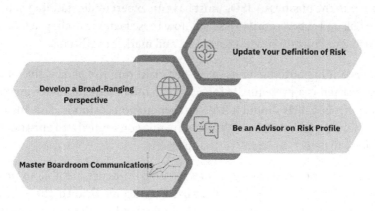

- Update Your Definition of Risk
- Develop a Broad-Ranging Perspective
- Be an Advisor on Risk Profile
- Master Boardroom Communications

Update Your Definition of Risk

CISOs have traditionally thought of risk as something that should be mitigated as quickly as possible. Security teams protect against risk by scanning systems and products, remediating vulnerabilities as quickly as possible, fixing misconfigurations, or applying patches. But, this mindset of risk as a technological requirement can be limiting.

Business leaders do not view risk as something that is always negative. I first learned in the IBM Office of the CIO that businesses take calculated risks constantly. For example,

- A business may choose to increase future profitability by accepting risks during an acquisition.
- Launching a product in a new market has a risk of failure, but it can also protect the business from a potential loss of market share.

> Security leaders almost always think of security risks in negative terms. When we think of risk, we think of an unmanaged cyber asset that adds to the attack surface.
>
> Instead of risk avoidance we need to update our thinking and communications to risk trade-offs. What is the opportunity for the business if we choose to accept or transfer a risk?

Develop a Broad-Ranging Perspective

The CISO must create a 360-degree risk perspective to become a strategic partner to the business. CISOs must have an expert understanding of business risk and cybersecurity risk, and how these factors are shaped by their industry, organization size, customers, and market conditions.

Understanding both business and cyber risk from the perspective of the organization is a prerequisite for a CISO to offer strategic advice on security controls. CISOs should not lessen their grip on customer data. Instead, they should understand which assets are mission-critical and enhance the capacity to detect threats as early as possible.

CISOs with the greatest degree of executive influence are able to proactively identify emerging risks.[5] They use a 360-degree vision of the business to help senior decision-makers with understanding risks and tradeoffs. Modern CISOs make it a critical priority to gather data on leading indicators, develop multiple courses of action, and build consensus around risk appetite "left of boom," or before an incident occurs.

Be an Advisor on Risk Profile

True collaboration on enterprise risk appetite means aiding senior leadership with clear information on tradeoffs and emerging risks. Considering the organization's risk profile is how the most effective CISOs create effective dialogue around risk appetite and shared responsibility.

---

5   Olyaei, S. (2020). The Key Drivers for an Effective Security and Risk Leader. Gartner.

Creating an Organizational Cybersecurity Risk Profile	
Question	**Examples of Measurement**
What drives value for the organization?	• Market position • Customer satisfaction • Financial performance • Growth trajectory
Which threats and vulnerabilities have the greatest impact on our attack surface?	• Legacy systems • Human error • Employee disengagement • Competitive landscape • Threat actors • Software quality issues • Ineffective processes
Do we have foundational controls to protect our critical assets?	• CIS Controls • The Cyber Defense Matrix
How effectively do we monitor and detect cyber incidents?	• Meantime to detect (MTTI) • Vulnerability criticality and age • Supply chain and software supply chain controls
Can we respond to a cyber incident and recover?	• Meantime to respond (MTTR) • Results of tabletop and recovery planning exercises
Are there unmanaged or emerging risks?	• Critical Asset and Product Inventory • Attack Surface Modeling • Ontologies and Knowledge Graphs • Third party vendors or M&A

Master Boardroom Communications

Briefing a board of directors is an art that requires a CISO to compress a lot of information effectively into a very short amount of time. Boardroom communications are also a mandatory part of the CISO's responsibilities. Board members are generally non-technical executives who provide oversight of risk management, especially risks that could lead to brand destruction.

My experience leading an executive briefing center at IBM helped prepare me for the pressures of boardroom conversations by teaching me key success tactics. I learned to compress complex technical information, focus on business value, and front-load my key message. A CISO should prepare for the unique pressures of board communications in a short briefings format, where there might be a total of 15 minutes to cover a huge amount of complex information.

Typically, a CISO will report to the board of directors on an established cadence, with an additional cadence of oversight delegated to another body such as the audit committee. Communications with any supervising or oversight body should always be tailored to the audience.

It is important to remember that a board of directors is not there to approve or disapprove of the CISO's security strategy or to hand out money. Instead, they are there to ensure the CISO and other executives are upholding the responsibilities of their role in a risk based way.

How to Communicate to the Board of Directors

1. Be Concise

You might have a total of 15 minutes to brief the executive board on security, but it's crucial to deliver a clear overview of your key message in the first 90 seconds. It is challenging to consolidate all of the work your team is doing into 3-5 concise slides, but it's also incredibly important.

2. Optimize for Required Reading vs. Boardroom Conversations

It is important for a CISO to carefully optimize their presentation around what should be covered in the boardroom and what documents should be submitted to board members in advance as required pre-reading activities.

Ensure your presentation is comprehensive, but optimize for what topics create the conversation you want to have with the board.

3. Anticipate Questions

Be prepared to address common questions and objections by being prepared with recommendations and a clear mapping to how your advice can drive value to the business, as well as what resources you need to achieve your recommended plan of action.

4. Be Prepared with a Tactical Plan

I recommend coming prepared to not only justify your recommendation but also explain why it is likely to work. You should be informed of the benefits of your recommended approach in comparison to other options to address any objections.

5. Have a Clear Call to Action

Underline your key recommendations by being clear about gaps or risks in the program. Strive for transparency without being unnecessarily alarmist.

Board members are not interested in the minutiae of security programs or a detailed history of solution lifecycles. Instead, they want to receive concise and expert advisory briefings that are tailored to the interests of the greater business strategy, using resources like the organizational risk profile I shared above.

A CISO is expected to provide a comprehensive and data-driven look at the organization's cybersecurity posture, maturity, and regulatory issues to better inform executive decisions around potential new products, go-to-market strategies, and partnerships.

What to Communicate to the Board of Directors

Communicate effectively about risks to business objectives and cyber assets to brief the board of directors in a way that is relevant and impactful. Consider focusing your board-level conversations on the following talking points to select the 10-20 most important KPIs for your security program.

Risk	Visualize the quantitative results of risk assessments and your recommendations, including a clear view of the top risks, risk appetite, and risk tolerance.
Program Health and Maturity	Benchmark your security program against industry peers and competitors and offer recent data from tabletop exercises. Any significant internal incident should generally be reviewed, as well as any resulting board-level discussions or lessons learned about incident decision requirements.
Program Metrics	Provide significant metrics across the security organization as well as security sub-domains such as cloud security or security operations, with insight into how these measures are trending.
Emerging Threats	Inform senior leaders of the evolving threat landscape by briefing recent events, trends, and potential impact. Educate the board on the global threat vector and provide insight into your own threat landscape.
Compliance Posture	Deliver a status update on your compliance, audits, and regulatory status.
External Partnerships	Proactive collaborations with industry groups, regulators, law enforcement, or intelligence.

Responsibility 5:
Continuously Adapt to an Evolving Landscape

Increase the Strategic Value of Security

As digital innovation accelerates, organizations are experiencing unprecedented cybersecurity risk, including expanding attack surfaces and threats. There is more demand than ever for the CISO to become a strategic partner to business units and help the organization avoid risks on the road to innovation.

I always emphasize to aspiring and emerging CISOs that this is a big, broad, and strategically-crucial role. I also believe that the CISO's strategic importance will continue to grow within their organizations as we face an expanding threat vector and new digital transformation pressures.

There is no clear roadmap for how to become a CISO, although I have observed that the most effective CISOs among my peers have undergone broad technology and business rotations in their early careers. As CISOs, my peers and I are also currently defining what it means to be effective in an evolving landscape. This requires a lot of agility, relentless curiosity, and fearlessness to adapt and experiment.

Continue to Expand Your Role

The CISO role is still being defined and expanding. Effective CISOs have the opportunity to assume new responsibilities within their organization. I find this exciting and energizing since I have always been in pursuit of new challenges in my career.

Because the CISO touches so many different functions in their day-to-day work, I have observed that there is a natural expansion happening within the roles of leading CISOs. It is a natural evolution for many CISOs to assume responsibility for information technology (IT), cloud, or physical security. Countless other CISOs are growing in their roles and assuming ownership of specializations such as fraud or privacy engineering.

The expansion of the CISO role is intriguing, and I see endless possibilities for business and technology domains to become part of what is considered

5. Continuously Adapt to an Evolving Landscape

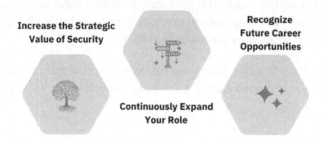

Increase the Strategic Value of Security

Recognize Future Career Opportunities

Continuously Expand Your Role

core security responsibilities. CISOs are embedded experts in so many business areas that expansion is a natural result of effective performance. Expertise in data tagging and classification can easily lend itself to ownership of data governance or focus on cloud security can also help expand into cloud operations.

Recognize Future Career Opportunities

What does an effective CISO do next? It depends on their appetite for new challenges and interest in continued growth. I don't think that CISO is my final career destination. An evolution towards increasingly important roles in technology or business leadership is a natural career move for many CISOs.

Sometimes, a logical evolution for a CISO is to become a CIO or CTO, although this seems to be increasingly less common in today's organizations where the CISO and CTO are often peers. In an innovation-rich business climate, a promotion to Chief Product Officer can increase the CISO's influence and build on their existing knowledge of strategy and growth.

More and more often, I observe CISOs becoming Chief Security Officers or Chief Trust Officers. Since the CISO is already a natural agent of internal and external trust, a promotion to formally lead trust initiatives often makes sense.

The Modern CISO is a Courageous and Collaborative Leader

The CISO is an incredibly vast and strategic role - but it's also one of the newest roles on the core executive leadership team. There is no clear path to becoming a CISO and even fewer instructions on how to excel when you finally land in a Chief Security Executive's seat. Today and tomorrow's CISOs face the challenge and opportunity of an evolving landscape where they must set strategic priorities in mid-flight.

The modern CISO is an essential executive, whose strategic priorities must be closely aligned with enabling business innovation at both speed and scale.

Summary - 5 Strategic Responsibilities for the Modern CISO	
Responsibility	**Recommendations**
Build 360-Degree Partnerships	• Strengthen internal relationships • Enlist, educate, and align stakeholders • Create shared outcomes • Be proactive about external engagement
Be Intentional About Security Talent	• Create an actionable succession plan • Be creative in recruiting talent • Create diverse, global teams • Recognize, reward, and rest your talent • Contribute to a stronger talent pipeline
Embed Security into Business Workflows	• Enable innovation at speed and scale • Start left • Create seamless security experiences
Create a Dynamic Approach to Risk	• Update your definition of risk • Develop a broad-ranging perspective • Be an advisor on risk profile • Master boardroom communications
Continuously Adapt to an Evolving Landscape	• Increase the strategic value of security • Continuously expand your role • Recognize future career opportunities

The industry needs CISOs who are relentlessly curious and collaborative. Emerging CISOs should gain the broadest set of experiences possible, have the confidence to operate without a well-defined roadmap, and be proactive about forming partnerships.

The CISO is still a deeply technical role that requires incredible expertise in both legacy and emerging technologies. There is little question that a CISO needs direct exposure to engineering, infrastructure, automation, analytics, and other technology verticals. But, the most strategic CISOs will thrive in a role that is much more than just tactical and technical. The modern CISO is a courageous leader who continuously embeds security into the business and unlocks new streams of value for the organization.

ABOUT LATHA MARIPURI

Latha is Chief Information Security Officer at Uber, where she oversees cybersecurity and privacy engineering for the company globally and its subsidiaries. Latha has a Bachelor of Science in Computer Science from Manhattan College and a Master of Science in Engineering from the University of Michigan. She is also on the Board of Directors at JupiterOne.

Prior to Uber, Latha was the Global CISO and Deputy CTO at News Corp. Latha was also a global business and technology executive at IBM. She helped shape the IBM Security division, has launched numerous highly profitable solutions globally, and led enterprise innovation initiatives. She has extensive experience in driving tech strategy, market research, product management, engineering, business development, and M&A.

Revolutionary
Leadership, Rebellious
Opinions, and
Knowledge Graphs

CHAPTER 2

Revolutionary Leadership, Rebellious Opinions, and Knowledge Graphs

by Jasmine Henry

Revolutionary Leadership, Rebellious Opinions, and Knowledge Graphs

Jasmine Henry

I never considered a career in technology growing up. It first crossed my mind as a possibility when I was 17, sitting in a college statistics course. I had an embarrassing commitment to my teenage identity as a *deep* and *edgy* person at 17, since I posted Mayakovsky poems about inciting revolution on Facebook and wore black nail polish. But, at that moment, I was just overwhelmed by the elegance and logic of statistics. This moment even had a soundtrack since someone in the class had failed to silence their LG flip phone before class. A hollow-toned, electronic ringtone version of "Big Poppa" began playing.

I charged into my stats professor's office when class ended and informed him I planned to be a statistician. He typed something into Ask Jeeves (now, Ask.com) and told me computers would soon make statistics careers obsolete, so I should really do something else with my life. I hold absolutely no grudges against this professor since he was an amazing human being, even if his advice was not informed by Google's seminal MapReduce paper.[1] After all, it *would* be seven more years before Harvard Business

---

1   Dean, J., & Ghemawat, S. (2008). MapReduce: Simplified Data Processing on Large Clusters. Communications of the ACM, 51(1), 107–113. doi.org/10.1145/1327452.1327492

Review Press declared data science the "sexiest job of the 21st century."[2] It would be at least another decade before the cybersecurity industry became painfully aware that security problems had a lot in common with big data problems, or that cybersecurity has a collective need for analytics skills and solutions.

How I Decided to Be a CISO When I Grew Up

If my short-lived dream of being a statistician was my first choice, then my second choice was to become a PhD in Slavic Languages and Literature. I funded a study abroad in Crimea by working three jobs simultaneously to support my full-time studies, including an internship where I used SQL and R to analyze giant data sets. I remember occasionally thinking about a career in computer forensics and then rejecting it as an impossible idea. At the time, I didn't know those types of jobs existed in the private sector and doubted I would be a good fit in a three-letter agency.

I supported my dream of becoming a PhD by earning money working on computers. One day, I received a letter from the most prestigious graduate school in my field. They were *pleased to inform me* of my acceptance but without funding. It wasn't personal since department funding had evaporated in the wake of the 2008 financial crisis. Even at 22, I knew it was foolish to take out loans for a PhD in Russian, so I shredded the letter and began applying for post-college jobs in an abysmal employment market. I landed in a Tier 1 help desk job for about 18 months, where I was mistakenly convinced that I was not moving the needle toward future goals. It was the perfect first job in retrospect.

Over the next few years, I moved from support to Technical Program Manager (TPM) work. Looking back, I wish I had fought harder to do exclusively engineering work instead of TPM, but I am also grateful for broad experiences. Research shows that many technical women are pushed strongly toward management or operations instead of working in roles that effectively utilize their math and science skills.[3] This was also a natu-

---

2   McAfee, A., & Brynjolfsson, E. (2022, March 11). Data scientist: The sexiest job of the 21st Century. Harvard Business Review. hbr.org/2012/10/data-scientist-the-sexiest-job-of-the-21st-century

3   Fouad, N. A., Chang, W.-H., Wan, M., & Singh, R. (2017). Women's reasons for leaving the engineering field. Frontiers in Psychology, 8. doi.org/10.3389/fpsyg.2017.00875

ral direction since I excel at technical documentation and data analysis. I remained vigilant about maintaining a balanced skillset by doing a lot of side projects and home labs. Around 23 or 24, I officially decided I would become a CISO when I grew up. My third-choice career has not changed in the last decade.

Listen Carefully, But Reject Advice That Doesn't Serve You

I returned to grad school at 25 to study Informatics and Analytics because statistics were elegant; I thought analytics was the future of security. I worked full-time and studied full-time, and slept very little, leading global teams of cloud-native developers. DevOps was not considered security work at the time, but I have always loved doing projects with an element of scale. Plus, I convinced my bosses to let me do free side projects that involved risk assessments, audits, and architecture for more security exposure. I was determined, even if hiring managers told me frequently that I lacked the workplace experience with 'actual security technologies' like *routers* to do security full-time. I ignored their advice and kept up my homelabs.

If you fast-forward about five years and one-and-a-half graduate degrees, I had not only broken into security, but I had achieved all the major hallmarks of a security professional, like terrible sleep habits and blurred lines between work and hobby. I had become a regular attendee at Black Hat and the RSA Conference. Next, I became Director of Security at a high-growth Series A startup. Being a baby CISO confirmed that I still wanted to be a CISO when I grow up, but it also made me realize that security in its current form is impossible, especially if you listen to advice that does not serve you.

Today, I work in a role that blends everything I care about, including hyperscale, security, statistical analysis, and cloud-native development. Security problems are increasingly similar to cloud and analytics problems, and I'm doing applied research that inspires me. My path was not straightforward, but I got lucky after three decades of rebellious opinions and tenacity.

The hardest part of security is breaking into security. The other hard part about security is all of it, especially doing it effectively. The security community is filled with some of the brightest and most dedicated people I know, who work tirelessly to protect their organizations, and burn the midnight oil mentoring, volunteering, in Capture the Flag (CTF) security exercises, and on homelabs. Many of us are unconventional thinkers and personalities who defied all odds to get to our current roles. My peers give me hope for the future.

Overview

This chapter is a blend of experience, research, and theory. It discusses what I learned as a startup security leader and research discoveries from my graph-based analysis of 372 million cyber assets. It also shows how I use knowledge graph data models to solve hard security problems.

The story has a subtle theme of rebellion and revolution. I believe we should constantly reevaluate what is still valuable and relevant, even if it means a departure from how things have always been done.

The industry needs people with grit and weird ideas to lead security teams. Research shows that 'rebels' like myself can foster breakthrough discussions, especially if we are open to new perspectives and dissent. Transparency and open dialogue are my approaches to people leadership.

I hope the end result is a realistic picture of what it could mean to do security well at cloud-native scale and what we, as individuals and as an industry, could choose to do better.

Part 1: Revolutionary Leadership

I still want to become a CISO when I grow up after serving that function in my prior role. I created a security function at a cloud-native startup and scaled security, privacy, and compliance from Series A to Series C. The startup grew from around 40 employees to over 200 employees, and I helped sign many large, trusted brands as customers.

Every successful startup will eventually realize a need to invest in security. At cloud-native startups, security is frequently a customer-driven motion. You typically need to provide evidence of security controls as part of the due diligence process performed by potential customers. Before a Fortune 500 signs a tiny startup as a technology vendor, they require questionnaires, evidence to support your answers, and copies of your InfoSec policies. If you are lucky and sign the customer, your contract might demand you quickly pass a series of audits.

I don't mind if security at a startup is often a customer-driven motion. It would be nice if security was done perfectly from day one. However, everyone has to start somewhere, and "before Series B" is not a terrible time to create a security charter. A customer-driven security motion also has some benefits to baby CISOs. You are usually guaranteed enough resources to pass audits. You can justify improvements in security controls by stating they are "an audit requirement." Most importantly, a customer-driven security motion builds customer value, and customer value is never, ever bad.

I was a solo practitioner during the first months when I owned security at the startup. I completed many customer questionnaires and built an entire set of security policies. I deployed a core set of security technologies, including a graph-based Cyber Asset and Attack Surface Management (CAASM) solution, security training, endpoint detection and response, and a secure access service edge (SASE) solution. It's possible to spend less than this, but all of these technologies scaled wonderfully. I eventually grew a small, global team of wonderful security practitioners and worked hard to create partnerships with other units.

Moving Mountains by Nurturing New Cybersecurity Champions

During my first six months as Security Director, I also passed three audits to hit contractual obligations for our customer: PCI DSS, SOC 2, and ISO 27001. I was told it was a career-defining move to pass three audits so quickly with almost no resources, but it was not actually that difficult. I relied significantly on extreme collaboration across teams and created shared outcomes with DevOps and product engineers. Some of the most dedicated people I have ever worked with sat in our virtual audit war room for hours of observation interviews with the audit firm.

I also passed audits by being ridiculously scrappy at various points. For example, I discovered a colleague in operating system engineering had won national IEEE awards and pen testing competitions as a recent undergrad student. I didn't even know that penetration testing was a competitive school sport in some world regions, but I had an answer to an audit requirement that I could not do myself. Kalpaj met all audit criteria for qualification, and he was also sufficiently neutral since he did not report to our cloud or security teams. So, I informed him that he was volunteering to be our pentester. Kalpaj did a brilliant job on manual testing and a written report, which turned into a long, productive mentoring relationship. I took a similar approach to scope out rising champions to help with backups testing, internal audit, and countless other requirements.

Bootstrapping a security and compliance function is never an ideal first choice, but desperate times are an opportunity to shine as a leader. My greatest leadership strength is my scrappiness and advocacy for rising talent. I find people with incredible problem-solving abilities and collaborate with them on tough problems. When they succeed, I am obnoxiously persistent in recognizing their contributions to the executive team. When asking people to do an extreme amount of work, sweeten the blow significantly by being a mentor, introducing them to mentors, and endorsing their efforts very loudly in public spaces at work.

The Right Attitude Toward Compliance is Very Unpopular

InfoSec professionals on the internet quickly emphasize that security is not compliance. They proclaim that checkbox approaches are not secure. While these know-it-alls are technically correct, an all-or-nothing approach to security is impractically expensive for most cloud-native startups. Behavioral psychology teaches us that an all-or-nothing mindset or black-and-white thinking is the most common cognitive distortion. Compliance is not nothing; it is much better than nothing.

Security leaders have a responsibility to drive as much improvement as possible. Compliance may be your first security target, and if you're smart, you will use compliance as a business tool if that best serves your circumstance. Frameworks like SOC 2 and PCI DSS define bare-minimum standards. They can be an effective baseline for cloud-native startups - especially when passing an audit or maintaining interim compliance is a customer requirement. Investors may also ask to evaluate your audit reports as part of due diligence, which is another opportunity to prove the value of security.

Passing a few security compliance audits will force you to document your systems, deploy intrusion detection and file integrity monitoring, train all employees, and enforce total coverage of endpoint protection. Those and other requirements are not bad places to start. I also firmly believe that ISO 27001 is pretty wonderful. If anyone managed to do ISO 27001 perfectly, they would have extreme rigor in their security management system.

So, all the tech bros with a Twitter account and cognitive distortions are technically correct when they say compliance is not the same as security, and checklists are bad. Compliance frameworks offer a varying degree of rigor and some glaring loopholes, like cloud-native startups can fake compliance just long enough to pass an audit. But, these approaches invariably result in expensive technical debt. Compliance is much better than no security, and it's also a valuable business tool. In an ideal world, compliance would be the outcome of effective security.

Positioning Security as a Revenue Center

I spent a lot of time building relationships with sales leadership and building a reputation for being extremely good at completing technical security questionnaires for prospective customers. I was fast, efficient, and someone who could create momentum in deals. I started spending increasing time face-to-face with customers during the sales process. I articulated our security, privacy, and compliance posture to contribute to annual recurring revenue (ARR).

I do not usually look like other technical executives when I get face-to-face with a CIO or CTO on Zoom. I am a woman in her mid-30s with blue hair and tattoos on my throat and both hands. But, I was good at using security to build customer trust since I cared about the customer's perspective, and I could also justify each one of our controls and explain our posture in great depth. I relentlessly measured my impact on revenue and worked tirelessly to change perceptions of security from a cost center to a revenue center.

I provided sales training as a security leader. I built a beautiful security and compliance website page and a whitepaper that explained our posture. I even convinced our sales leadership to start regularly adding compliance to customer agreements and could brag that 35 percent (and, eventually over 50 percent) of our revenue was security-driven.

Changing executive perceptions to view security as a revenue center is mandatory work for security leaders, perhaps especially startup leaders, since all of us are under-resourced. Creating customer trust is a valuable skill, especially if that effort comes from the right place of really caring about your customer and your security posture. When you have proof that security drives ARR or helped close a funding round, you are much more likely to have adequate resources.

Earning Customer Trust with Information Assurance

Startups are under a lot of pressure to compete with more established companies and must convince customers that going with the startup is not a risk. The pressure to quickly create a reputation for trustworthiness is not isolated to startups. Many huge companies create internal organizations to quickly take new cloud software products to market.

I genuinely empathize with customers who have questions about my employers' security posture. Supply chain risk is terrifying, and they are doing the right thing to assess our impact. We are responsible for proving we are secure enough for our customers to trust us. Security leaders have a vital role in ensuring that the business is competent, consistent, and accountable via cybersecurity assurance.

Assurance requires understanding what customers expect from security and how these expectations vary by customer audience. Empathy and understanding are how security leaders make a case and deliver meaningful proof of security.

Making a Cybersecurity Assurance Case		
Audience	**Common Security Expectations**	**Relevant Types of Proof**
Executives	• Security improves product agility and innovation. • Security impacts business viability. • Security drives profitability.	• Continuous Building and Testing • Security-enabled Business Opportunities • Security Impact on Revenue
Customers	• The vendor actively manages security vulnerabilities. • The vendor is personally invested in my success and security. • The vendor consistently behaves in secure ways.	• SBOM, vulnerability bulletins • Security-focused product onboarding • Access to real-time evidence of confidentiality, integrity, and availability
Employees	• Secure behaviors are convenient. • Security cares about my employee experience. • Security is about reward, not punishment.	• A mature DevSecOps practice • Town Hall meetings, anonymous security reporting channels • Security champion programs and security incentives

I created several real-time dashboards to demonstrate security posture and navigate executive conversations. One was a real-time display of our General Data Protection Regulation (GDPR) posture that demonstrated which of our cloud assets were located in North America, APAC, and Europe. I also tracked high-risk deployment events, data breach costs, AWS resource utilization, etc. Creating tailored artifacts for cybersecurity assurance helped me consistently make the case for trust.

Creating Relentless Transparency with Colleagues

Security has an incredible responsibility to serve internal customers, or colleagues, especially as we gain more and more influence in executive decision making. We have a responsibility to protect the happiness and productivity of our coworkers, perhaps especially our engineering colleagues since we often act as technical advisors in executive decisions. We are most effective at advocating for others when we create a culture of relentless transparency.

It is not easy to create security controls that make people happier and more productive. It is impossible if security leaders are not good at *interactive communication*. I worked hard to facilitate authentic dialogue, open-ended questions, and constant listening when speaking with global colleagues.

I was very intentional about transparency for many reasons. Transparency is a prerequisite to collaborating on shared outcomes. It is genuinely important for leaders to be transparent during times of uncertainty and change, which is always the case at hyper-growth startups. Last, many of my engineering colleagues came from open source (OSS) backgrounds and still valued OSS principles like community, privacy, meritocracy, and transparency.

> I once published a policy that stated employees might need to pay for a replacement laptop if their work-issued equipment was stolen due to negligence several times in one calendar year. This policy was intended to control genuinely extreme patterns of negligent behavior.
>
> After publishing the laptop theft policy to Confluence (an internal wiki), my phone began blowing up. Lots of people wanted to tell me how they felt about this policy. And honestly, I took it as a massive win that people trusted me. I was happy to talk to them about their feelings, fears, and opinions. I wanted to have these conversations, and I significantly preferred that employees call me instead of their manager, HR, or my manager. This felt like proof that I had established radical transparency and open dialogue about security.

And, I Struggled in a Few Areas, Too

Many individuals in security from marginalized backgrounds reach their first security leadership position by being far more quantitative than anyone else. We are excellent at what we do in order to be taken seriously, and we make decisions using a lot of data. When we grow to a position of influence and leadership, there is a shocking moment where we must become more relationship-driven to be taken seriously.

I remember the exact moment when I realized I needed to pivot toward people. I had stayed up *very* late making a slide deck with 35 radar charts to show how a year's worth of security recommendations impacted our risk posture in different control areas. I was exhausted and unhappy with the outcome of the meeting. It is generally a terrible idea to try and cover 35 radar charts in a 30-minute meeting. Also, I had recently started reporting to a new executive, and a lot of charts blindsided him without much context or an underlying relationship.

I wish I had easy advice about navigating the boy's club that is the executive suite. I don't. I very intentionally got better at small talk in my early 20s by learning a lot about professional football and starting to follow it. I've learned to distill my data presentation significantly into fewer, simpler charts. I have also learned the art of "nurturing ideas."[4] Instead of surprising an executive with 35 radar charts, you should consider planting a seed and watering the idea over time and consecutive one-on-one meetings.

Studies show that my experience is not singular. Women leaders are more likely to struggle with navigating C-Suite relationships since we have fewer demographics in common with the majority. This results in fewer opportunities to build relationships since we are less likely to be invited out for drinks or golf. Really, we should all consider the inequalities of relationship dynamics and make a serious effort to plan workplace networking and bonding activities that include everyone.[5]

I Also Borked Any Sense of Boundaries: Don't Be a Yacht CISO or a 24/7 CISO

Back in grad school, I heard whispers about a CISO at a huge company that was remediating a massive, extremely long-term data breach. The CISO's immediate response was to abandon his team, fleeing for an extended vacation on his yacht. I told myself that when I became a CISO, I'd sleep on the floor of our security operations center during an incident.

---

4 Credit is due to my mentor Dee Young for helping me articulate the art of nurturing ideas, as well as standing by patiently while I learned why it matters so much!

5 Rosenzweig, J. (2021, December 16). Four Reasons Women Still Struggle to Advance to and In the C-Suite. Toolbox. www.toolbox.com/hr/diversity-inclusion/guest-article/four-reasons-women-still-struggle-to-advance-to-and-in-the-csuite/

I do not own a yacht, and I was not a yacht CISO. I was an *extraordinarily available* young CISO. I did redlines for customer contracts on vacation. I had meetings from 7 AM until 11 PM since my team and I had an 11 hour time zone differential. I tried to consolidate evening meetings to two to three days per week a few times, but I did not try hard enough.

I also did not sleep on the floor of a physical or virtual SOC since I went even further, staying up all night to help investigate weird false positives from cloud security tools, even when it was an exercise in futility since many cloud threat detection systems are a black box. I justified this stuff by telling myself it was a startup, and I did not have the resources to do just one thing. I had to do all the things, and this type of extreme behavior was not good for my health.

The right boundaries are probably highly individual, but they are almost certainly BETWEEN the yacht CISO and the 24/7 CISO. Do not hide from the FBI on your yacht. Do not be a CISO who *doesn't even sleep* on the SOC floor since you are awake doing non-critical incident response documentation. *Both options are bad.* Revolutionary leadership is extreme ownership and advocating for your people, but it is not doing the most for years on end. Be self-aware of your warning signs and take respite as often as possible.

Part 2: Rebellious Security Opinions

I had done an effective job of scaling security from Series A to C at the startup, but I wanted to change the world. I believe that security in its current form is untenable. I wanted to learn from a leading CISO and contribute to industry knowledge of cloud-native security. I went to work for my favorite vendor, the graph-based CAASM solution. I genuinely believed that graph models could solve some of security's biggest problems.[6]

At JupiterOne, I am exposed to security being done in incredible ways. I am learning how to do security more effectively and optimize for emerging use cases, which is exhilarating as someone who wants to build a series of world-class security programs. I am also doing some incredible research,

---

6   In case you are wondering, I still firmly believe that knowledge graphs have amazing potential for solving our collective alert fatigue, and part of my plan for the rest of this year is to explore that.

including my recent work as lead author on the 2022 State of Cyber Assets Report (SCAR). Recently, I analyzed nearly 400 million cyber assets from almost 1300 organizations and found that the security landscape is really complex. In fact, it's running a lot of bright, dedicated people into the ground.

I Didn't Want to Write About Burnout, But Here it Is

Honestly, I think we're all a little tired of burnout as a topic. It isn't because we aren't burnt out; it's because the idea of being burnt out takes up way too much space in security publications and conference agendas. I often joke that security professionals aren't here for the money, and it's true. Most ways to earn a middle-class wage are less arduous than security. Studies show that security teams are expected to work eleven hours more each week than any other team, even product engineers.[7] The fact that the "security all-nighter" is a REAL thing for anything besides purely voluntary reasons should horrify all of us. Regularly staying up overnight for work is not okay. Occasionally staying up all night for a LAN party is probably acceptable if it is your choice.

My research shows that the average (mean) security team has a backlog of 120,561 findings. 98 percent of these findings come from two sources - cloud security tools (46 percent of total) and vulnerability scanners (53 percent total). A much smaller percentage comes from endpoint detection and response, bug bounty programs, and penetration tests.

120,561 should be a horrifying number to my peers in security, but it isn't. I get one of two responses, either "yup" or "actually, that seems low." I cannot imagine a world in which it is normal for anyone's backlog to have 120,561 things in it. Can you imagine if a Doctor had a queue of 120,561 patients or a development team had 120,561 change requests? I can imagine it, and I can also imagine the physician or dev raising a middle finger and immediately leaving to work for a more reasonable employer.

Even if we weren't dealing with an unmanageable number of findings, we're also dealing with an absolutely unmanageable attack surface that must be defended or tested, depending on where you sit in the organization. The

---

7 Reclaiming hours lost to cybersecurity incidents. Tessian. (2021, December 13). www.tessian.com/research/ciso-research

average security team is responsible for over 160,000 cyber assets, including tens of thousands of devices, network components, apps, data assets, and user identities.

The reality of our attack surfaces gets even more unreasonable when you consider that security professionals are just 0.46 percent of the U.S. workforce - or an average of 1 security employee for every 200 employees. If every company represented in my research were average and asset security responsibilities were divided equally, one security person would be responsible for 252,000 assets.

It isn't psychologically healthy to try and tackle the weight of securing hundreds of thousands of assets or findings, at least not with the traditional skills we learned during security certification. For the first time in history, an entire asset lifecycle can take place without human intervention, so we must view automation as a first and last result. Manual security methods do not scale to assets created through automation. The challenge now is to figure out how to turn 120,561 findings into a more reasonable task list by correlating enough data points to understand risk.

We Should Redefine Cybersecurity Skills

One of my graduate school professors described his first job working in technology for a major U.S. based automotive manufacturer in the late 1970s. He wore a belt bag of floppy discs, walking the halls to provide hands-on support to a select percentage of employees whose jobs required a computer. Just over 40 years ago, a company's entire device asset inventory could be worn on a belt. Trying to wear an 18-gram floppy disc for each of our device assets today would be impossible for anyone to do for an 8-hour shift. With an average of 32,190 device assets per organization, your belt bag would weigh over 1,277 pounds.

Legacy IT technologies like laptops, premises-based servers, routers, gateways, and smartphones are a relatively tiny part of the security team's cyber asset mix responsibility.[8] Instead, our asset inventories and attack surfaces contain a lot more cloud devices, apps, data, and identities that

---

8 Physical devices are still an important security consideration because they are generally used by employees, who are unpredictable. As a mentor Michael Howard says, "humans are the biggest piece of malware on your network."

relate to each other in complex ways. Managing the new attack surface requires a new generation of security professionals with skills in analytics, data visualization, and cloud.

My CISO Says Supply Chain Risk is Like a Mountain of Manure

The media loves talking about supply chain risk and Log4J, but I think very few of us know the extent of third-party exposure in our environments. On average, just 8.7 percent of the code that runs in an enterprise is developed in-house. Homegrown code typically has a relationship to one or more change management trails, such as pull requests. That means over 91 percent of the code running in the enterprise is third-party code, including open-source code repositories and third-party applications.

Complexity is an understatement. We're in the thick of what my CISO, Sounil Yu, calls a predicament. A predicament is a problem that cannot be solved with current solutions; it can only be managed. In the late 19th century, large cities like London experienced a predicament when piles of horse manure formed on the streets, impacting water quality and creating disease risk. While these excrement mountains could be managed with shovels and wheelbarrows, the manure mountains weren't really solved until horses were replaced with automobiles.

It would have been unreasonable to ask the good people of Victorian London to get rid of their carriage horses and start hoofing it across town. It is similarly unreasonable to just get rid of third-party code - can you imagine how quickly businesses would crumble without applications and open source libraries? We can only manage this solution with vendor consolidation, software bill of materials (SBOMS), and real-time inventory of assets and asset relationships. But, we are definitely neck-deep in piles of third-party risk; I appreciate Sounil's analogy to describe a bizarre supply chain landscape.

Intentional Inclusion is a Safety Issue

I once attended a CISO dinner where a peer admitted he had never considered the idea AI could be biased. I was sitting in the corner with several other women security leaders; we all audibly gasped and started whispering in horror about how *one cannot simply trust AI.*[9] To use security technol-

---

9   6 months later, I have heard several CISOs say this.

ogy in safe and ethical ways, we need to consider a diversity of perspectives and consider how years of systemic privilege can create blindspots. We must become very effective at listening, considering new perspectives, and facilitating open dialogue.

To say that diversity is an issue of life and death is not an exaggeration, either. Just ask Emily Ackerman, a former PhD student at the University of Pittsburgh. She found herself unable to maneuver her wheelchair onto a curb due to a motionless grocery delivery robot at the end of the side-walk. "I found myself sitting in the street as the traffic light turned green, blocked by a non-sentient being incapable of understanding the consequences of its actions."[10]

The experience, which Ackerman described as "dangerous" and "dehumanizing" occurred because the technology hadn't been programmed to consider the safety of disabled individuals. Safe and accessible technology cannot occur in a vacuum. It can, however, occur when tech is designed and used by teams with a broad set of experiences.

As leaders, we have a responsibility to create teams filled with diverse perspectives since the very safety of our populations depends on it. This responsibility is not going away, especially since the cybersecurity industry is facing an imperative to automate everything and deepen our adoption of technologies such as machine learning and AI. While leaders and hiring managers have an extra responsibility to foster diversity, everyone can be intentional about inclusion. As Dr. Meg Layton has said, if you have a few spare hours, you can boost other people's voices if you have a social media account or review papers.

We should be intentional about surrounding ourselves with diverse perspectives and avoid being in an echo chamber. I am increasingly conscious of the risk of being in an ivory tower, especially since I'm now in a research-focused role at an organization that does security extraordinarily well. I am privileged to have a peer network of many excellent engineers and security leaders. CISO Andy Ellis advised me recently to fight the echo chamber effect by doing hands-on volunteer work to secure a non-profit, and I intend to follow his advice.

---

10 Ackerman, E. (2019, November 19). NCDJ. ncdj.org/2019/11/my-fight-with-a-sidewalk-robot/

Why Security is Actually a Big Data Problem

Digital transformation has permanently changed the enterprise technology landscape. The onset of the pandemic was a major moment for security teams since the pandemic created a shift towards speed in enterprise software development. Enterprises had to stand up solutions for remote work or telehealth overnight at the onset of the pandemic, which showed executives that overnight development was possible. It was the end of 6-18 month product development cycles.

Being able to deploy new features very quickly has changed how enterprises architect their products, increasing the adoption of serverless architectures and microservices. This evolution has significantly increased the number of cyber assets that security teams must identify, manage, and secure.

Static IP addresses comprise fewer than one percent of network assets, while network interfaces are a huge percentage - a respective total of 267,029 IPs and 15,782,226 network interfaces. Network interfaces are used by modern DevOps teams to route traffic between subnets by hosting load balancers, proxy servers, and network address translation (NAT) servers, and, apparently, static IPs are used very rarely.

It is not possible for security teams to intimately know each of their cyber assets when they are personally responsible for several hundred thousand assets. Instead, security practitioners need the ability to query, understand changes, and ideally, identify enough interrelated data points to identify the most toxic combination of risk. Risk is generally a perfect storm of critical assets with misconfigurations, overprovisioned users, and sketchy findings.

Why It's Actually Really Hard to Answer Basic Questions About Security

It is infuriating to non-technical business leaders that security people cannot answer basic-seeming questions. It isn't for a lack of trying, either. **No security person ever has woken up in the morning and thought to herself "you know what? I don't give a flying Turing test about which of our EC2 instances (a type of cloud device) are exposed to the public internet."**

Mainstream media coverage of security incidents focuses on grave and basic errors, like a cloud database with a password of Admin123. While it is true that basic failures cause most security breaches, basic errors are not so basic and they are also not usually a single data point. It is generally several data points that line up like dominoes across multiple systems, users and policies. The Admin123 password only got media coverage because it led to a database that was misconfigured and because the database contained important data.

Understanding whether an EC2 instance is exposed to the public internet is a great example of a basic question with no straightforward answer and a lot of technical variables. It depends on:

1. If security rules permit ingress or egress traffic from the internet
2. If the EC2 instance is in a publicly routed subnet
3. If the subnet and VPC have an internet gateway or NAT provisioned
4. If the network ACL on the VPC or subnet allows the traffic
5. If the EC2 instance has a public IP assigned
6. If the EC2 instance is active

Risk is not a single data point, it is several data points that relate to each other from different systems. Security teams need the ability to quickly understand complex relationships since there are many, many data points involved in answering a seemingly-basic question.

The security landscape has all the characteristics of a big data problem since we encounter an incredible volume, variety, and velocity of data every day. The ability to "answer a basic question" requires really sophisticated correlation of data from a lot of different sources. This can be done manually in theory, but it cannot be done quickly if you are manually investigating.

Security is NOT Two Dimensional

Most of our security solutions are inherently two-dimensional. Our systems function like a spreadsheet or a relational database - they essentially provide data in a list format. What a list does not offer is complex relationships like the ones that occur in the real world. A list in one security system might describe a misconfiguration, but it does not allow you to see how this happened or what it means since those data points live in many other tools.

Security teams need the ability to ask questions and surface meaningful answers quickly. Essentially, we need to have the ability to use search engine-like capabilities at work and we should consider tested analytics approaches to create these capabilities in our environments. Knowledge graphs are a way to understand, query, and act on complex, real-world relationships.

Part 3: Knowledge Graphs

A knowledge graph is a model of an interconnected set of real-world objects and their relationships. It can also be referred to as an ontology. According to Ralph Hodgson, CTO at TopQuadrant, all knowledge graphs are defined by the following:[11]

Extensibility - A knowledge graph can accommodate a diverse set of data and metadata, and new evolutions of this data.

Query - A knowledge graph model can be inspected via a query to find answers to questions.

Semantic - The definition of the data is stored in the graph's data model.

Intelligence Enabling - A knowledge graph provides the ability to understand dependencies and other complex relationships between objects, including cyber assets.

---

11 Knight, M. (2021, September 15). What is a Knowledge Graph? www.dataversity.net/what-is-a-knowledge-graph/

Knowledge graphs are generally implemented by businesses when one or more of the following things happens:

1. A need to capture enterprise data across a wide range of technical or business contexts

2. A need to harmonize data from multiple sources according to a standard data model

3. A need to unify data classification according to a single standard

4. A need to understand the relationships between data, including complex dependencies

5. An increased need to facilitate analytics sophistication, including AI or machine learning

There is no one solution for security knowledge graphs. Instead, it's best thought of as a model. It can be adopted with a CAASM vendor, developed in-house, or deployed using several open-source tools (like Cartography, Cypher, TinkerPop, Gremlin, or Sparql). The approach you choose should have the following characteristics:

- A common graph data model that defines nodes (or cyber assets) and edges (or relationships)
- Integrations to capture data on assets, relationships, findings, and guardrails.
- Querying capabilities

What You Can Actually Do with a Graph Data Model

A knowledge graph model for security analysis is not an actual solution to the dumpster fire - for example, graphs cannot SOLVE supply chain risk, but it can help you find third-party risk. I have used the graph data model for security and feel it is a valuable tool.

One of the most straightforward use cases of a graph-based approach to security is to query for details about your cyber assets or users.

The queries below are J1QL, JupiterOne's domain-specific query language for security graphs. But, any open source graph query language such as Cypher, Gremlin, or SPARQL could work here.

Who is Jasmine?

```
FIND google_user
WITH email = "jasmine@example.com"
```

```
FIND github_user
WITH email = "jasmine@example.com"
```

```
FIND User
WITH email = "jasmine@example.com"
```

Does Jasmine Have MFA Disabled?

```
FIND User
WITH email = "jasmine@jupiterone.com"
AND mfaEnabled = false
```

These queries allow us to discover Jasmine is a Google user, a Github user, an active user, and whether she is using multi-factor authentication, or MFA (spoiler alert: yes she is using MFA, and it's definitely the good kind of MFA).

Understanding Direct and Indirect Relationships

Relationships are a significantly underrated source of insight for security practitioners. Consider the following question:

What groups is Jasmine a member of and what access does that grant?

In order to answer this question, we must:

1. Evaluate who Jasmine is

2. Inspect the existence of a user identity owned by Jasmine

3. Review the access groups Jasmine is a member of

4. Determine which access roles, including cloud access roles, are assigned to those groups

5. And finally, determine which cloud access policies are assigned to those roles.

It's a very difficult and winding task without a graph-based approach to security. With graphs, however, it's a relatively simple query:

```
FIND AccessRole
THAT ASSIGNED >> UserGroup
THAT HAS >> User
WITH email = "jasmine@example.com"
```

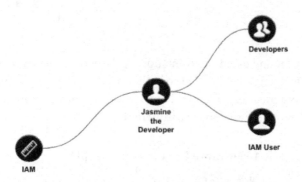

Relationships that cross service boundaries are the most confusing but also some of the most interesting relationships that can be discovered in security. Graphs are the ideal structure to discover and manage these complex relationships.

Understanding Relationships Between Users and Events

For the purposes of illustration, let's imagine an enterprise environment that meets all of the following criteria:

1. GitHub is used as a source control management service
2. Jenkins is used for continuous integration and continuous deployment
3. The cloud service provider is Google Cloud
4. There are several scanning services that continuously detect vulnerabilities

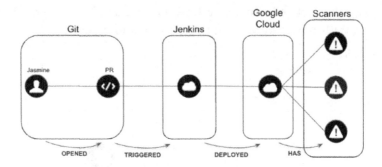

Uncovering user and event relationships can be accomplished with a single query; which engineer pushed code that resulted in a security vulnerability? Or, more precisely, which PR author was responsible for providing a resource that our scanner says is vulnerable?

A Few More Use Cases for Graphs	

Incident Response	• What is the Blast Radius?
	  • Is this device or instance still online?
	  • What other resources are in the same subnet?
	  • What data stores does it have access to?
	  • Is it behind a load balancer or auto-scaling group?

Security Ops & Engineering	• What instances, workloads, and apps are vulnerable? • Which developers and PRs introduced new findings this week? • How do findings relate to mission-critical deployments? • Which findings are on apps with production data access? • Which code findings impact internet-facing apps? • What are my vulnerable workloads with incident and event alerts?
DevSecOps	• What services and repos are part of this application? • What are the open-source dependencies or software bill of materials (SBOM)? • What developer opened the most PRs yesterday?

In Conclusion: 2 Theories on Revolutionizing Our Industry

Security is ridiculously difficult and I do not have all of the answers. I have learned from experience and I also analyzed 372 million data points to validate whether my experience was normal. Sometimes, the state of security and our day-to-day experiences as practitioners can feel a bit surreal, but that's just the reality of chasing a moving target and trying to protect an attack surface that is expanding and changing very rapidly.

I do not claim to have all answers, but I have two working theories on how we can collectively improve, based on both experience and research:

1. Leaders should be incredibly intentional about healthy workplace partnerships. Being empathetic and transparent when collaborating gives security leaders a huge advantage. Caring about others and listening allows us to drive more value, and eventually, create champions and cross-functional momentum that can move actual mountains.

2. Security is really hard, but we should reframe the problem and draw solutions from applied analytics. The problems we are solving at work are no longer just security problems, they are questions about automation, cloud, and big data. Knowledge graph models and other analytics approaches have considerable value for the new landscape.

I genuinely believe that cybersecurity leaders will collectively save the world, especially if we are proactive about learning from our peers in the security community. We do not need to reinvent the wheel every time or suffer in silence, we can share what we learned and collaborate with other practitioners at the forefront of rediscovering what it means to do security well. Learning from our colleagues, our customers, and our peers increases our effectiveness. Collectively, we are reinventing cybersecurity.

ABOUT JASMINE HENRY

Jasmine is Field Security Director at JupiterOne and lead author of *The 2022 State of Cyber Assets Report* (SCAR). Previously, she was a Director of Security at a different SaaS startup where she became a JupiterOne customer in September 2020. She is an accidental career specialist in applied graph theory for cloud-native startup security, but she firmly feels she could do *much worse* since graphs are great.

Jasmine has a Master of Science in Informatics and Analytics from Lipscomb University, and is working to complete a PhD in Information Science. She is on the board of directors for The Diana Initiative and a career village organizer for BSides Seattle, as well as a speaker at countless industry conferences and events. Jasmine has worked with Esper.io, IBM Security, HPE, the ADP Research Institute, Philips, the Tennessee Valley Authority (TVA), and other organizations in her career.

Security-as-CTO

CHAPTER 3

Security-as-CTO

by Aubrey Stearn

Security-as-CTO

Aubrey Stearn

> **You will never be in control of security's external cadence; however, the attack surface area is entirely your baby.**

Growing up as a Child of the Internet

I was born in 1984, the same year all the best films came out: *Ghostbusters, The Terminator, Indiana Jones, Beverly Hills Cop,* and *Star Trek III: The Search for Spock.* It was undoubtedly a year for fine vintage films! 1984 was also the year Ken Thompson outlined a method for corrupting a compiler binary on a *nix system in his Turing award acceptance speech. We've seen a resurgence of Thompson's technique with pirate versions of Xcode creating binaries with added malware. If there was ever a good example of not trusting the ground you walk on, it was my birth year.

Today, I'm a fractional or interim CTO. I don't have a formal education in technology; the best I've got is a UK A* GCSE in IT, or a General Certificate of Secondary Education. That means I spent most of my final term playing Pokémon, handed in my coursework the day before exams, and still got an A* (the highest possible grade). My system of choice for Pokémon was a No$gmb, an early monochrome Gameboy emulator for DOS.

Almost everything I know is built on experience and tinkering. Building a Gameboy DMG-01 emulator required me to develop a deep understanding of central processing unit (CPU) architecture. I learned about the architecture of CPU technologies such as microprocessors, including RISC, Itanium, and IA64. I also was able to understand how the 2018

MELTDOWN exploit worked, which was a hardware vulnerability that impacted many microprocessors.

I also learned constantly by directing my curiosity to search engines. If someone told me they were running Z-series mainframes in a data center, I'd wonder why anyone would run such a niche mainframe platform instead of more cost-effective commodity kits and start using a search engine for answers. I also trolled users on my college network by using the unsecured NET SEND command to broadcast messages about free pizza as well as other games of cat and mouse with a close friend. It worked until the college network admins got wise to our IP sources. Still, it made me wonder if my friend and I were very good or if the network admins were rubbish.

The only time I wished I'd gone to University was when I wrote a programming language to try and represent regulation and law as code. I wish I had taken computer science to learn graph theory, compiler design, language syntax, and all that jazz. Still, I was able to navigate most of this stuff on my own using search engines as a child of the internet.

Other early explorations included self-directed learning about Ghidra, an open source framework for software reverse engineering from the U.S. National Security Agency. I explored the Z80 instruction set from Gameboy for assembly programming. My love of legacy gaming led to hands-on experiments with the dynamic recompilation of Gameboy ROMs (computer files containing data from a read-only memory chip that are frequently used in the context of emulation).[1]

I don't think someone's educational background should be a barrier to getting in the door for a job in technology, especially if someone is curious and hands-on. Formal education should never be a factor in breaking through the glass ceiling. I simply obtained my education in a less formal way than some others.

Diversity in tech leadership is essential to propagate diversity of thought. Never let anyone hold you back, not even yourself.

---

1 Assembly language is assembly language, no matter what CPU you are using. I would 10 out of 10 go down this programming rabbithole again!

I'm Not <u>in</u> Security; I <u>Do</u> Security.

I have given a number of talks on cybersecurity from the CTO's perspective and most people remember my opening disclaimer: "I'm not someone who works in security but someone who does security."

I don't say this as an indemnity. Instead, my disclaimer sets the scene. My cybersecurity security experience comes from a practical place. I'm a hands-on practitioner, even though I deeply value the support, information, and education of cybersecurity researchers and academics.

As a fractional or interim CTO, I'm a gun for hire. My gigs typically fall into one of three categories; small, medium, or large.

1. Small

A very small technical team or no technical staff.

- I am very hands-on at small engagements. I often need to make quick judgment calls to balance security, business outcomes, and execution capabilities.
- For example, I may discover a small customer wrote a crap content management system (CMS) with hand-rolled security. I will make a quick call to bang an adaptive load balancer (ALB) with an identity

verification service and a web application firewall (WAF) in front of the homegrown CMS so the customer can keep executing.

2. Medium

A technical team of 12-50 people.

- I am relatively hands-on at mid-sized engagements. Often, I start by running a spike, defined as an extreme programming method to gather information or test how long future work will take. I use this information to build out a pattern the organization can adopt and industrialize.

3. Large

A technical team of 50-300 people.

- Being an interim CTO at large organizations is akin to steering an aircraft carrier. While a one-degree change in direction can seem meaningless at first, a slight shift in strategy can also create prominent issues over time that eventually require course correction.

- Steering a technical team of this size involves a lot of politics and cross-functional work to pull in stakeholders from different directions. To lead technology at a large organization, you need an advanced knowledge of risk and security. You also need an extremely advanced knowledge of corporate navigation.

There are different levels of backpressure (resistance) and challenges for a fractional CTO at each size of organization, which are a bit like a sliding scale. My personal sweet spot is the middle tier. I find working with technical teams of 30-80 people is a great place to operate since the corporate arteries aren't typically clogged with best-laid intentions or hundreds of audit policies.

I have experienced that documentation on cybersecurity policy, controls, and posture does not always yield desired results. Organizations with reams of 50-page documents don't always outperform smaller security teams, especially if a smaller team has the right tools. The best outcomes don't always result from the best intentions. Instead, the best outcomes come from equipping the right set of people with the right tools, and making sure they have enough room to execute on cybersecurity.

Consumability

"Consumability" is a crucial concept in cybersecurity. I define it pretty simply; consumability is a measure of whether the "doing people" ingest the information you feed to them. "Doing people" in technical organizations are typically developers and engineers.

Some cybersecurity compliance frameworks can be unhelpful to a culture of consumability, particularly if the framework results in excessively thick reams of policies and documentation.[2] Hundreds of pages of reading can overwhelm engineering teams, resulting in less-than-ideal security outcomes.

> Security can be meaningful to engineers, but only if it's consumable. Creating a culture of consumable cybersecurity can shift behavior in important ways.
>
> Products are more secure from inception when security means something to engineers. Consumable cybersecurity can result in organizations that are better-prepared to respond to ever-changing threats.

My approach to engineering is customer-centric and outcome-driven. We need to understand our customers to understand what to build. Enabling engineers to make the right decision requires us to create organizations where the builders can ask risk-based questions, understand the business, and know the customer.

To illustrate this idea, consider a digital home mortgage company. Downtime may be a very small risk to this type of business. If the web application is unavailable and customers cannot make a mortgage payment, it may have a minimal impact on company revenue or reputation. Most likely, customers will just try to pay their mortgage later.

---

2   In my experience, some frameworks are easier for engineers to consume. I find NIST 800-53, COBIT, and SCF have minimal adverse impact on engineers, especially compared to some alternatives.

Understanding risk tolerance and customer expectations allows engineers to create frameworks for distributed decision making. These guidelines help teams of builders take risks that are tolerable to the customer. And, guidelines for decision making are also what we need to strive for to create consumable cybersecurity requirements.

Is the best way to deliver requirements for cloud security controls a spreadsheet with 900 columns? Probably not. **Engineers want to know what to do.** Abstract explanations of cloud controls that apply to a countless number of technologies are not consumable. 900 column spreadsheets may be comprehensive, but they are often not prescriptive. Engineers need meaningful examples and enough data to understand ideal security outcomes.

Deliverability

Deliverability is another important concept for effecting organizational change. When I start a new assignment as an interim CTO, one of the first things I benchmark is communications. *How quickly does it take for me to send a message to the whole team?*

The worst latency, or delay in message delivery, I've measured was three weeks. It once took three weeks for a message to flow naturally through a distributed global team. The message was dead simple: it explained the team would be using a real-time chat product instead of email. I measured the day-by-day trickle of people switching to the new product. The message was delivered, there was a three week period of latency, and finally the message was consumed by the entire team.

> **An Overview of the Internal Communication Lifecycle**
>
> Deliverability → Latency → Consumability
>
> It is possible to benchmark communications in an organization measuring latency, or the length of time between when a message is delivered and when it is consumed by the team.

Deliverability involves a very simple question, of whether it is possible to reach everyone. It also should involve another question about consumability: *"Did the message land? Did the memo about 137 new Cloud Controls memo get read? Was it consumed, based on behavioral or technical data?"*

Humans learn using one of four primary learning paths:

1. Visual
2. Auditory
3. Verbal, or reading and writing
4. Kinesthetic or tactile

Engineers are not all verbal learners simply based on the fact they cut code.

Consider how many of these four learning styles are well-suited to consume security requirements from a spreadsheet with way too many columns.

I think about learning styles because consumability creates better customer success. A business sets goals when I am hired as an interim CTO. I am hired to help deliver a product, fix technical debt, or grow an engineering capability. The magic to actually accomplish these goals comes from engineers, while my job is to debug and facilitate the process.

I can only form a plan to steer a ship in the right direction after reverse-engineering the issues that individuals and teams face. While I may give an order, the direction of an organization only changes if everyone is on board. And to win buy-in from everyone, I must deliver consumable cybersecurity information in ways that are meaningful to engineers.

The Language of Risk

I find security enablement conversations with businesses are easy. I ask organizations to define the cost of lost customer confidence. If preferred, this cost can be defined at an atomic level. We define what it costs to lose one customer or five customers.

Risk is both material and reputational, and both of these types of risk should be part of business conversations. It can be difficult to win support for security investment if you try to talk in exclusively technical terms with a CFO or COO. But, business leaders will always understand the language of risk.

> **Net present value** is an important part of the risk language landscape. The idea is best explained by the 2019 film *The Devil Has a Name*:
>
> "If you make more money doing it than it costs to get caught doing it, continue doing it."
>
> I advise organizations to consider net present value often by comparing the cost of new cybersecurity controls to the cost of documented risks.

On Zero Trust

As an interim CTO, I am frequently given a pitch in interviews. Potential employers usually tell me "this is just a temporary gig" and they "just need someone to hold down the fort". I roll up on Monday and prepare to start listening, learning, and asking questions.

It is not in my best interest as an interim CTO to wholesale rely on what people tell me, and certainly not if I don't combine listening with observation and investigation. I need the ability to look under the hood and draw my own conclusions. Specific challenges are always unique and the best leadership solutions are organic and holistic to suit the team, the time, and the place.

The Importance of Code Sympathy

Practicing security as a CTO gives me unique visibility into relationships between security and engineering teams. My biggest pet peeve about security culture is a lack of code sympathy, or an absence of first-hand understanding of code. I wager the biggest reason engineers distrust security teams is when they feel misunderstood. This can occur if a security practitioner gives instruction on application security, despite having no experience in code or cloud.

There is room for all types of skill sets in security, but security teams need at least some individuals with the technical experience to have code sympathy. It is troublesome to have a team with too many analysts and no one who can sympathize with code builders. I've had a few consulting gigs where I was primarily responsible for security and I found my technical mastery was met with skepticism. There can be deep tension between security and engineering. We must build security teams that have a capacity for code sympathy by making sure we have the ability to understand engineers.

Some Final Thoughts

It's easy to say "shift security left" and DevSecOps is our path to victory. But, the actions are a little more involved to actually shift an organization. First, we need to understand the real-world cognitive demands on our engineers and if builders have the capacity to take on security.

We should focus on creating security guardrails with room for engineers to operate, switch lanes, and work outside their comfort zones. We must also gently enforce the standards and policies that protect our organizations from cybersecurity risk.

> For cybersecurity to be effective, it needs to be deliverable and consumable. Does it cater to different learning styles? Does it reach the right audiences?

Capacity Matters

Engineers need enough free capacity to sustain the additional cognitive load of security responsibilities. Look holistically at how everyone in the organization delivers information, not just the security team. Effective security is a whole-team sport.

Situational Awareness Matters

If you have a threat intelligence capability but lack a software bill of materials (SBoM) or operational bill of materials (OBoM), then something has gone very wrong. Intelligence is useless without situational awareness.

Hire Engineers as Well as Analysts

Every security team needs some people who are ready to code and share pain with engineering counterparts. Consider how cross-functional teams with embedded cybersecurity engineers can move the needle. At one major tech organization, Site Reliability Engineers (SREs) from cyber and software engineering backgrounds spend 50 percent of their time cutting code and the other 50 percent of their time improving reliability and related capabilities.

Create a Well-Organized Security First-Aid Kit

Medical first-aid kits are organized in a specific way because they are often used in a state of panic or shock. Everything in a first-aid kit is easily identified and packaged neatly into an accessible and consumable box.

Consider creating a security first-aid kit for situational awareness by including well-packaged frameworks for decision making. Remember to strive for consumability because the people responding to cybersecurity incidents are usually different from the people who built the service. A well-organized security first-aid kit goes a long way to calm the initial panic of a security event and guide responders toward an acceptable risk threshold.

ABOUT AUBREY ELIZABETH STEARN

Aubrey Stearn is a transgender, 6'8" former cage fighter in London, England. She has rocked in roles such as CTO, interim CTO, Head of IT Ops, and Lead Developer. Aubrey has a huge passion for automation, since it allows her to do less while accomplishing more work in smarter ways.

Aubrey believes the DevOps movement has redefined our definition and expectations of engineers. She actively seeks to build super awesome teams of excellent people and advocates for testing in production. Aubrey also works to extract the value from failure so her teams can later succeed.

CHAPTER 4

Confronting Inherently
Flawed Systems

Confronting Inherently Flawed Systems

by Carla Sun

Confronting Inherently Flawed Systems

Carla Sun

Introduction

Everyone wants to believe that computing is pure and free from human flaws. I always say that the damn thing about computers is that they always do exactly what we tell them to do. A hugely-complicated decision tree of binary yes and no choices eventually leads to the deadlock or crash that forces us to consider "turning it off and on again." While yes and no should always "resolve" something, computing has become so complicated, and the moving parts so numerous, that it is inescapably flawed–just like its creators. Yet, much of tech lives in a state of delusion that computing can be pure and free of human flaws because its practitioners push for excellence in a true meritocracy without bias, politics, or emotions. When we look closer, we know that this is not the case. So the looming question is: how do we confront unexpected behavior in what is otherwise meant to be perfect?

I am not well-built for my social environment and consider myself somewhat of a human disaster. Unbeknownst to myself and my loved ones, I went undiagnosed with a neurobiological disorder for most of my life. My system does not produce enough dopamine, enabling the brain to act and operate like an average adult. I am developmentally delayed, impatient, compulsive, hyper-focused, overwhelmed, bored, and lazy all at the same time. Combine this with stereotypically high expectations of growing up A.B.C. (American Born Chinese); tiger mom included, I am a constant failure. Everything I do is a struggle and a constant grinding of the gears. So how did I, a local human disaster, make sense of one of the most chaotic parts of security in Incident Response?

In rare moments of clarity, hyperfocus, or disability aids, I built systems to over-correct and overcompensate for the failures guaranteed to occur in my daily life. What If we accept that computers are also unreliable and often temperamental beings instead of being perfect and perfectly predictable? If computers can be subject to unexpected failures at inopportune times, we can learn from these systems and coping mechanisms to deal with disasters and the unexpected.

In helping make sense of my ideas, Jasmine Henry at JupiterOne pointed me to a phrase that perfectly captured my mindset and the processes to keep my head above the water. She called it *predictive failure mitigation*. My thoughts, feelings, and memories constantly fight for my attention and are often defeated by my hyper fixation on failure.

Humanity and computing will always be intertwined because humans wrote the first line of code. Even when we get to the point of code writing code for us– to err is to be human, and computing follows the same human flaws. My constant exposure to unexpected behavior from my undiag-nosed disorder empowered me to resolve unexpected external behaviors. Ironically, this equipped me to approach security incident response in ways that I didn't realize until I started writing this chapter.

Messy, Disorganized, and Forgetful

For many of my possessions, unless they are so heavy that I can't readily move them, I easily lose them. The number of times I've locked myself out of my car or home, the number of badges I've had to ask my environment team to replace, or the number of jackets I lost as a kid –and continue to misplace as an adult–nothing is going to save me from being forgetful. We all experience these symptoms sometimes, but for people like me, the fre-quency and severity are detrimental to daily living. Even with disability aids, my absentminded behavior and tendency towards guaranteed failure can't be resolved. So, what's someone like me to do?

There's a saying: If something wasn't in the first place you checked, make sure to put it there every time. This works great if you're nice, neat, and consistent. For me, this ends up being a heap in which, yes, the paper I spe-cifically need is in a stack of various books, documents, half-finished proj-ects, sketches, stickers, fabric samples, junk mail, and magazines, probably the bottom of the third major "group" from the top. This doesn't work as soon as you add somebody else into the mix, obviously, as sometimes my partner also needs that specific piece of paper.[1]

When Marie Kondo's organization method rose to fame, the first episode was an emotional roller coaster for me. The first step, she'd advise, was to dump all of the contents into one pile. My anxiety kicked in immediately. Wasn't the giant pile the opposite of what I wanted? Wasn't my already existing giant pile the source of all of my judgment, criticism, and the starting point of many fights, frustrations, and tears?

So I looked inwards. I'd get so fed up and angry at myself that I'd end up hyper-focused on the problem. I observed the behaviors, defined expected behaviors, and documented the unexpected behaviors. As forgetful as I am, long-term planning is dubious. Instead of death by a thousand little mistakes as I suffer daily, I accidentally poured a lot of energy into survival by a thousand little improvements.

My badge kept falling off my reel, I'd get a new reel. The new reel would unclip from my pocket, so I got a lanyard. I kept losing my lanyard, so it always stayed on my neck at work. I lost my lanyard at home, so it went to the same pocket in my work backpack as soon as I got home. I lost my backpack at home, so I'd put my backpack next to the front door. When I stopped fighting myself in trying to fit a square peg into a round hole, when I stopped trying to be like everybody else and wear my badge on my hip on a reel–then I finally, finally stopped losing my badge.

I didn't feel triumph, but I did feel relieved. As these little unconscious systems became more apparent to me, I started to desperately cling to whatever I could notice and embrace that I would fail and account for it. For my entire life, it felt like I was dying by death from a thousand cuts. The best managers of my life always went through my accomplishments and showed them in a new light– progress by a thousand little improvements.

The combination of these two things–always assuming that failure was inevitable but casting my mitigation efforts as a thousand little improvements (rather than a thousand little cuts) ended up being the trick. Always assuming failure can be a foreign notion in some aspects of computing. As

---

1 I'm forever grateful to you.

a quality assurance engineer, all the test cases I ever built only accounted for the happy paths, with everything working as expected. But on a personal level, I realized that I had to live with constant failure and struggle, and that mindset evolved as I engaged in my security career. I always assume that we have been compromised at work (to the horror of one of my CISOs). *So, how do we use this attitude of predictive failure mitigation for dealing with the unexpected in security?*

Solving for Unexpected Behaviors

So there we were, trying to resolve incidents across multiple countries, disciplines, teams, and time zones, and all of the essential resources were all over the place. An external team managed the permissions to access resources, and they didn't have pager service level agreements (SLAs) as intensive as ours. Response times were slow because we were constantly waiting for the right people to pay attention to our requests to get the proper access. We were rebuilding to-do lists repeatedly with every incident I managed. The process was slow, clunky, and required a lot of energy.

This all drove me absolutely insane, so my hyperfocus kicked in. My documents and notes are *all over the place* at work, but how was I able to keep up as an individual and not get fired thus far? Like the rest of the world, we moved into cloud-based documentation management at some point in which I could use the search function. Why were we relying on outdated systems that required the whims of an entirely different team to enable us? So, I moved our resource sharing system into the cloud. I removed a gate-keeping entity and took that management off their already overloaded plate. I could manage the permissions of all the resources and grant them as necessary, and if I had time to automate it, I wouldn't have had to pay attention to it.

Now, because everything was in one place, I'd eventually notice patterns in how we did things. I began to templatize all of the most common resource formats. When we expanded to a team of IMOCs (incident managers on-call), each manager could copy and paste the template folder and fill everything out like a worksheet. I noticed there were usually three simultaneous streams of work during an incident: an engineering workstream for mitigation or elimination, an investigation stream for evidence of exploitation and magnitude of impact, and a notification/communication stream for compliance obligations. I wrote out a simplified workflow to demonstrate how these three main workstreams were interrelated. As the dataset grew, we noticed patterns and built better playbooks and checklists for repeated or similar incidents. We organized and sent repeat and similar incidents directly to a managed risk register. Whenever we could make the process more efficient, we updated the template.

Like everything else in engineering, I broke everything down into bite-sized problems. Like the famous divide and conquer algorithm, I successfully solved small problems one by one. Putting it all in a heap made it obvious where the shortcomings were, where the failures in the process were likely to occur, and what to then do about it. Sometimes, the only way to resolve a monumental list of unexpected behaviors was to throw out the notion that it was "always done this way." If I always assumed that things would fail, I could curb it sooner rather than later with templates, playbooks, and historical logging.

Returning to Marie Kondo's pile of potential despair, I noticed a few behaviors. For example, she was kind to the people she was helping. She answered every question without judgment, with a gentle, guiding voice, breaking down the giant pile into one decision per item: keep, throw away, or donate. We can't boil the ocean, but we can do it a cup at a time. Kondo understands that organization doesn't come naturally to everybody. Her rules are guardrails, and like a good, mindful recursive algorithm, if you keep at it, it eventually scales well, especially when you start to parallelize resources. This was progress by a thousand little improvements.

Finding Order in Chaos

My eighth-grade science teacher didn't have assigned seating on the very first day. She introduced herself, talked about the different parts of science we'd cover for the year, and then gave us an exercise. *"Put yourself in alphabetical order by last name,"* and then she sat back in her chair and watched. The first half of the first row attempts to bubble sort themselves into some semblance of a mini alphabetical order for their section. It's horribly inefficient and slow.

I am slowly going insane towards the last row as I see nobody being helpful or even taking control of the situation. We are paralyzed. There are so many students in the room; surely somebody can do this. I am horribly impatient, so I get up and ask the whole room, *"whose last name starts with an A?"* Letter by letter, we gradually sort by our last name until the whole room is in alphabetical order. Other students catch on and start sorting themselves by the next letters in their last name. As we finish, my teacher congratulates the class and points at me casually. She explains this exercise tells her who her lab table leaders will be. I am mortified. I hate attention, and my impulsive nature and impatience have put me in the spotlight again.

Coincidentally, my big mouth also landed me my first Incident Response (IR) position. I mention that I am familiar with software releases because of my Quality Assurance (QA) days, and I know about managing web application vulnerabilities. The anxiety to get things done and not fail pushes me through decision paralysis. My empathy and fear of failure force me to build decision workflows and checklists. Rejection sensitivity, people-pleasing, and low self-esteem enable me to work without ego. I mindfully take care of my teammates in incident rooms and ultimately finish my tenure as an incident response lead relatively unscathed.

IR is a high-stress, high-emotion role, laying bare all the egotistical personality flaws of the tech industry. Tech believes that it is truly objective, free of emotion, a genuine meritocracy, and decisively correct–and that's the problem. Every time there's a bug, deadlock, or unexpected behavior, it's because of flawed human programming. I love to tell everyone that the damn thing about computers is that they do exactly what we tell them to do. Those who understand will tiredly nod, already thinking about the next test case that will account for this previously undiscovered path.

In the book *Thinking Fast and Slow*, Daniel Kahneman describes two systems in how we think. System 1 is the emotional system, and system 2 is the logical system.[2] Those who assume that they think with system 2 more often rely on "gut feeling" than actual objective evidence, thereby actually relying on system 1. It makes them more biased and more likely to act on emotion rather than hard evidence.

Constantly being corrected as a kid really fueled my need to be correct, so

2   Kahneman, D. (2011). Thinking, fast and slow. Farrar, Straus and Giroux.

I anxiously double-check my facts and work. Constantly being told that I am emotional makes me double down on relying on data to make my decisions. I notice those who criticize that I bring up sources, charts, and data are often the people in power who are never questioned. They claim to take my suggestions at face value, but I trust my own experience (including my data and analysis) rather than their perception of mine.

Learning from the Mistakes of Others

"Smart people learn from their mistakes. But the real sharp ones learn from the mistakes of others." [3] Every incident response program I encounter in tech is a recreation of other industries with more dire consequences. For example, the post-mortem process comes from medicine where doctors convene and discuss how the death occurred, and what could have been done better. Red teaming comes from war games and military practice exercises to ensure maneuvers are done correctly. Firefighters use life-sized dummies and fire in buildings to mimic environmental scenarios and test firefighters in high-pressure situations.

All of these lessons are written in blood, but in tech, the only loss is monetary in most cases. Not only do we get to traipse around claiming that we're engineers (when more traditional disciplines of engineering include certifications, tests, and consequences greater than a bad performance review), we act like we invented the damn wheel when responding to our monetary losses. In our hubris, we poorly reinvent incident response procedures from other industries. And we, with our silly outages, hardly take our work seriously enough to understand why they bother to stick to hard and fast rules in the first place. Without life or death consequences, tech is fairly consequence-free (though I applaud GDPR for trying to hold us accountable). I don't believe the old system is working, but can I find the confidence to change it?

When I first met some of my beloved Canadian colleagues in person, I noticed they all wore a ring on the pinky finger of their dominant hand. They explained to me that all engineers in Canada are given this ring at

---

3   Mull, B. (2006). Fablehaven. Shadow Mountain Publishing.

graduation.[4] The legend is that the rings were originally made from the first Quebec bridge that collapsed due to poor engineer oversight. The ring touches each design when an engineer signs off and reminds the engineer that mistakes are costly.

There's an interesting principle known as Chesterson's Fence.[5] In order to remove a rule, we must understand why it exists in the first place. Only then can we be permitted to remove the rule. Tech blindly adopts some techniques without knowing the history or reasoning behind why it exists. This is especially apparent for security incidents or removing cultural habits without understanding their benefits. When tech attempts to fix response techniques, we rarely understand their origins. There's value in reinventing the wheel in order to understand it, but our understanding is clouded without context or history.

I began to research failure mitigation in other industries to see where tech learned how to respond to unexpected behaviors. History and context gave me the ammunition to understand and alter the systems that weren't working for me. My partner has a private pilot's license, which enabled me to focus on incidents (well, accidents) in the aviation industry. Here's what I learned.

Airborne interlude

Modern aviation is a fairly conscientious venture with a good safety record. Sadly, this culture of safety is built on the bones of those lost to horrendous accidents in the past. When an accident occurs, the industry applies diligence by listening to these lessons, even as they recede into the past, and saying: never again. We start by looking at aviation safety from the viewpoint of air traffic control.

On our last vacation before the pandemic, my partner picked a beautiful vacation spot for us in Tenerife, Spain. My only request was somewhere warm since it was cold in March. While on vacation, a fabulous, jet-setting colleague of mine asked over Instagram, *"How did you know about Tenerife?"* I had no clue, so I asked my partner. A slight grimace later, he

---

4   History: Order of the Engineer. Order of the Engineer. (2019, December 13). order-of-the-engineer.org/about-the-order/history/
5   Rickard, M. (2021, October 31). Chesterton's Fence. matt-rickard.com/chestertons-fence/

mirthlessly explained: "I know about this place," he tells me with a guilty face, "because one of the world's worst airplane disasters happened at the airport here." What? I pause while drinking my coffee to avoid spitting it out. A lovely English-speaking couple next to us pipes up. One of them also knew about this famous airport disaster.[6] It turns out that the airport we'd landed at days earlier was the site of the deadliest aviation disaster in history. A combination of foggy weather, excessively heavy ground traffic, and miscommunication led to the collision of two jumbo jets and the loss of 583 lives. One jet thought it was cleared to take off while another (hidden by fog) was still on the runway. The second jet realized the first was taking off but couldn't clear the runway in time. The legacy of this incident lives on in numerous changes to rules on radio phraseology (e.g. the word "takeoff" can only be used when explicitly cleared for takeoff or when such clearance is canceled) as well as spurring changing attitudes to in-cockpit hierarchies (now any crewmember, regardless of rank, is encouraged to challenge the Captain if something seems wrong)—all of this to ensure that such a mistake never happens again.

Aviation is quite safe these days in the U.S., and I believe this is because of the way the NTSB (National Transportation Safety Board) conducts its investigations. The NTSB was purposely evolved to be free from influence and focus solely on passenger safety. "Because the NTSB has no formal authority to regulate the transportation industry, our effectiveness depends on our reputation for conducting thorough, accurate, and independent investigations and for producing timely, well-considered recommendations to enhance transportation safety."[7] The number of hull losses significantly dropped off somewhere around 2011.[8] Whenever my partner flies, he straps checklists to his thighs before we start take-off procedures. While he was prepping the plane, I flipped through a few checklists. He explained the checklists reduced potential mistakes and allowed him to timely and procedurally troubleshoot as issues arose. The checklists were borne of previous failures that led to the potential or actual loss of life. The

---

6   Final Report of KLM Flight 4805 Investigation. FAA Safety. www.faasafety.gov/files/gslac/
    courses/content/232/1081/finaldutchreport.pdf
7   History of the National Transportation Safety Board. NTSB. www.ntsb.gov/about/history/Pages/
    default.aspx
8   Salas, E. B. (2021, August 5). U.S. air carriers: Hull Loss Rate 2000-2019. Statista. www.statista.
    com/statistics/1031922/us-air-carrier-hull-loss-rate/

NTSB, free from being beholden to funding, laws, or operations of transportation, can focus on the main goal of passenger safety. This mindset has strongly influenced how I conducted investigations in security incident response.

So, having looked at how aviation handles the aftermath of crises, is there anything I can take back with me?

Clearing the Runway

The process of Air Traffic Control (ATC) juggling simultaneous take-offs and landings reminds me of releases and how multiple concurrent incidents can be seriously confusing. During a computer security incident, armed with a curl command to determine if we fixed an issue or not, there was a ton of confusion because the 401 we were expecting was giving 500s instead (originally we were getting 200s). It turned out that a separate availability incident was in progress, affecting whether or not we could see if we had pushed our fix or not.

In another incident, I had temporarily taken down something that actually coincided in time with another, unrelated, outage. My teammate helpfully wrote, after both outages, that whatever had happened earlier that morning wasn't us, so the root cause was still unknown. During the post-mortem, I brought up that exact message when they attempted to pin that incident on us.

"Clearing the runway" doesn't need to happen on a routine basis in our line of work, but when something breaks to a serious enough degree, it's a lot damn easier to validate a hotfix when everybody briefly stops. Removing variables and breaking down the problem into a single focus point really helps. In an aviation emergency situation, ATC is willing to clear all runways for a stricken aircraft to make an emergency landing. They ask how many souls are on board and how much fuel is left so they can proactively prepare for worse-case medical staff or firefighting resources. ATC prioritizes the stricken aircraft over all others regarding the right of way, delaying other take-offs and redirecting airplanes to maintain altitude or land elsewhere. Leadership can look in, enable, unblock, and grant exceptions as needed. The whole runway is clear for landing to reduce the chances of additional unexpected behaviors exacerbating the issue. History has taught me again and again, to clear the runway if we need it, otherwise, there might be too much going on, especially if the information of the telemetry is constrained, like confirming a vuln fix, or what the dials are saying on a malfunctioning aircraft that can only be communicated by the pilot.

Why do we stop other releases when there's a priority x (PX) or severity x (Sev X) incident, a junior member of my team asks me? Well...

Prioritization

Clearing the runway was a very interesting lesson for me about prioritization. I realized something when I did my own private, monthly post-mortems (thank you medicine) and metrics. We were overwhelmed and taking too many incidents that I didn't think deserved the panic and alert that opening an incident caused. My boss gave me feedback that it was exhausting to see yet another incident open up. I went to my mentors, a lovely group of fiercely intelligent women that helped me with every bit of challenge that I faced in IR, and asked them what I should do. My Data Protection Officer (DPO) at the time gave me excellent advice. "Build a program with the means that you have to the ends that you want." If I didn't want to prioritize an incident, I was free to do so. Again, throw out the way we've always done things if they're not working.

I thought I was expected to see the resolution of every report that I received. I needed to get to the end of my rope to throw out "the way we've always done things" and make a better, more focused system where I could clear the runway for the important stuff. I suffer from rejection-sensitive dysphoria. Rejection occasionally makes me think that my world is ending. I did not want to dismiss someone who reported something they thought was concerning. I ran my triage process, rated the concern, and directed them to a simplified, 5-step worksheet for incident reporting and a post-mortem report. I asked them to follow the steps and follow up with me, which was usually required when I had a higher priority incident. My empathy for rejection made me not want to reject these security-minded folks. I thanked them and hoped that not rejecting their concerns would continue to make them feel acknowledged and appreciated.

My fear of rejection (and of making others feel the same way) also made me take on incidents that initially seemed like they were in scope but didn't feel right. I triaged it, but the CVSS (Common Vulnerability Scoring System, an open source, globally-used framework for scoring the severity of a vulnerability) score didn't match the urgency of the trusted reporter, a product counsel that I had worked with closely before. I put aside my feelings until I was overwhelmed with a cotemporal incident that clearly had a much higher priority. I took a moment to figure out why it "didn't feel right" of the two and realized that one of the incidents did not have the security control failure as a root cause– an already determined fact.

A customer misunderstood a setting and asked for logs in response to the mistake. I deemed it a privacy-only incident since there were neither failing security controls nor was there engineering work required beyond providing logs to the customer. I appreciated and enjoyed working with every product counsel in the past, but I knew that I was hitting my limit. Have you ever told a lawyer "No"? Have you ever shit your pants as I did at that moment?

Because my product counsel was smart and understanding, they recognized their need for their own incident response process. I was honored that they trusted me to execute and acknowledged my need to defend my scope and focus on security incidents in which a security control had failed. I gladly consulted their chosen incident responder when they found the capacity to build out their own program.

Breaking Decision Paralysis

My impulsiveness has led me into roles of significant responsibility, both in my eighth-grade lab and within IR. It forces me to be good at improvisation because now I have to save my own butt from my big mouth. Most security incident responses don't have a game plan by default. We're going in completely blind–though perhaps not at much as the 8th graders trying to sort themselves by name.

I'd start throwing out plans and suggestions in what I describe as "confidently unconfident." This made incidents so much easier. "Sanity check," I'd declare as I asked what I thought was a stupid question. I felt enabled to ask because mistakes slow down incident resolution times. My fear of failure trumped my lack of self-esteem to deem my question unworthy.

Miscommunication, like the Tenerife disaster, could make problems worse. It made me demand the confidence to ask questions by habit, especially those perceived as "dumb."

I'd get multiple direct messages during regular meetings from people thanking me for asking a "dumb" question because they weren't sure either. Improv gave us the first game plan and kept us open to suggestions, feedback, and criticism. Together, the teams crafted plans that satisfied all requirements of major stakeholders in the incident room. Clear communication made our response times faster. What originated as a lack of confidence and self-esteem to ask these questions ended up helping reduce the collective decision paralysis of an incident response room.

Fighting indecision also happened in my daily life as an AppSec engineer, usually concerning ownership. A bug bounty report came through, was confirmed, and off I was to hunt down the responsible team. The endpoint should have been owned by another microservice but was currently sitting in the wrong codebase. The engineer smugly told me that I should make the other team fix it, but the other team wasn't claiming it either. Annoyed and impatient, I stated that the vulnerability was already exploited, that it was an active embarrassment to the brand. If nobody owned it, we should just delete it. The engineer quickly called in the product manager, and magically coding a resolution to the vulnerability was prioritized.

This inspired me to use a lot of wild suggestions to force people to make a decision. It's like using a coin toss when you can't decide; whichever side you're hoping for is probably your answer. In all seriousness, telling someone to delete it would get somebody fired, but it forced them to think about how important it really was. Did we have to keep it? Who actually gets fired if we follow through with Carla's wild suggestion? Well, I have my reason to ask to delete it; something's already gone wrong if the security person has to come hunting. Suddenly the responsible party emerges, and the issue is prioritized. This slightly evil technique has resolved so many related abandon-ware issues. I dislike that it's effective, and I can empathize with their decision paralysis. I back up my priorities with a transparent triage system since, again, data is key.

Miscommunication Due to Hubris

Landing a plane is arguably one of the most dangerous moments during a flight. Ever wonder why they ask you to put away your devices? Your chances of escaping after a crash are higher if you're not distracted and ready to take orders from the flight attendants. Commercial flights have at least two pilots, and if either pilot deems the situation unsafe during a landing, the plane is supposed to give up, climb and attempt the landing again. This is called a "go around." The Asiana Airlines 214 crash in San Francisco concluded that ultimately, 1.5 seconds before the crash, a co-pilot requested a go-around, but it was too late.[9] The NTSB's investigation determined that someone perceived the plane was too low and slow before the call to go around, ultimately causing the plane to crash into the sea wall at SFO. The investigation concluded that the automatic flight system was ultimately at fault. However (and this is purely speculation on my part), given that the plane was visibly not set up to execute a safe landing, did power dynamics in the crew play into how delayed the request was to go around?

Growing up Asian, it's fairly common to be perceived as disrespectful if you question your elders or seniors. This is commonly observed in a lot of cultures, including those of the pilots. Did an inability to question a superior or captain delay a junior person from speaking up in time? NTSB's recreation of the event shows that the aircraft was far too low and slow, a dangerous combination when landing, when approaching the airport, for around a full minute of time.[10] If the aircraft was in danger for that long and if a go around in the last few seconds was never going to be successful, why didn't anybody speak up sooner? In another incident in 1997, a jet crashed into terrain on approach into Guam due in part to incorrectly flying a low visibility instrument approach into the airport; though the first officer and flight engineer requested they abort, they only did so six seconds before the ultimate crash.[11] Again, why didn't anybody speak up sooner?

---

9   Accident Report: Asiana Airlines Flight 214. (2014, June 24). NTSB. www.ntsb.gov/investigations/AccidentReports/Reports/AAR1401.pdf
10 KPIX CBS SF Bay Area. (2014, June 24). NTSB Animation Details Asiana Flight 214 Crash. YouTube. www.youtube.com/watch?v=baLL8N-d4xE
11 Accident Report: Korean Air Flight 801. NTSB. www.ntsb.gov/investigations/AccidentReports/Reports/AAR0001.pdf

Throughout my life, I never fit the mold of a skinny, smart, focused, quiet Asian girl. By the time I was leading IR, I knew that I was never going to, and started to embrace just how differently I thought and acted. Over Zoom, working with EMEA hours in the bay area, and especially during the pandemic, I quickly learned to wait 13 awkward seconds in case somebody had a thought or was blocked by internet delays. I always wanted to make sure that everyone has a chance to talk, either live, through direct message, or through an anonymous survey. I don't need to be right to see to the end of an incident. Anybody can question our approach, and we can change it or explain it to satisfy all criteria and concerns. I can live with myself knowing that I do not need to steamroll others to get the job done. Every time somebody starts a question with "this may be a dumb question", it's usually the only time I'll interrupt. I'll tell them there's no such thing as a dumb question in my incident rooms. Allowing all questions builds a psychological safety net in the incident room, while reducing miscommunication, misunderstandings, and mistakes.

I'm so lucky that my lessons are not written in blood. I do hope that the lives lost reinforces the lesson of the go-around rule: any pilot in the cockpit is permitted to question a landing, regardless of their seniority.

Sadly, speculation about the power dynamics in the cockpit brings in another concern– the Bystander effect.[12] There are so many people in this situation, surely somebody else will do something. (On Asiana 214, there were 4 pilots in the cockpit). When we expanded IR to train up other IMOCs, my very first piece of advice is to actively battle the bystander effect. In my first few situation rooms, I presumed that everybody would know what they needed to do, I didn't really need to direct people. What I saw, unfortunately, was that people were lost. The bystander effect was happening in my 8th-grade science classroom, and I speculate that the same thing happened in Asiana 214's cockpit. There are so many of us; surely somebody will bring it up, somebody will do something.

My impatience impulsively puts me in the spotlight to start leading. I've been told many times that I'm a natural leader (which I dislike), but it gets

---

12 Hudson, J. M. & Bruckman, A. S. (2004). The bystander effect: A lens for understanding patterns of participation. Journal of the Learning Sciences, 13(2), 165-195. https://doi.org/10.1207/ s15327809jls1302_2

things going, lowers response time, keeps me sane, and at least satisfied that I did what I could. Those 13 seconds waiting on Zoom were painful every time, but as soon as somebody piped up, or they passed without concern, I knew that I was giving space to the people helping me resolve the issue at hand.

Blameless Post Mortems and the NTSB

I was accustomed to enduring mood swings in my personal life, but when the pandemic hit, I'd never seen such dead situation rooms. So many people were experiencing depressive symptoms for the first time. I couldn't even be mad. I had gone through this so many times on my own. I'd remind people, "Don't forget to eat", because many times had I accidentally skipped a meal or forgotten meds in a whirlwind of hyperfocus. "This can wait till tomorrow,"; I'd tell the dedicated engineer who was working east coast hours, and it was already 9 o'clock my time on the west coast. How many times had I stayed up all night, hyper-focused and researching obsessively about something because it was the only good, productive thing going on in my head?

Having lived all of the same issues myself without the dark cloud of the pandemic, I could recognize when people were blocked emotionally or by priority. It became a default question to ask, "what's the status, are you blocked by anything?" It also made me recognize when folks were making bad decisions based on system 1, or their emotions. I could politely prod and question bad takes since I also believe in the golden rule: treat others the way you want to be treated. I had a lifetime of rejection-sensitive dysphoria experience to arm me with the emotional sensitivity to do it right. Whenever people apologize to me for rescheduling, if the reason is health or kids, I say the same thing every time. Self (which includes family) > health > wealth. It can wait. When folks communicated their blockers to me, I worked to assist, unblock, or find another resource. No computer security incident is worth the sanity of my teammates.

The last thing that the NTSB and my unwitting lessons in emotional empathy taught me was to ensure that post-mortem reports were blameless. Probable cause and hearsay statements from NTSB reports are not admissible in court.[13] Blaming folks is usually unproductive, and the NTSB's ultimate goal above all else is passenger safety. It made me extremely mindful, especially in fear of my own rejection-sensitive dysphoria, that I made sure to never admonish anybody, even in a joking matter, about the source of the root cause. Even folks that admonished themselves for missing it in a pull request, I'd stop and redirect their thoughts. What'll we do differently next time? What can we do to make sure this doesn't happen again? Like my favorite CTO once said, we should never waste a good incident. Git blame, a troubleshooting utility, gave me the exact time that we introduced the vulnerability and nothing else.

Decoupling blame from a postmortem allows us all to absorb the lessons without feeling self-conscious or guilty for mistakes we may have made in the past. A friend of mine previously read a post-mortem about one of his colleagues getting successfully socially engineered for information. He listened to the recording out of curiosity. One day, he answers the phone himself and immediately recognizes the modus operandi of the caller, mimicking the call he heard. His boss is concerned, ready to take over, but my friend is confident. He's got this. Being the beloved troll he is, he strings the social engineer along for a very, very long time before eventually hanging up, giving his department a laugh.

I often quote other news reports of breaches when I convince somebody that something is worth scrutinizing. Learning from history should be uncomfortable, and it should motivate us to trust our pattern recognition and respond in a way that has proven successful. Reading up on history makes me that much better at my response to problem solving, especially during my Incident Response days. I hope to carry forward these lessons so that fewer people have to suffer. Fear, uncertainty, and doubt should never be used in convincing people to do what's necessary for security. History, data, and removing emotion from the situation should clarify what needs to be done. The irony that my excess of emotions made me better at recognizing it in others was weirdly empowering. I have become immune to inappropriately emotional responses. The NTSB has inspired me a lot in conducting myself as an incident manager on call.

---

13 Hofer, S. & Nguyen Worthy, M. (2020, June 30). What information from an NTSB report is admissible evidence in court? JD Supra. www.jdsupra.com/legalnews/what-information-from-an-ntsb-report-is-31087/

Conclusion

Over time, I learned to adapt to my chaotic life. My daily personal and career life is still a struggle, but life's uncertainty optimized my flaws to take it on, even during the deep collective trauma of a pandemic. I hope to honor the sacrifices and lessons learned by those in disaster response: firefighting, aviation, FEMA, and the like. I have learned ways of problem-solving; they don't have to be chaotic, even if I am.

ABOUT CARLA SUN

Carla Sun is a Security Engineer with the Product Security Team at Gusto. She was previously a Security Incident Response Lead at her former employer. Prior to that, she was an Application Security Engineer and Quality Assurance Engineer.

Carla's brain chooses to fixate on learning from history and to apply these lessons to daily life, whether it is to prevent web application security vulnerabilities or to protect her houseplants from her cat. She is a lifelong bay area resident. Her random musings can be found at twitter.com/crapcarlasays

For the Love of
Frameworks: Creating
Relevant, Reusable
Patterns for Security

For the Love of Frameworks: Creating Relevant, Reusable Patterns for Security

by Lonye Ford

For the Love of Frameworks: Creating Relevant, Reusable Patterns for Security

Lonye Ford

Security has changed a lot since I got my start as a 19-year-old. Cyber was anything but sexy back then. Nobody was inviting us to write books or speak on any platforms. They didn't even want to see our faces—we were the 'NO' team. It's a different story now, of course. People get how vital security is to the business, creating safe ways to work without putting the organization in danger.

Cyber careers have also morphed drastically in recent years, evolving into many different skill specialties. Today, saying you want to go into cyber-security is like saying you want to be a doctor. *What type of doctor? A brain surgeon? A dermatologist? A dentist?* Cyber is the same way: Are you assess-ing the security of the cloud environment? Are you focusing on how we protect our water systems or the orbits of our satellites? And the world itself has morphed alongside cyber, especially with the rise of the Internet of Things (IoT). When everything is connected, everything needs to be secure. Because of this, cybersecurity is what I would call a hybrid career field. It's a field where you must have domain expertise then overlay the security perspective. Just as much as your dermatologist isn't the correct expert to perform brain surgery, your cyber expert developing policy isn't the appropriate person to run your pen tests.

As the CEO of Arlo Solutions, I help defense-sector organizations create new strategies to assess, authorize, and review cybersecurity risk to the information systems and organizations. It's an exciting place to be, solving entirely new problems no one has tried before, such as: *How do you assess the security of an unmanned aerial surveillance drone? How do I assess data/code traversing the cloud network to a fighter jet?* My answer: you use a framework.

In a cybersecurity landscape that's constantly changing, I believe that it is critically important to create comprehensive, scalable frameworks for risk management. You could say that I'm a frameworks junkie. While compliance gets a bad name sometimes, the fact is that safe and repeatable processes save lives in government and many other sectors. Whenever aviators go into an airplane, they go through a checklist: *Do I have everything I need in my flight jacket? Have I gone through all my safety checks? Am I ready to take to the sky?* The agencies I work with must focus on a variety of laws, policies, and regulations, but they also need to be able to share information. A checklist—or a framework—can help them balance those requirements to combine innovation with safety.

My work energizes me to create new patterns for risk management in emerging spaces and by the opportunity to have a tangible impact on the security of these organizations.

My Cybersecurity Journey—From the South Side to the U.S. Air Force to the Corner Office

Two very different environments have shaped my life and career. The first is the South Side of Chicago. I'm proud of my roots in this predominantly black neighborhood, but I'm also conscious of my lack of exposure to successful women of color in business and politics. Without role models like these, you can become less aware of the possibilities for your future. Still, it was comforting to be around people who looked like me, spoke like me, moved like me, and listened to the same music. That changed a lot with the next step in my journey: the U.S. Air Force (USAF).

I grew up in Chicago, but the Air Force helped raise me. My first duty station was this crazy place called Aviano, Italy. I was such an anomaly there. At the same time, it showed me just how small my tiny portion of the world had been. Exposure to other people and things opened my mind; it helped give me the resiliency and determination to be successful. As a veteran, I'm so proud and grateful for the role of this organization in my life.

My Air Force service began on the help desk. No offense to help desk technicians, but this is truly starting at the bottom, and that's a fantastic place to be. You gain experience and visibility across the gamut. As a service-oriented person, I like to help people in every capacity, so I loved that kind of work. It also led to my first leadership role at age 21, leading a 24/7 help desk operation servicing 7,000 customers. Over time, I expanded into system administrator and network administrator tasks—at one point, I was a cable dog, pulling CAT5 (cable for computer computer networks) through buildings—and then got my start in a cybersecurity role for program offices within the Air Force Intelligence community.

After getting all this valuable cybersecurity training in the Air Force, I decided I wanted to get into the retail space and became the general manager of a Sears department store when I returned home to Chicago. I have tremendous respect for people who start in professions like retail and I was still finding my way through the transition back to civilian life, but retail at that level was not for me. Next up was banking, but it wasn't as comfortable a fit for me. The military instills the mindset that your success is based on the mission's success, which conflicted with the banking industry's intense monetary focus.

Finally, I landed in defense. I moved to the Washington, DC area, took a job with the Defense Information Systems Agency (DISA), and supported government contracts with the U.S. Department of Defense (DoD) CIO, the U.S. Army CIO, and the U.S. Air Force CIO. As my career progressed, the time came to start my own business.

I had been doing club promotions on the side in the greater Washington, DC area. My partner in that business thought I would hit it off with his wife, so he introduced us. He was right. A week after we met, we had combined our names, Arlene and Lonye, into "ARLO" and had the name for our new company: Arlo Solutions, LLC. The rest is lightning in a bottle. Today, Arlo offers intelligence, cybersecurity, program management, and strategic communication solutions to the U.S. government. In August 2021, we were listed at #153 on the Inc. 5000 annual listing of the nation's fastest-growing private companies. In February 2022, we were named to Inc. Magazine's Annual Vet100 list of the nation's fastest-growing veteran-owned and veteran-operated businesses.

Frameworks: The Foundation for a Healthy Risk Approach

After starting with a technical focus, my cyber career has progressed toward risk management, frameworks, and systems assessment. I have supported the Department of Defense through multiple cybersecurity assessment and authorization frameworks. I started my framework support with the DoD Defense Information Technology Security Certification and Accreditation Program (DITSCAP), then the DoD Information Assurance Certification and Accreditation Process (DIACAP) and more recently the National Institute of Standards and Technology (NIST) Risk Management Framework (RMF).

Once I was introduced into the world of NIST cybersecurity standards, guidelines, and best practices, I was hooked! What an amazing body of work, did I say I was hooked? Now, coupled with my extensive experience in conducting assessment and authorizations for the DoD and the NIST Standards, I went to work on producing streamlined methodology to implementing Risk Management specifically to the agencies I supported. For example, I lead the authoring of the Air Force Fast Track process which is a methodology used to grant an Authority to Operate (ATO). This process was developed to significantly reduce the timeline to authorization and get crucial capabilities to the Air Force's warfighter faster. Arlo Solutions brought that vision to life by leading the development of the details, processes and guides that would make up this process. More than one year later, the Fast Track ATO process is the primary risk management mechanism for IT and cybersecurity acquisitions for the USAF. This was the first time, that I am aware of, we integrated the assessment of the technology in an operation relevant environment within the assess and authorize process. The Fast Track ATO process allows cybersecurity leaders the discretion to make an authorization decision based on review of a combination of a Cybersecurity Baseline, an Operational Assessment (e.g., Penetration Testing) and an Information Systems Continuous Monitoring

Strategy. The goal of the Fast Track ATO processes is to facilitate operationally informed risk decisions versus decisions based only on compliance checks. The success of the Fast Track ATO process is transforming the USAF's risk management process by fostering risk-based decision making based on operationally relevant assessments. Obtaining new technology no longer requires seemingly endless paperwork and up to a year of time.

The foundation of the Fast Track process is based on the NIST RMF standards. So, I guess you can say I stand on the shoulder of giants. I'm not developing these streamlined approaches to assessing risk from ground zero, but from the collaboration of stakeholders across academia, government and private sector via NIST engagement.

Collaboration is a crucial part of developing frameworks and cybersecurity in general. Security can't work in a silo; it requires a lot of research and talking to many people. My current focus is on DevSecOps and creating repeatable processes for assessing and authorizing code in rapidly changing environments, including code transitioning over to the aircraft. *When we start talking about Dev, Sec, and Ops, guess what?* That means I need to develop something beneficial for all those different perspectives. This is challenging because we've worked too long in our silo to communicate well with the organization. We need to learn to evaluate a business case versus just saying no to something.

When I develop a framework, my goal is to also develop guides, templates, procedures from multiple different perspectives... develop a holistic approach. The goal is to have the appropriate data in order to facilitate decision making from senior leadership. I also want to ensure that the individuals responsible for conducting the assessment have what he/she needs in order to provide risk based recommendations. I also ensure that the developers understand the security requirements as well as statutory requirements that will need to be implemented in order to be accepted on to the larger enterprise. In other words, I have to translate from English to Spanish, to French and Amharic (figuratively speaking). I take a cradle-to-grave approach. Sometimes, I feel like I'm an artist and I'm going into the booth to create this masterpiece. It truly lights me up—it's my rap over a dope beat—and I love it!

What's Next for Our Industry

As I look at the industry, it excites me that people now respect the importance of cybersecurity to the business and recognize security risk as part of business risk. It was often challenging to get decision makers to understand this in the past. This might have been due to cybersecurity teams focusing too much on saying no, which shut down conversations or sent them in unhelpful directions. In reality, "no" isn't always the most secure choice—especially when compelling business needs force a "yes" anyway, even an insecure one. The better answer is yes, but...

Now that security is more integrated into the business, the strategic question is how to enable change securely. Senior business leaders need help making risk-based decisions. Integrating developers, ops personnel, and decision-makers to create policies and thresholds is a complicated landscape. Frameworks help by providing a context to navigate those choices with a full understanding of their implications.

I'm an optimistic person in general, so I'm proud of what the government is trying to do in cyber. It's incredibly difficult to change the culture and align the government with industry standards all while complying with mandates and laws. We need to create frameworks that mesh with a long list of compliance regulations in our highly integrated world. We can move, change, and evolve faster without getting into trouble with clearly defined processes in place. Better GovSec makes better government innovation possible with better service for the people. As a service-oriented person, that has always been my goal.

The Future for Rising Leaders

Despite what you might hear, entrepreneurship is definitely not glamorous. For the first four years in business, Arlene and I didn't pay ourselves. It takes a certain level of obsession to become successful, and your motivation has to be something more than just money. If you're just in it to get rich, you'll give up on it as soon as you think of an easier way to do that. You need a foundation of doggedness: no one stops you until you reach your goal, and you learn every lesson along the way. We never had a "plan B" because total failure was never an option.

Don't get me wrong, we failed often, but we recovered fast and used those failures as learning lessons.

As a successful woman entrepreneur in cybersecurity, it's important for me to acknowledge the implications of identity in our field. Still, it doesn't come naturally to me to talk about myself in those terms. When you come up in the government, you don't necessarily talk about your differences. You don't talk about sex, race, religion, or color. You talk about your knowledge, skills, and ability. Instead of highlighting me as a woman, highlight me as a cybersecurity expert.

At the same time, people who did not fit the traditional profile of a cybersecurity professional needed to conform to fit in for a long time. There's real value in leaning into you and what you can bring to the table. I owe a lot to the male leaders I've learned from, who have given me opportunities by making room at the table. But as a woman leader or entrepreneur, don't try to lead like the man leads. You lead how you lead; that might mean being softer, more of a collaborator, or a caregiver.

Success comes down to knowing what you're doing and building the right team. As you're building your career, take every opportunity to put yourself in situations that make you uncomfortable and take every opportunity to collaborate. If you get a seat at the table, open your mouth and talk. Nobody did you a favor inviting you there—you earned it because of your hard work and expertise. You deserve to be there. Know it and own it.

ABOUT LONYE NICOLE FORD

Lonye Nicole Ford is co-founder and Chief Executive Officer at Arlo Solutions, LLC located in Washington, DC. Arlo offers Intelligence, Cybersecurity, and a full range of cutting-edge Program Management and Strategic Communication solutions to the United States Government.

With over ten years of duty in the United States Air Force, Lonye acquired both love and expertise in Cybersecurity and Information Assurance. Her career began as an Information Technology Specialist, including her first leadership role at age 21, leading a 24/7 help desk operation servicing 7,000 customers.

As a government contractor for 20+ years, Lonye led large teams and managed projects and portfolios ranging from $2M to $1.5B. She developed a myriad of innovative solutions and policies that were implemented at the highest level in the government, including co-authoring the Air Force Fast Track Risk Management Framework (RMF) process and assessing, developing, and streamlining the United States Department of Agriculture RMF process.

Lonye holds a Master of Business Administration degree and maintains a CISSP certification. She also supports underprivileged communities in the Washington, DC, and Chicago metropolitan areas and partners with UrbanPromise, a nonprofit youth organization in Camden, NJ. She aspires one day to organize her own legacy nonprofit.

CHAPTER 6

Teaching is a Shared Responsibility

by Dr. Meg Layton

Teaching is a Shared Responsibility

Dr. Meg Layton

Pulling Back the Curtain

There is a misconception about cybersecurity — some even say a myth—that cybersecurity is hard. Cybersecurity is some black magic that only the wisest programming wizards understand, or only for the solitary hacker in the basement shut off from all humanity. The reality, however, is far different and cybersecurity as a concept is not particularly difficult to grasp. Security is based on human concepts such as trust, confidentiality, integrity, and risk. Cybersecurity is at the center of the human connection to technology in sharing these human concepts. This unites everyone and allows people to talk about cybersecurity with a level of empathy. Everyone has experienced issues of trust or confidentiality when it comes to technology.

In the OWASP Testing Guide v4 foreword, Eoin Keary famously warns that "security should not be a black art or closed secret that only a few can practice."[1] OWASP (Open Web Application Security Project) is an online community known for freely-available methodologies, tools, and documentation about Web Application Security. It's notable that a member of the OWASP global board is making security more approachable and encouraging developers to know and understand security secrets. As technology becomes more ubiquitous and available to people, the mystery surrounding "the cybers" falls away, and the concept of security as a shared responsibility gains ground. "Security is everyone's responsibility"

---

1   Keary, E. (2015, July 29). Foreword, Testing Guide 4.0 - Release (4th ed.). OWASP.

becomes a mantra that many can relate to as cloud computing is widely adopted and the C-Suite expands with defined CISO roles.

Dorm Security

Let's use the example of "dorm security" to illustrate how security is a concept of shared responsibility. When you are at home, you are responsible for your own security. Whether you leave the door open or lock the deadbolt, the only impact is to you. Your computer is your responsibility. Choosing to use a password or not protect your internet access point is an individual choice.

In comparison, you'll find that the doors are locked at a college dorm unless you have the key to access. Your security now depends on you and everyone else in the dorm, with the key to the front door. If you decide to prop the door open for pizza delivery, you risk yourself and everyone else in the dorm. The control of security has been expanded in that you have been entrusted with their safety and your own. This is comparable to the responsibilities users have on a shared network, such as a corporate or university environment. If you "leave a door open" by circumventing security controls, you have the potential to impact the entire corporate environment. Being secure ultimately depends on fundamental human relationships and trust rather than physical controls to make the environment secure.

In 2018, the National Institute of Standards and Technology (NIST) published a booklet entitled *Cybersecurity is Everyone's Job* as part of the initiatives in the National Initiative for Cybersecurity Education (NICE) Working Group.[2] In simple terms intended for a general audience, it guides organizational departments and functions in what measures and controls they can influence and what actions they can take to make the organization more secure. The opening line in the introduction states, "We are the greatest vulnerability in any organization" and urges everyone to take shared responsibility for security. The booklet compares the responsibility of cyber hygiene to that of public health; as one should wash their

---

2 Uenuma, M., Cone, S., Judge, K., Jarrin, P., Mastro, R., & Woskov, S. (2018, October 15). Workforce Management Guidebook. NIST. nist.gov/itl/applied-cybersecurity/nice/workforce-management-guidebook

hands, one should be responsible for cybersecurity. The booklet stresses that although technology and talented individuals are essential, the organization "cannot be secure without all individuals doing their part, across all business functions, technical and non-technical."

It is important to realize that the business of securing the organization extends beyond the technical team and includes items an organization depends on, such as software. How can the shared understanding of security as a critical component be extended to learning to ensure a shared responsibility throughout an organization?

Exploring the Kolb Learning Model

Exploring learning models and learning loops helps to understand some of the challenges of building shared security responsibility. It is generally accepted in learning style theory that individuals may prefer different learning strategies and these influence how effective learning is, as well as how comfortable they are when learning occurs. In a learning style model made popular in the 1980s, Kolb explored how a person processes information.[3] Kolb explored factors of perception, such as concrete experience or abstract conceptualization, and information processing by active experimentation and reflective observation. Kolb identified learning style groups and learning modes, leveraging how discussions, analysis, experimentation, and theory all influence how we learn.

The four learning stages identified are Concrete Experience, Reflective Observation, Abstract Conceptualization, and Active Experimentation (Kolb, 1985).[4] Kolb further identifies four learning styles: divergent, assimilators, convergers, and accommodators. The definitions of the style most preferred correspond to how comfortable learners are. Kolb's theories further posit that individuals should progress through all four stages in learning fully. John Dewey's claim that learning must be grounded in experience is at the heart of Kolb's learning cycle. The theories say the way we learn

---

3   Kolb, D. A. (1984). Experiential Learning: Experience as the Source of Learning and Development (1st ed.). Prentice-Hall..

4   Harb, J. N., Durrant, S. O., & Terry, R. E. (1993). Use of the Kolb Learning Cycle and the 4MAT System in Engineering Education. Journal of Engineering Education, 82(2), 70-77. doi. org/10.1002/j.2168-9830.1993.tb00079.x

best is to incorporate how we do things with how we think about things. While not everyone will learn best with exactly the same exploration of these facets, incorporating these facets into learning experiences can be vital to ensuring continued learning. The individual's learning style affects the organization's knowledge and influences effective continuous learning. Understanding these learning models and theories can ensure that the message of accountability for security is delivered effectively.

Kolb Learning Styles

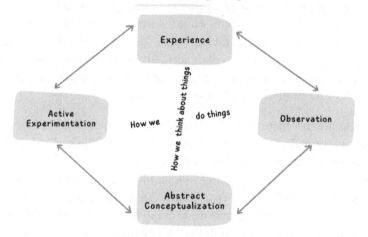

"Security is everyone's responsibility" is especially valid for the secure development lifecycle. Some estimates indicate that insecure coding causes close to 80 percent of security vulnerabilities. Many curricula remain focused on the technical traits of coding and don't spend enough time teaching developers to think through the potential implications of insecure code. Security vulnerabilities can be costlier than traditional software bugs to fix or even discover. This trend is likely to continue with the explosion of digital sensitive data or personally identifiable information. With the potential of significant ramifications with broad impact, why is security often not a developer's first concern?

Expanding the Developer Mindset

There are a couple of reasons why security is not at the forefront of a developer's mind. The first is the shroud of mystery that often surrounds cybersecurity. The thought follows that if it is hard to do, it is also hard to take the step for protection. In conversation with a developer trying to explain how important it was to ensure appropriate protections, I was explaining why it was important. I explained using a simple hack as an example, although I explained it in manual terms. (I would explain about password cracking using brute-force. Attackers would use multiple passwords against the same username to access a system.) I remember the developer asking me, "That is so hard; why would anyone do that?" He did not seem to grasp that while we explain the hacks in manual terms, the tools to automate them are not particularly difficult to find. Many programs use basic concepts, and users do not necessarily need to understand things in-depth to check for issues or flaws in software.

To overcome this mental block, I like to use examples of just how easy it has always been. I explain using an old movie, one of the hacker favorites: *WarGames*. If you're not familiar with this classic from 1983, a young high school student uses his computer to look for a new game prototype and accidentally accesses a U.S. Department of Defense computer, nearly triggering World War III. The movie made many tech enthusiasts more aware of some of the easy access to tools that can disrupt security. There's a great scene in this movie where our hero starts war dialing (using a machine to make calls) to find a machine that will answer his modem. With the insert of a (very large) disk, he types a few numbers for area codes and prefixes and lets the computer do the rest of the work. The viewer can watch as the computer dials and hangs up on different people and businesses like Saul's Fish Market without ever being aware that they are being targeted by technology. He eventually leaves and returns to a printout of possible targets of machines that have talked back to his modem—all after typing a few numbers into his program.

Describing this scene often helps people understand how easy it is to type in a few numbers and let the program do the rest. It also helps illustrate that while maybe war dialing isn't a thing anymore, people are still trying to access systems in ways that probably are unexpected. It also helps to dispel the myth of the ever-changing threat landscape. While the tools and technology may have changed over time, the actual threat has remained the same – the machines have information someone wants – and someone will do their best to get it. In this regard, the threat landscape hasn't changed at all.

The second challenge for a developer is a mindset shift. Developers purpose-build their code to meet a need and function in a specific way. A specific functionality has been requested, and ideally, the code delivers this. It becomes difficult to visualize that the code may be used for something not originally intended. This is one of the reasons that lack of input validation is a common software flaw. With purpose-built applications, the developer thinks, "enter a username here and then X happens," without thinking through secure coding practices. The developer is not considering "what if it's not a username? What if someone enters a recipe for cocktails instead? Or what if they enter a command that means someone should launch a program?" If asked what happens if someone enters something else, developers often reply, "the code wasn't built to do that." It is challenging to conceptualize someone using the code for a different purpose than what was intended. In reality, code is much more of an "if you build it, they will use it" kind of tool. Much of code is repurposed to do something different than originally intended, and developers would benefit from considering other possible applications.

The third reason that security is not at the forefront of a developer's mind is the curriculum. Developers focus on and are rewarded for delivering on functionality, even if it introduces a potential risk. Understanding how to code securely is as important as understanding why it needs to be done. **Secure coding practices during software development cycles are important to ensure security is an everthought, not an afterthought.** While current SDLC practices refer to "shift left" to move security earlier in the development cycle, it should always be present in the mind of the developer. However, injecting it in such a way that the importance is understood and the lesson persists can be challenging.

Case Study

At one point in my career, I managed a team of software developers who were responsible for building a program to be used by incident response teams. The developers were very good at what they did, both on the user interface side and the database developers. What they did not understand was what incident response teams would do with the product. They had read the documentation and knew the use cases and persona— but did not...*understand.*

Once this challenge was identified, I became a training mentor and gathered many of the developers in a room for a week to teach incident handling and some hacking techniques. At the end of the week, a small capture the flag (CTF) was held for the team to see what they could find! As real hands-on training, the developers completed the incident response portion using the product that they were coding. I started the course with a walk-through of customers, then issued a challenge that I could get their personal information in six steps by working through the customer list. This was used to demonstrate that my own data and their own data were impacted by every move that the team made. I wrote in large letters at the front of the class: **Security of your information is my responsibility; security of my information is your responsibility. People that you protect depend on you.** This helped set the tone that what we were about to learn impacted not the "unknown and faceless customer" but could impact someone they knew.

A couple of very memorable moments came from this training experience. The first is our UI team, who came to me on the second day and said to me, "Goodness, our UI sucks. How would someone respond to the situation you just used? We didn't show anything important." Good question. (The next release solved that problem.) The most memorable moment, however, was when I started exploring Structured Query Language (SQL) injection attacks. I tend to walk people through this in three steps: explain what it is, demonstrate why it matters, then how to correct it, and finally let them do it themselves. For the uninitiated, SQL is used to communicate with common relational databases and is used by developers, database administrators, and applications themselves to manage, move and store the data being used by databases around the world. SQL injection is sort of exactly what it sounds like: someone is entering data that the application treats as code (injecting instruction). Essentially, tricking applications into executing unwanted commands. This is an old vulnerability from the 1990s but is still pervasive today. It is in the OWASP list of top 10, although recently has slipped down the list.[5]

The easiest way to show why it matters is with examples, and while SQL injection can be done manually, automated tools like SQLMap can make things happen very quickly in the right environment.[6] For this class, we used the Metasploit modules. Metasploit is a well-known open-source penetration testing framework, and many standard techniques have been automated within the framework to allow for testing quickly.[7] We got to this section right after lunch, and in talking with the development team, I had one of the folks in the front row turn white and leave the room. I followed the developer into the hallway and asked, "Hey, is everything okay?" The developer turned to me and said, "I am fine. But I have to go fix something in the code. Right now. Today." We hadn't gotten to the "how to fix it" part, but this illustrated that the developer already knew how to fix it.

Up until that moment, it was not seen as important enough to stop to fix. By connecting the ease of exploit to the code error and starting with the mission of protection, the mindset shift became clear; security is, without a doubt, the developer's responsibility. The methodology connected how we do things with how we think about things: concrete experience with examples and story, reflective observations with technical tools showing, abstract conceptualization explaining the risks, and active experimentation with hands-on learning and a CTF at the end.

Security is a Shared Responsibility

Accountability and responsibility for security are one of the most important tools we have in securing the environment. Removing the mystery surrounding cybersecurity, making it more accessible, and connecting on the human level can be a game-changer in ensuring that everyone is dedicated

---

5   Top 10 Web Application Security Risks. OWASP. owasp.org/Top10.
6   sqlmap.org
7   metasploit.com

to the same mission. Developers can help by accepting their role in securing software, ensuring security is considered from beginning to end of the SDLC, and taking measures to ensure that they stay up to date on the latest techniques and exploits. Organizations can help by stressing that everyone takes an active role in security, understanding different learning models, and incorporating human connections and stories into their training to ensure that everyone is connected to the mission. Educators can help ensure that the connections are made beyond the technical "here is how to do this" checklist and skills to the human side of the technology and explore security with all four styles of the Kolb models. With everyone connecting and continuing the lessons to allow for lifelong learning, cybersecurity can truly become a shared responsibility by everyone.

Security is a shared responsibility, and that message takes on additional value when you share the learnings within your own community. A community is developed by shared experiences, shared values - and for it to sustain, the community members must be able to contribute as well as draw from resources. As security professionals, it means that to fully participate in the community, we often "get what we give". The further I get in my security career, the more I understand that it is part of my responsibility to ensure security learnings are demystified and more accessible to those that desire to learn more, no matter at what stage of their career the learners have found themselves. When I find something especially inspiring, useful, or have a story about teaching you'll find I use #NextgenInfoSec hashtag on social media - I invite you to join me in sharing your learnings with the community, and sharing the responsibility for bringing up the next generation of security professionals - demystifying the trade, and making security for all a reality.

ABOUT DR. MEG LAYTON

Dr. Margaret Meiman Layton (Meg) is Head of Security Architecture and Engineering for Children's National Hospital. She discovered her passion for security at the height of the dot-com era, while Director of IT for a telecommunications company doing business in Africa.

In 2001, she joined a startup that was acquired by Symantec. Meg was at Symantec for nearly two decades in various roles, most recently Director of Engineering for the Cyber Security Services unit.

Meg has a Doctorate of Information Assurance from University of Fairfax; a Master of Science in Telecommunications and Computing Management from Polytechnic University of New York University; and a Bachelor of Arts in Political Science from Albertus Magnus College. Meg maintains mulltiple certifications, including CSPSS, CSSLP, and GIAC for Incident Handling, Forensic Analysis, and Penetration Testing. She is CNSS 4011 and 4012 certified.

Meg lives in Virginia with her husband and children. She volunteers with Women in Technology, Women in CyberSecurity, and Women's Society of Cyberjutsu. Meg is also a Technical Mentor for CyberPatriots, a scouting badge counselor, and an Adjunct College Professor of Information Security, Computer Forensics, and Risk Assessment. You can find her on Twitter @vamegabyte

Tearing Down
and Retraining
Muscle Memory

CHAPTER 7

Tearing Down
and Retraining
Muscle Memory

by Tracy Bannon

Tearing Down and Retraining Muscle Memory

Tracy Bannon

Raging Against Muscle Memory!

If you Google "muscle memory", .56 seconds later you will get a listing of "about 63,900,000" entries. Scrolling through just the first page gives two distinctive opinions. The first is muscle memory is important to reduce decision-making time; the second is it takes at least 3-6 months to break muscle memory.

What does this have to do with changing the way we approach cybersecurity? Muscle memory exists in every organization and has the potential to help or greatly hurt a team's effectiveness. Let's start by defining muscle memory: **"the ability to repeat a specific muscular movement with improved efficiency and accuracy that is acquired through practice and repetition"** [1]

Living with a soccer coach means I'm exposed to training and athletic speak every day.

My role with any client, sponsor, or organization generally lasts less than 3 years. I am not a CISO, rather I am a chief architect and software engineering leader keenly aware of the foundational role of cyber security and resiliency. With each new client, my first step is situational awareness and

---

1   Merriam-Webster. Muscle memory. merriam-webster.com/dictionary/muscle%20memory

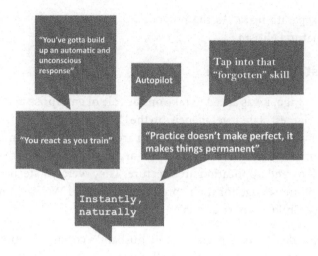

understanding the capabilities, instincts, and relationships of the group or situation. It is similar to starting a new high school soccer season and meeting this year's players. The time starts with intros, a few stories, and banter to get a feel for personalities and understand if anyone has played together before, then break out into a few small-sided games. The coach is looking for muscle memory and if it needs to be retrained.

Trust as a Foundation

I consistently find the biggest obstacle to addressing cyber resilience is not technical, but rather a lack of trust. While there are many technical challenges, organizations where a pervasive sense of trust exists fare much better.

My career as a software architect and engineer requires that I am keenly aware of the security needs and requirements of my clients. I have spent years focused on solving complex government challenges with software that involves private and sensitive information about taxpayers, the health and wellbeing of children enrolled in enabling government programs, and data that help our warfighters protect us as a nation.

While there are many policies and stakeholder-related security requirements, the pattern I repeatedly encounter is that cyber security is carved off as a separate team. As the proverbial protectors of the castle, there exists a natural elitism.

The First Day of Practice

A few years ago, I was asked to take on the role of enterprise architect for one of the largest state-level agencies in the US. The architecture leadership team was already in place, including 10 architects with varying specialties: information architecture, database architecture, enterprise services architecture, and application architecture. They were all steeped deeply in domain knowledge for their "product line": Child Welfare, Integrated Eligibility, Child Support, and so on.

On my first day, I took a page from my husband's coaching approach and started with intros, stories, and small-side games. I brought together the architects and the senior engineers to get to know them, their superpowers and to understand their products and lines of business.

From a title and specialty perspective, it was quite a diverse group gathered around the conference room: data and database architect, infrastructure architect, network engineer, middleware engineering lead, application architect, performance testing leader, enterprise services operations, and even document management subsystem engineer.

Missing from the table was anyone focused on security. Maybe some of these guys are "T-shaped" I wondered? The gaggle of tech pros discussed their roles and how their teams operated. As the conversation progressed, it became obvious that the organization was comprised of rugged individualists with their own approaches and language. I was stepping in to lead a colony of cowboys.

"T-shaped" means having a mix of breadth and depth allowing for more horizontal collaboration and sharing than traditional "depth only" specialists.[2]

---

2   Howard, C., & Chansler, G. (2015, February 9). Fitting to the T. IT Briefcase. itbriefcase.net/fitting-to-the-t

What does it mean to be T-shaped?

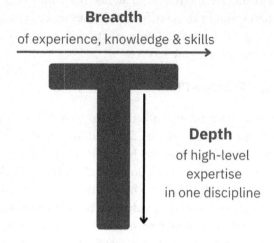

Breadth
of experience, knowledge & skills

Depth
of high-level
expertise
in one discipline

I felt like I was watching an international soccer team made of individual star players. These stars could occasionally pass to one another, but usually, they were concerned about moving the ball to goal themselves.

Observations: Skills, Alliances, and Elitism

The credentials of my team were impressive and included academic degrees, certifications from industry, corporate awards, and time served. There is some merit to understanding the journey of the individuals, though ultimately a team is defined as an interdependent group of individuals working together to achieve a goal.[3] In getting to know the individuals, there were definitely excellent individual skills.

I could spot the alliances right away, guys who had shared war stories from over their many, many years together. Their familiarity with one another could masquerade as trust. This group did not operate as a unified team; they operated as a loose federation of individuals lacking a common goal and shared mission.

---

3   Thompson, L. L. (2007). Making the Team: A Guide for Managers (3rd ed.). Pearson..

Missing from the room was cybersecurity. Over the years, the cybersecurity group became more and more insulated and isolated. Their funding and their corporate sponsorship had taken a different approach by funding constant training and certifications. They met as a group, wrote whitepapers, and published mandatory edicts and standards. In essence, they had their own private-club jerseys.

Preseason Practice Plan

Leading means mentoring and coaching. I sat down for dinner with my husband (who is an Ops guy by day) to draft out an initial practice plan. Any coach will tell you that you hope for and envision an undefeated season, and you start with the foundational building blocks. My team did not have all the skills needed. The security organization needed to be at the table; security needed to **voluntarily join the team**. Our organization needed to have a **shared mission**. That mission needed to be defined using a **common language** to help set shared expectations. These rugged individuals needed to have a sense that we were part of the same team. We needed to build trust with one another and with me.

Extending an Invitation

The distancing and regimented separation of the cybersecurity pros has always rubbed me the wrong way. Why? Am I anti-specialization? No; I am totally in favor of individuals choosing to dive deep and be the resident expert. Do I want exclusive ownership? No; I want reasonable shared responsibility. You see, I'm not a typical architect and I don't fit the profile of a typical software engineer.

I have always sought shared knowledge, shared responsibility, and having complete visibility and understanding of all aspects of any product, solution, or digital platform that we design, deliver and operate. Add in that I thrive on building a sense of community, and you have a sense of why my approach to cyber has raised eyebrows and caused turf wars.

I spent time with the leaders and mid-level pros from the security team and was able to make the case for them to "help the architects and the delivery teams". While it was true that help was needed from the security team, the time was not right to make formal changes to add security directly to the architecture group... at least not yet. Security would be in the room as we recalibrated.

The Shared Mission

It's ironic that we all make fun of mottos and mission statements that became trendy in the late 1980s. However, the techniques for crafting mission statements sow the seeds for buy-in, inspiration, and a common language.

Taking into consideration this government agency's imperative and legal charter, I rallied the team together to define a plausible and attainable mission statement aligned to the agency's mission. This was not without eye-rolls and murmurs of "more touchy-feely crap." Keeping focus on the task, we spend a morning together defining our purpose, our values, and our goals. Many of the individuals I've met during my career have been drawn to work with the government because of their values and the core purpose of the agency. The hours can be long and the pay does not always keep pace with our cousins in the commercial space.

As we started to openly discuss why we were drawn to that agency and that team, some core elements and emotions surfaced. This agency has the responsibility to find and protect abused children in need of effective child protective services to prevent any further suffering. It was also immersed in providing rehabilitative services to children and parents to restore the integrity of family life.

That is what we were called to do! Each of us had a shared responsibility to align business agility with technical agility to protect children and restore families. Can you think of another domain with such a need to secure data and have cyber-resilient solutions supporting the agency?

A Common Language

After a few more days of quiet and inquisitive observation, it was time to pull the team together and establish our definitions and language. I often start by collaboratively laying out a common set of definitions, the rationale, and the impacts. The first step is checking if the organization has existing definitions or if there are corporate policy or statutory regulations that define some terms and procedures. Often, policy or corporate definitions are focused on siloed assignment of responsibility. This reflects the slow evolution from waterfall to agile, or worse, reflects the organizational structure.

This phenomenon of codifying an organization's structure in the processes and the resulting software is often called Conway's law, taken from Melvin Conway's description written in 1968: "Any organization that designs a system (defined broadly) will produce a design whose structure is a copy of the organization's communication structure."[4]

With markers and post-it notes in hand, we began to map out the existing structure and called out the historic context for how it had evolved. Coupled with our wonderful shared mission, the initial posturing began to break down. We laid out clear and succinct definitions of agile laying flat that there was no one on the team that defined it the same way. We did not prescribe the brand of agile or any named methodology. The focus was on core values of the agile manifesto.[5] It was not without heated debate that continued to highlight the depths of the lack of trust. It did, however, provide honest dialog and considerations for valuing the left more, but not ignoring the items on the right.

More Value		Less Value
Individuals and interactions	over	Processes and tools
Working software	over	Comprehensive documentation
Customer collaboration	over	Contract negotiation
Responding to change	over	Following a plan

DevSecOps Fireworks

The next term to address was DevSecOps; this is where the fireworks began and justifiably so. DevOps is not simply "Development + Operations", nor is it simply "Development + Security + Operations". These terms carry across people, processes, technology, and culture. They are foundational

---

4 Conway, M. E. (1968, April). How Do Committees Invent? Datamation. melconway.com/Home/ Committees_Paper.html

5 Beck, K., Beedle, M., van Bennekum, A., Cockburn, A., Cunningham, W., Fowler, M., Martin, R. C., Mellor, S., Thomas, D., Grenning, J., Highsmith, J., Hunt, A., Jeffries, R., Kern, J., Marick, B., Schwaber, K., & Sutherland, J. (2021, August 10). Manifesto for Agile Software Development. Agile Alliance. agilealliance.org/agile101/the-agile-manifesto/

to emerging digital transformation for software and software-intensive offerings.

Most of the team had wildly different definitions and very limited experience with DevSecOps. Generally, their experience was on applying some time-saving automation to their slice of the software development lifecycle. As an organization they had struggled to implement what you could call a pipeline, falling back to the muscle memory of deployment checklists, scans, and putting the quality assurance (aka testing team) in the cross-hairs for any defects.

I put on my architect's hat to drive and started by exposing the current state (the baseline), then working on a reasonable target vision. I also asked everyone to take 30 minutes before lunch to sketch, draw, or copy a DevSecOps image that spoke to them personally. We would share these over a working lunch as inputs to crafting a succinct shared definition.

Driving ownership of the definition means we did not adopt any one suggestion. We started as simply as possible with the "ole infinity loop" drawn on the whiteboard. Together we discussed how all the humans in the process should think about and react to each of the chevrons. We also needed to create our own shared understanding of where and how security fits into modern software engineering.

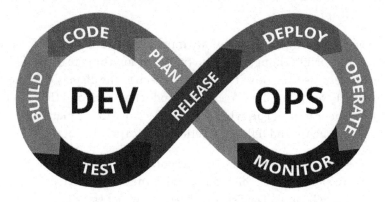

Basic DevOps infinity loop as a starter template[6] [7]

6   DevOps. Office of the Chief Software Officer, U.S Air Force. software.af.mil/training/devops/.
7   Nichols, B. (2021, March 29). The Current State of DevSecOps Metrics. Carnegie Mellon University SEI. insights.sei.cmu.edu/blog/the-current-state-of-devsecops-metrics/

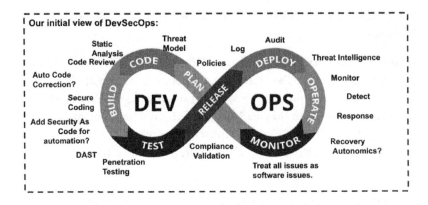

A sketch of our initial ideas for adding security to DevOps concepts

Who Is Responsible for Security?

The tension and tug-of-war opinions during our discussions on security highlighted that there was universal concern about security. This was a +1 situation, everyone is concerned about security. I breathed a sigh of relief. The discussion also highlighted there are differing opinions on who has responsibility for a holistic cyber security and resiliency culture.

Who is responsible for security? My immediate gut instinct is to shout out "EVERYONE!", though I don't actually say anything to start. If I had immediately asserted this, it would have been to the dismay of some on the security team, the developers, the product owners, and those living in "the cyber castle". (The cyber castle is the ivory tower metaphor that is heavy in theory and light in practical application and action.)

The assertion that cyber is shared responsibility is becoming a more familiar response across the industry with the rise of DevOps concepts and its doppelgänger, DevSecOps. These approaches bring with them excellent patterns and practices that need substantial rigor and learning. At the heart of DevSecOps is constant feedback and the ability to respond quickly to discoveries, situations, requested or necessary changes. This type of rapid response requires a team that shares the same mission, can see risk and take bold action, speaks the same language, and inherently trusts one another. (Sounds like an emergency response team or perhaps a soccer team, doesn't it?)

Ultimately I believe security is a child of quality and it is a quality attribute. You may be familiar with the calling quality attributes the "-ilities". The origins of this definition are my training with Carnegie Mellon's Software Engineering Institute (SEI).[8] From that perspective, I've found the definition of quality attributes and ruthlessly prioritizing them another mechanism to drive cyber wholeness, regardless of the type of software or methodology being used. Quality includes both the features that delight and engage the end-users, as well as keeping the users, the enterprise, and all data safe.

As part of our ongoing discussions and ideation, it's important to gain agreement on this concept as well. Can you claim to have a quality service that meets mission objectives and user expectations without a holistic cyber mindset? Clearly not, and we needed to build those collective relationships and opinions so we could move from ideas to actions.

Why Are You Spending Precious Hours Talking?

This was a real question from the overall executive leadership. The expectation was that as a new leader I would *impose* my wisdom in the form of practices and processes, based on successful efforts with other similar organizations. The realization was that when we had met and discussed my joining their organization, they had only heard the sentences that they wanted to hear, especially the CIO.

So it was time for a frank, transparent discussion. This conversation could not be siloed with only the CIO, it required bringing the executive leadership team together, along with their senior staff and trusted advisors.

---

8   Reasoning About Software Quality Attributes.
    Carnegie Mellon University SEI. resources.sei.cmu.edu/library/asset-view.cfm?assetid=513803.

Walking a fine line to keep the trust and integrity of the team's debates, and sharing my own observations, I laid out the four transformational elements necessary to any sustainable success:

1. Shared vision

2. Blended team

3. Common language

4. Trust

About 10 of us met as I answered questions, gave insights, and laid out specific actions and activities to address those four transformational elements. How would success be measured? It is a combination of qualitative and quantitative data. Qualitatively, meet with the individual team members, ask questions, and listen. What are their pain points, opinions or worries? What is exciting about the growing consensus and team building?

Using anonymous surveys can be helpful if the intended audience is not too small, implying a lack of privacy and ability to speak openly. It is a relatively fine line. Quantitatively, we can also look at indicators such as hours worked, defects by type by environment, scan results, and number of hand-offs in a particular value stream.

A new technique that I intend to begin leveraging is called measuring HumanDebt. Duena Blodstrom, CEO of People Not Tech, has a series of measurable and detectable indicators on psychological safety, a cornerstone to building a culture of courage based on honesty and trust.[9]

Another Day, Another Definition: Cyber Resiliency & Cyber Security

Our team's shared mission and objectives required a few more definitions and rally points for continued growth. Shifting from traditional security-team scans of a final project before go-live, to having a cyber-centric culture, required some definition finessing.

Expanding our lexicon to include cyber resilience was a cornerstone definition. Cyber resilience is not an alternative to cyber security, but rather

---

9   Blomstrom, D. (2022, January 27). The HUMANDEBT™. People Not Tech. peoplenottech.com/articles/the-humandebt/

an expanding universe of principles and capabilities tied into and aligned with modern software engineering and DevSecOps.[10] Cyber resiliency is the concept of ensuring operational and business/mission continuity. For my team, and with the support of the executives, a bit more whiteboard time was warranted to make an investment in discussions that drove us to action.

Using inputs from industry experts as a launching spot, we agreed that **Cyber Security** cannot mean impenetrable defenses. The reality is that breaches and attacks will happen. The enemy is ever-evolving using new techniques and exposing more and more attack vectors and surfaces than ever. From script kiddies to organized combatant nations, we need to expand the definitions. **Cyber Resilience** is our ability to prevent, respond, and recover.

The team rallied and agreed we needed to prepare, respond and recover from cyberattacks and data breaches while continuing to operate effectively. Like every topic, every technology, and every new idea, it was going to be too easy to get overwhelmed with the universe of guidance from CISA's Cyber Resilience Review (CRR) assessment (developed by the Department of Homeland Security) to CERT services (from Carnegie Mellon's Software Engineering Institute).[11] We opted that we would get smart together using NIST Cybersecurity Framework quick start.[12] This discussion proved to be powerful and haunting, exposing a rawness: wildly mixed opinions on who actually had "security smarts."?

Security Smarts

A small surface crack started to show in our newly formed team. Folks who hailed from the legacy security team lacked street credentials as developers and engineers, yet pushed out secure coding standards. In the past, they

---

10 Alkove, J. (2021, November 3). Cyber security is no longer enough: businesses need cyber resilience. World Economic Forum. weforum.org/agenda/2021/11/ why-move-cyber-security-to-cyber-resilience/

11 Assessments: Cyber Resilience Review (CRR). CISA. www.cisa.gov/uscert/resources/ assessments

12 NIST. (2016, May 24). Getting Started with the NIST Cybersecurity Framework: A Quick Start Guide. CSRC. csrc.nist.gov/Projects/cybersecurity-framework/ nist-cybersecurity-framework-a-quick-start-guide

had provided lengthy word documents on a SharePoint site. Occasionally, a proposed-code review checklist template was suggested.

This came directly from the land before Agile where silos dominated the landscape. The developers and engineers were the recipients of heavy-handed guide books that read like legal policy without reference implementations (that is, production quality samples) or automated tests.

The architects and engineers who grew up as hands-on developers focused on the requisite software engineering needed to meet the end-user needs (provided via requirements and focus groups). They also addressed some of the cross-cutting concerns such as performance and maintainability. (Long ago, these were called "non-functional" requirements but I prefer the definition used earlier, that is, software quality attributes or the "ilities".)

This lack of respect and understanding of the shared nature of security manifested in a battle that I needed to take on and shed some blood for; provide security tool access for developers and delivery teams. To get to that point, I'd have to double down on building more trust.

Institutional Mistrust: An AntiPatterns

I often turn to a book called, "Antipatterns: Managing Software Organizations and People".[13] The structure and easy consumption appeal to my inner software architect and my love of design patterns. My book is dog-eared, with myriad highlights. One of the first I landed on in brainstorming how to address this systemic situation: **Institutional Mistrust**.

Institutional Mistrust

In many organizations, there is a general lack of trust in the abilities and motives of every job function, business unit, and person; this is human nature but sometimes it pervades the culture so much that it is effectively institutional.

- Colin J. Neill, Philip A. LaPlante & Joanna F. DeFranco, *"Antipatterns: Managing Software Organizations and People"*

---

13 Laplante, P. A., Neill, C. J., & DeFranco, J. F. (2011). Antipatterns: Managing Software Organizations and People. Taylor and Francis Group.

Institutional Mistrust is classified as an Environmental antipattern that has its roots in communication, culture, and honestly. Some of the dysfunction that is symptomatic of this anti-pattern include:

1. Tasks that are duplicated because the results from one group are not trusted by another group

2. Energy is lost with the pointing of fingers

3. Good staff level

Addressing **Institutional Mistrust** on my team needed a crawl, walk, run approach. First, I needed to take responsibility for my work and assume the best in people. Second, I demonstrate model behavior by being trustworthy myself and setting and holding others accountable, helping others to do the same. Finally, the one that would bring the most backlash AND the most reward, refactoring to distribute responsibilities.

Building Human Trust

When we speak about trust in the context of cybersecurity and cyber resiliency, it is usually referencing machine-to-machine trust, or a belief of a machine or sensor to act dependably, reliably, and secure in a given situation.

I am talking about good old-fashioned, elbow-to-elbow trust. In the age of zero-trust architecture, a generation of script kiddies, and surge of cyber espionage, there is an absolute role for trust among the team, the executive leadership, and the entire organization.

There are multiple psychological studies that provide frameworks or equations for how to build trust. In 2000, Charles H. Green wrote a book titled "The Trusted Advisor" where he outlined an equation for trustworthiness.[14] His equation defines the components that need to exist in order for someone to be perceived as trustworthy and for others to extend trust.

The 4 components are:

1. Credibility has to do with words and ideas and how someone expresses and shares.

---

14 Green, C. H., Maister, D., & Galford, R. M. (2021). The Trusted Advisor: 20th Anniversary Edition. Free Press.

2. Reliability are deeds and actions and while it is action oriented, it does include an emotional element. Does the person understand my unique context?

3. Intimacy has to do with a sense of personal and psychological safety; Do you believe that confidences are kept?

4. Self-orientation deals with how much someone is self-absorbed OR are externally altruistic and empathetic.

The components of the trust equation are as follows:[15]

The Trust Equation

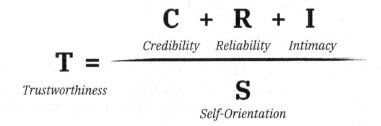

$$T = \frac{C + R + I}{S}$$

T = Trustworthiness

C + R + I = Credibility, Reliability, Intimacy

S = Self-Orientation

Establishing trust requires both someone to present trustworthiness and for someone else to extend an offer of trust. To diagnose and understand the steps to take for my team and the organization, we would need to display trustworthiness. Clearly this team of senior architects and engineers had credibility, were well educated, and credentialed.

Reliability was, at times, suspect for many as this was often not within their control. Their ability to "make good" on their word was often at the whimsy of redirection by others. To address this, we would need a shared and transparent cross-organizational backlog. This was a tremendous sticking point! The existing fiefdoms needed reassurances that the intent was not to seize total control, but to protect the team and give them the necessary buffer to deliver on time and as promised.

---

15 Understanding the Trust Equation. Trusted Advisor . (2020, April 27). trustedadvisor.com/why-trust-matters/understanding-trust/understanding-the-trust-equation.

Intimacy includes understanding the context of others, both specific to the unique domain (child welfare, health care, military, fintech), and the contextual surroundings for the project or program and its impact on individuals. To build intimacy, we must understand one another's role, responsibilities, and cognitive load. As the adage about empathy goes, "You can't understand someone until you've walked a mile in their shoes".

This was not limited to our team and also included the senior executives. They needed to openly share and champion for the actions and vision of the team. Doing this empowers us to propagate trust across the entire department vertically and horizontally. My approach is to build momentum and trust from the top down. Model the positive behaviors you want to ultimately see manifested in a new culture built together. As our team continued with open dialogue, we also needed to problem solve together. With the right guidance, scaffolding, and buffering in place, the team begins to display trustworthiness and extend trust to one another.

I must admit that an undertone existed that attempted to paint me as a "diva demanding full control". I responded with transparency, empathy, and modeling the behaviors I wanted to see in others. I'll concede this was difficult at times; more than once I left for the day with a heavy heart. Bootstrapping myself each morning became my own personal mantra.

Challenge #1: Access to scanning tools for delivery teams

Fundamentally we all agreed that defects needed to be surfaced as quickly as possible to give developers context to quickly address the issue. In my experience, this needs to include any tool that developers can use to quickly uncover defects and flaws. Making this a self-service event removes dependencies on others for handoffs and makes the process as effective and as timely as possible.

This presented an obstacle for us to solve. All security tools and scanners were reserved for the security team and not available to the development organizations. With the dual purpose of building trust through joint problem solving and to enable self-service code quality improvements, I proposed we solve this together.

Step 1: Show how rapid feedback speeds delivery of secure, quality code

The development teams had been toying with test-driven development (TDD) and educated on automated testing. We selected a product team to use as our shared experiment. "Win or Learn Fast," is the phrase used by Cyber pro, Nicole Dove. Replacing the term "fail fast" became our battle cry.

For the pilot development team, I asked that unit test code be subject to code reviews until developers and team leads cut their teeth on quality and appropriate unit tests. This was viewed as my being too controlling and a few choice sexist slang terms were heard in the hallway chatter. To address the chatter I was consistently open and honest, demonstrating repeatedly that my "self-orientation" component was negligible, with complete focus on the success of the humans in the mix, the teams, and the organization.

I mentored the architects and engineering leads to jump in to take on a user story and code unit tests as well. My point was that you'll have ineffective code reviews if you've never done it. We use the opportunity to execute some pair programming as a type of "trading places" game. This allowed our security pros to demonstrate they could do more than push out security coding manuals. It was a bit stressful; I hate it when I make silly logic errors or when my code is not textbook elegant. I had to do the very thing I was asking of others. At times it was embarrassing, and on a few occasions, I knew my face was a bit flushed, but together we had fun. The shared lesson demonstrated the faster the delivery team had feedback on quality and defects, the more effectively and quickly defects and issues could be addressed.

Step 2: Demonstrate accelerated feedback with self-service tooling

After demonstrating value on rapid code reviews, the next step was to rally for self-service scanning. This proved to be quite difficult! While we were well on our way to tearing down transitional swim lanes across the team, the overall organization and funding were organized so that only the security team could be allowed licenses to the security scanning tools.

Truth be told, there were some lightweight territorial attitudes and fears of no longer being necessary. Much like operations, teams may fear they will be less necessary when replaced by the automated deployments, the security team feared that they would be less necessary. The reality is the opposite! When operations and security are freed up by automation or shared execution by others, they are now free to dive into the more difficult challenges. Both teams could also start working more predictable hours.

It took a few months and negotiation on funding to eventually provide access to the paid version of Burp, Fortify, and other scanning tools. In the interim, we held OWASP lunch-and-learn sessions and encouraged using free versions to fine-tune their skills.

Challenge #2 - Developer Access to Production

Embracing shared responsibility for the health of production was another necessary step in our evolution as a Cyber-centric and DevSecOps-savvy organization. In the past, developers were completely banned from any access to production. They had reacted by creating what I call "Easter egg" health reports. These were screens that were obfuscated from normal navigation, but that provided functional health metrics, such as the number of cases currently opened or time in queue for addressing an issue. Overall, development teams had clandestine and well-intended workarounds to address their lack of access to production monitoring.

This surfaced a fundamental mistake in our team building. While we asked operations to participate on the team, I was so excited by the growing relationship with security that we didn't passionately pursue operations in all discussions. The doors were open, but we didn't send the proverbial follow-up note and calls to court them.

Operations had a laundry list of reasons to exclude dev production access, including fear of developers having access to PII data. Debunking this particular opinion was relatively simple. We had a shared cyber faux production access and production data was routinely ported to non-production environments for performance testing, as well as debugging of production defects.

This surfaced a historic lack of trust based on the distance between the historic teams and the strength of the bricks used to route the swim lanes. Residual opinions by the security team held a view of the developers and delivery team that they were more worried about pushing fast features, even if the quality was low, and had "no clue" what security really entails. There was an undercurrent that only operations could be trusted to protect production.

The muscle memory for Ops included NO access for anyone. A multi-stepped process was needed to move forward. First, operations were often left as uninvolved, except for being provided roadmap dates for go-lives along with hardware and software specifications. The enterprise often treated Ops as doers and not as thought leaders and considered them reactive and not pro-active. While it may have been true that operations were often **forced to be reactive**, the culpability was horizontal.

Improving quality (feature and cyber) improved the lives of the Operations team and we negotiated for access to operations dashboards for a select set of senior engineers. There was also an agreement that all "Easter Egg" monitoring would not be hidden but openly discussed and secured.

Challenge #3 - Protecting Lower Environments

While we tout using DevOps principles to commit code to the main branch and have it automatically progress through the pipeline to production, there is a need for a mirror production-like environment, especially when about to go live with a new solution or ecosystem.

The number of features to be included in a minimum viable product for a new constituent-facing capability can be fairly extensive, even when taking an agile mindset. While pitching blue/green (A/B) environments was considered a bridge too far to start, I was labeled as wearing rose-colored glasses and endured discussions explaining the costs associated with hosting production and all the accouterments.

Muscle memory was too great with historic environment names, ownership, and usage. The muscle memory of how they went live in the past with new systems meant they did not buy into the need or cost to secure "pre-prod" (pre-production) in the same way.

As the new pipeline started to mature, features were being released into pre-prod and almost instantly pushed into the new production location as well. Pre-prod would be used for performance and load testing and possibly some traditional user acceptance testing. Keep in mind that in any organization, there are generally different identity, credential, and access management solutions for development and testing than for production. I needed to expose the need to have a complete parity environment that was managed with identical rigor and security concerns as production.

As luck would have it, a formal request was made to expose pre-prod to internet traffic for senior stakeholders, funding suppliers, and quite frankly, political leaders to "try out". Think of this like a traditional user acceptance testing environment but open to the internet. I knew we needed to expose the security risk and targeting of pre-prod. It required two steps to expose the danger.

Step 1: Familiarize Stakeholders with Real-time security dashboards

First, I educated the stakeholders about security and analytics dashboards by simply adding basic Google Analytic tagging to an existing LIVE health and human services related website. Using a simple java script added to the inherit base page, the stakeholders would be able to see real-time dashboards. Here is a sample custom HTML tag to capture a visitor's IP address.[16]

```
<script type="application/javascript">
function getIP(json) {
dataLayer.push({"event":"ipEvent","ipAddress" : json.ip});
}
</script>

<script type="application/javascript" src="https://api.ipify.org?format=jsonp&callback=getIP">
  </script>
```

With the stakeholders' permissions, I had my team configure Google Analytics dashboard application on the mobile devices of the attendees. We then set about getting the stakeholders comfortable with navigating the dashboards. They were shocked to see foreign IPs hitting the login page for this solution. Using the geolocation feature, we watched the map highlight hits from Israel, Germany, and Romania. The identity expert and the network firewall expert both explained how the current capabilities were secured.

---

16 Kravitz, A. (2021, February 25). Get Visitor IP Address with Google Tag Manager. Mixed Analytics. mixedanalytics.com/blog/visitor-ip-address-google-tag-manager/

Step 2: Shock and educate

As everyone in the room proudly discussed our seeming ability to thwart production attacks, I had the team help the stakeholders toggle to a different environment: pre-prod. Surely this would be uneventful. What we saw not only mirrored production but was busier. More foreign IPs were targeting the pre-prod environment. Given the rather poor practice of using production data for pre-production performance testing, the exposure risk was evident.

This showmanship was a dangerous step to take given I was still new to the overall enterprise and battling ill-founded perceptions. Using the trust equation, I doubled down on keeping my TQ (trust quotient) high by focusing on self-centeredness (that is, not being self serving) and credibility components. This exercise was needed to shock stakeholders and even some on the team into unifying. It worked.

Summary

Although the bulk of this chapter took place with one agency, I have repeated these techniques and steps with other teams, other organizations, and other clients.

- First, establish a shared vision. If one has been written down already, revisit as a team since everyone in the organization and the effort must support and believe the vision.

- Second, define your language together. Recalibrate and redefine when necessary, breaking down barriers and forging new ground together. Look at the makeup of the team and think like a coach. Do we have both breadth and depth with cross over? If not, recruit!

- Finally, build trust using the trust equation. Be bold in modeling your behaviors and even more so, mentor others by taking them aside and helping them grow.

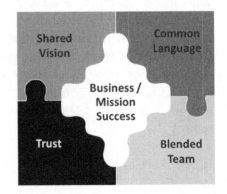

Cultural building must balance a shared vision, common language, blended teams, and trust to enable success.

One Final Story: Anatomy of a Failure

I would not be an honest or real individual if I didn't share failures as well as successes. Perhaps failure is too strong. We were eventually successful in reaching production, providing new capability at speed, and we learned much along the way. As Nicole Dove says, "Win or Learn!"

In 2018, I had the opportunity to work with one of the US Military Services. The scope of work was to conduct an experiment with the outcomes being a working prototype and the associated RMF package that would be necessary to operationalize the prototype if warranted.

> NIST Risk Management Framework, or RMF, helps ensure organizations are able to address rampant cybersecurity threats by providing "a disciplined, structured, and flexible process for managing security and privacy risk." [...] a framework is just that: a frame of reference from which to adapt according to your needs and situation.[17]

I saw a clear path to a WIN! The architecture was straightforward and the high-level mission objectives and subsequent quality attributes (scalability, security, maintainability, performance) were known and prioritized.

The vision was clear and shared, we had a well-focused and shared lexicon, the team was blended and we had initial trustworthiness displayed by all on the team. With my coach's hat on, I realized we needed to extend the team to have the RMF package creation team, as well as experienced RMF evaluators associated with the team, so we could begin building out our RMF package incrementally. What I did not take into consideration was the difficulty in fighting muscle memory associated with RMF.

RMF is based on a waterfall mentality. When a *project* is completely designed and ready for production release, a full "package" is created and

---

17 Tracy, R., & Price, G. (2021, April 13). The Risk Management Framework is Dead. Long Live the RMF. www.nextgov.com/ideas/2019/06/risk-management-framework-dead-long-live-rmf/157717/

submitted for evaluation and approval. I enthusiastically invited the RMF group to participate in early design and build as partners.

We underestimated the impact of being matrixed by another organization. Their home organizational structure had too much power and lacked the interest to change. While the mid-level and boots on the ground were interested, they were not given the top cover they needed.

As their coach, I underestimated the amount of pre-season training to help them. The pace of change was too much for this small and part-time group to consume. With limited time to complete the experiment and even more budget limits for upskilling, the path to closure became clear. We resigned to complete the technical build of the experiment and conduct all the requisite tests and such, then enlist the rag-tag group of RMF folks to create the RMF package and shepherd it through the evaluation.

In the end, the overall experiment was considered a success. It met mission objectives and laid the foundation for moving to a cloud-based ability to spin up new tenant-centric, vessel-specific environments for training purposes. It was not without some loss of credibility and a lower overall trust quotient, however. My zeal to help others work in a nimble and agile way had actually increased my self-centeredness. I was hell-bent on rapid new ways of working and had failed to extend intimacy in the form of contextual understanding to the RMF team.

You can learn from both good examples and bad examples. My goal in sharing this final "failure story" is for you to see the importance of the truth quotient, the need to think like a coach, and the tremendous strength of muscle memory!

ABOUT TRACY BANNON

Passionate Architect!!! Tracy (Trac) Bannon is a Senior Principal in MITRE Corporation's Advanced Software Innovation Center. She is an accomplished software architect, engineer, and DevSecOps advisor having worked across commercial and government clients.

Tracy's architecture specialty emphasizes cloud native, decoupled architectures, DataOps/xOps, and DevSecOps. Understanding complex problems and working to deliver mission/business value at the speed of relevance is job one!

Trac walks the walk and talks the talk. She's just as passionate about mentoring and training as she is about architecting sustainable ecosystems! She enjoys community and knowledge building with her teams, her clients, and the next generation of technologists by guest lecturing at universities, leading working groups, and sharing experience stories.

Trac is a featured speaker and panel moderator at industry events holding certifications from Microsoft, AWS, DevOps Institute, PMI, Scrum Alliances, and the Software Engineering Institute (SEI).

CHAPTER 8

Your Greatest Vuln
Culture of No

Your Greatest Vuln: A Culture of No

by Breanne Boland

Your Greatest Vuln: A Culture of No

Breanne Boland

Some time ago, I started working in a wonderful, well-functioning security team. I don't believe in dream jobs, but I do believe in the effects of diligent, careful work, and I got to benefit from it for months. Other teams across the company respected us, and even though we were part of a sometimes-onerous process for helping people do their work more securely, people liked talking to us. We were well regarded and—dare I say—popular. People knew we couldn't approve everything they asked for, but they also knew we would explain why and help them to choose more secure options for their next project.

The trouble with a good, distinctive team culture is that, like so many microclimates, they are vulnerable to change.

In our case, the culture of yes shifted sharply to a culture of no across several upsetting months. We were ordered to decline the requests of more and more of our colleagues. Unlike a mature security culture, we no longer worked within an acceptable amount of risk. People knew that if they came to us they would have their requests denied, and they wouldn't get much information about why. We were buried in work because people kept leaving our team. I didn't have the power to change things, so I could only watch and, when the decay bit too deep, plan my next steps. When hiring managers asked why I was looking for a change, I made the usual professional-grade excuses about seeking new challenges and wanting to learn more, but I told the truth to a handful of hiring managers I trusted.

"If I stayed any longer, I was going to become worse at my job."

This is because there are several problems with existing within a culture of no and being obligated to support and propagate it. *No* leaves no room for complexity. *No* gives you fewer options to think around, and across time your critical thinking skills atrophy. *No* and its predictable recitation means your colleagues will stop seeking the advice of the security team because drawing your notice won't get them anything they want and will get them several things they don't. If your job can be done by a simple function that returns the same negative string every time, you're not a very good security engineer.

Fostering a culture of no in your company's security org, more than anything else we pour hours and so much money into preventing, is the biggest risk you're facing. Because it means people will make choices without consulting you if they can get away with it, and because they'll think twice about informing you of concerns. This means you'll lose valuable hours when you could be responding to an emergency quickly and effectively. Your company may or may not draw the attention of nation-state actors, but you absolutely will work with other teams across your company and rely upon them for the information you need to do your work. If they're unsure about bringing it to you, your chances of success diminish considerably. Few outcomes are worse than the fatal misstep of teaching your colleagues to fear the team tasked with helping them work more securely. The good news is that it doesn't have to be this way.

A Visit to a Culture of No

Let's pretend you're on a security-adjacent engineering team and on an otherwise ordinary afternoon, a pop-up interrupted your work. It appeared for just a second and disappeared, quickly enough that you didn't get to read it. You think you saw the word "download" and what could've been a progress bar, but it all disappeared so fast that you didn't have time to take it all in, let alone screenshot it. You took a quick look at all processes running on your company machine, and everything seems normal, but you're unsettled. You were hoping to finish one more task before afternoon standup, but there's no way around it: it's time to go ask security.

You walk across the office with your laptop under your arm wondering who'll be there to answer your question. It looks different over there; they sit in a separate section of the office away from the rest of engineering, and it just feels a little less friendly. You tried posting in their channel and even sent a DM to their lead, but you didn't get an answer and didn't want to do anything else on your laptop without knowing for certain it's safe. Still, you're not very happy to be doing this; the last time you had to talk to someone on the security team, you were greeted with a joke about your programming language of choice and your preferred equipment. He feigned surprise when you said you hadn't heard of a recent breach he mentioned. Not the worst, but just enough to make you reluctant to engage again.

You find the lead of the team sitting solo among the group of desks. You open your mouth to start explaining what you saw, but the lead talks first. "Did you finally switch to a real programming language?" he says. You know that to make this work, you're going to have to laugh and pretend to be in on the joke, but suddenly you're too tired to go through with it. "No," you say. "I was looking for someone else. I'll just email instead." The lead says something else as you walk away, but you don't catch it and don't want to.

Back at your desk, you think about the mystery popup for a moment longer before deciding to put it out of your head. They probably have tools for detecting stuff like this anyway. You recall one of the nicer members of the team—maybe if you bump into that guy later, you'll mention the popup. Maybe.

If the security team is hard to deal with, people will hide things from them rather than having to deal with them. And if they are an obstruction, people will find another way to deal with their problems, but it might not be the way the security team would prefer. This can be a simple matter of Jira tickets not being filed correctly or something more complicated like missing the first signs of a devastating breach. Either way, the team won't know until it's too late.

A Visit to a Culture of Yes

Let's try again.

You're trying to finish one more task before standup when you're interrupted by a surprise popup. It's tempting to put it off—you just need to make one more test pass, and then you can finish the code submission. But you remember the last engineering all-hands when the head of the security team talked about how there was nothing too small to report and no deadline that was more important than working securely. "We're always glad to look at anything you think is worth looking at," he said and seemed to mean it. The security team has a good working relationship with engineering and the VP of engineering nodded when the head of security said this.

You pick up your laptop and cross the office. Two members of the security team are there, looking at a single monitor and talking intently about something.

"Am I interrupting?" you ask.

"Never!" one of them says. You've had lunch with her before; you're not friends, but friendly. "How's your dog?"

You smile and open your laptop to show the new dog picture that you made your wallpaper that morning. "I saw something weird today, though."

"What did you see?" the other security team member asks.

You tell them what you managed to glean from the quick flash of the mystery popup. The security people look at each other. "I think that sounds like—" and he says something you don't know. It sounds like software. "Have you bumped into that yet?"

You admit you haven't.

"Oh, it's really cool," your sometimes lunch buddy says. She explains how it does laptop governance, keeping software up to date, and ensuring certain programs can't be installed. "Want to see what it looks like on our end?" She offers you her seat, and you sit between the two team members as they show you the admin panel. Then they bring up some documentation and show you what it looks like when configurations are synced and it looks exactly like what you managed to see earlier.

You thank them for the introduction and then apologize for wasting their time.

"If you wonder about it, it's not a waste of time," one of them says. "Thanks for asking us. We'll put something in the engineering channel about it because I bet you're not the only one who was surprised at noticing that."

And they post something in the engineering channel about 15 minutes later, tagging you as the person who brought it to their attention and including a clear screenshot of the popup you missed. And apparently, they made an emoji of you with sparkles? Within an hour, there are ten comments on it from people across the company saying they'd also seen something but didn't want to ask.

At standup, you explain what's between you and your completed task, which is immediately understood. Afterward, you come back to your one finicky test, get it to cooperate, and create the PR (submit your code). It's accepted that afternoon.

And someone from your team uses your sparkly new emoji on the automated message saying it's been merged.

Cultivating a Healthier Alternative

Security has a reputation as one of the saltier corners of technology, which is understandable considering the ongoing news; we unavoidably have to deal with risks we didn't cultivate and mistakes we didn't make. This built-in adversarial dynamic can compound itself when you join a team that leans into it, fostering an "us vs. them" approach to the work that makes difficult days easier with gallows humor and camaraderie. The trouble is when it spills into the everyday and makes the work you're trying to do harder or even impossible. It's a short-term gain that can hinder your long-term progress.

To do this work well and to serve the people we do—and this is a service role, make no mistake—we have to cultivate a culture of yes.

A culture of yes doesn't mean agreeing to everything people suggest; we all know that a secure product, infrastructure, and culture are impossible to achieve that way. But we have to say yes to our colleagues. Yes, we can work with you. Yes, we want to understand why you want to approach your problem in the way you're proposing. Yes, we will talk until I understand the original problem that led you to an approach that might not be working so well. And yes, we will give you the information you need to do your job.

Yes, we respect you as the authority of your problem, and we appreciate the chance to help you meet your goals more effectively and safely.

A culture of no cuts off this flow of information and goodwill before it can take root. No, I will take what I want from what you said and ignore the bigger picture. No, I won't consider that there are almost always reasons behind decisions, even ones not working so well today. If you won't do it my way; no, I won't help you. Possibly worst of all, no; you don't need to know that.

Would you be excited to explain something difficult to someone like that?

Lots of people come into new workplaces with old scars from cultures of no. I've witnessed it as a certain timidness in presenting a question, either privately or in a meeting. It also appears as being afraid of getting in trouble, which is an idea best left in childhood. Our colleagues have their jobs because they're qualified and interested in the work. If one of them needs security help but holds back because some misguided person in their past made them feel insecure or incorrect, it's in everyone's interest for us to do better.

The good news is that even if you're mired in a culture of no that was built in a years-long effort to elevate security to the role of dictator, you can still fix it.

Recognize If You're Marching in a Red Flag Parade

Before we get to the cure, let's talk a little more about how to diagnose the problem. Like all security problems, we can sometimes cause further harm if we try to address a symptom thinking it's the cause. We can do better by working to properly understand the problem before we act.

If you've been steeped in a culture of no for a while, you may not be able to see how it manifests right away. If you're new, it can be tempting to try to downplay what you're experiencing, if only because interviewing is hard and the thought of doing it again so soon after taking a new position is exhausting.

One tell is that the security@ and phishing@ aliases are quiet. Ideally, these should receive a steady stream of forwards with regular false positives, because that's what aliases like this are for. If they're quiet, maybe your company isn't large enough to be noticed by spearfishers, or maybe your colleagues don't trust that writing to your team will be fruitful.

It's also useful to watch how other teams interact with security. Do members of your team leap to mockery as a default, even if they say quickly that it was a "joke"? Do they say or even suggest that there's only one correct way to do something? Do they feign surprise? If your teammates are engaging in any of the troubling behaviors outlined in the Recurse Center's social rules, you likely have a problem.[1] Same if you hear even one joke about the team being "scary": something's not right.

It's also useful to watch how communication with the team works. Is there an unofficial "friendly" member of the team that people on other teams try to talk to first? Do people reach for DMs over communication in open channels even for non-sensitive issues? Are cross-team meetings quiet, even furtive? Are your teammates secretive about tools or upcoming work for no good reason?

None of this means an unredeemable situation, but it may mean your security team is doing more harm to their cause than good, quite possibly without meaning to. A risk with hiring security-interested people is they are attracted to the glamorous problems: breaches that make news, vulnerabilities that result in common vulnerabilities and exposures (CVEs), and all the accolades and exciting stories we all love hearing. The problem is that while glamorous problems are certainly a part of the work, it's not the majority of what's needed to keep a company operating safely from day to day. Unless you are a researcher or part of an especially aggressive red team, your work is going to be more about people than computers a lot of

---

1   Social rules. Recurse Center. www.recurse.com/social-rules

the time—and, yes, how people use those computers. Not everyone on the security team may understand this, but fortunately, this can be fixed too.

Take Red Flag Inventory

Once you've gotten that early sense that something's not working right, the most difficult parts of turning around a culture of no are figuring out exactly what you're dealing with and explaining to others what you're perceiving. This gets even more complicated because creating a culture of yes generally requires a lot of directed, consistent effort, but a culture of no seeps into the negative space left when you're not putting that effort in. This means that a culture of no can take root without anyone intending to work that way. I've known wonderful engineers, ones I still count as friends, who created a culture of no without meaning to. Pushing back against this kind of culture requires both offensive work to create the culture you want and defensive work to prevent the kind of culture you don't. And figuring out where to put time and energy is easier if you have an inventory to work from. Let's talk about some ways to do that, from the easiest and lightest to the most complex.

The best way I've found to start on this work is meetings. Yes, I know; most of us already have too many meetings on our calendars. I'm writing this almost two years into the pandemic and the world is well into the accelerating Zoom deluge. However, my distaste for more *Brady Bunch*-style people grids is massively outweighed by my desire to make a culture that works. Make that switch in yourself and it gets better.

If you're new, one of the very first things to do is figure out how people talk to each other in your company. Is it a "let's hop on a quick call to figure this out" culture? Are important conversations spread across a hundred tightly focused channels or a handful of more general ones? Is a lot happening quietly in group chats? Are changing opinions or spicy takes primarily expressed via emojis and reactions? Whatever it is, you need to become fluent in it or find someone on your team who can explain what's going on.

And you'll need to figure out the right places to be because the next step is sleuthing. You've already gotten a sense that something isn't working right; now keep listening and figure out who in the engineering org isn't benefiting from your team's work in the way you want. This can be someone who asks pointed but useful questions in Slack, or it can be someone in the all-hands who's making a confused or annoyed face when your team's giving an update. What you're looking for is someone who isn't getting what they need from your team. This person is an authority on at least one version of what your team isn't doing right, and they're your new mentor.

If coffee or walks outside the office are available by the time you read this, do that. The meeting needs to be lightweight (so not lunch, and not some terrible agenda-devoid hour-long block they have to endure) and ideally on neutral turf. If mobility's an issue, somewhere in the office can work, but make it private and somewhat different from a normal meeting: bring tea, offer a snack, or start with a disarming story. Put them at ease early by telling them, either in the invitation or in a DM, exactly why you're meeting and what you'll be asking. You want to make it clear that something different is happening. Once your new resource friend seems to get that you're trying something new, start asking about their history with security at previous jobs and then work your way to their experience with your team specifically. This may mean not taking notes because framing it as a more casual conversation draws people out better. In that case, just block time to write things down after.

Questions to Ask Over Security Coffee

- What's a time in this job or another where you learned something from security? What worked about that for you?
- Could you tell me about a time you approached my team for help with something and didn't get the response you wanted? What did you expect, and what actually happened?
- How do you like learning about what other teams do? What's a team that does this really well here?
- What's the best way for you to reach out to another team about a difficult problem?
- Do our current communication norms work for you? What's worked better for you at other jobs?
- What could our team do that we're not already doing?

If you found the right person, they'll answer expansively and may even be excited, because sometimes these problems arise when these questions have gone unasked for too long. If they're not forthcoming, that's OK: learn what you can, and figure out the next person to talk to. If you think a reticent person has further useful things to say, check in with them again in a few weeks. Sometimes it takes a while to build up trust.

Your other resource is to find the person who seems most scared of security. This may be a relatively new dev, or it may be someone who works with sensitive resources but doesn't consider themselves "technical." Earn their trust using the methods above, assure them that *you* need *their* help, figure out what could help them feel more comfortable with security-adjacent work and dealing with your team, and then work as hard as you can to make that happen. If you make things better for the person having the hardest time, you'll make things better for everyone.

The goal for this phase is to learn what's been going on so far. A great bonus is establishing important relationships as you continue this work. Not every meeting will result in the need for regular one-on-ones, but some will. Ask them if you can check in with them as you continue this work. Monthly can be a good starter cadence, but you might do it weekly or biweekly if your team is working more directly with this person and their team. Match the cadence they want, and use it to provide accountability for your work for them. Even if you don't need the accountability for your own progress, you'll get the benefit of regular check-ins on your efforts and—if you're lucky—the feeling of growing trust with a colleague as they see you following through on your promises and integrating their feedback as you do.

You may need to initiate a lot of meetings to find your key resource people. Depending on the size of the org, your intros may number in the dozens. Take your time with this because it's important to get it right.

This part of the work is also meant to get you and your changing team in front of people whose perceptions of the security team may have been unchanged for years. The goal is to find the people most affected by your team who have been the most disappointed, and then keep listening to them and asking more questions. They'll shape your strategy at every turn and sometimes surface smaller problems that you can fix quickly, which contributes to establishing trust. Never underestimate the long-term power of a quick fix at the right time, done when you said it would be done.

Not all suggestions from people outside of your team will be relevant to your goals or even attainable, and this is fine too. Part of establishing this trust is telling them what's possible from your team. Stay honest, and your alliances will get stronger.

Increased Transparency Helps People Like You

While you're executing your careful campaign of individual contacts, you can and must take your work wider. Take your early sense of what's blocking your cultural goals—secrecy, stinginess, being difficult to approach, or something else entirely—and figure out how to foster conversations that push against that. At a company where people knew they relied on my team but couldn't explain what exactly it was we did there with the fidelity we wanted, I had success with "Ask Us Anything" meetings. After starting the job, I found that my team of well-intended people with decades of engineering experience had turned into an opaque entity for the rest of engineering. By creating a monthly venue where people knew they could safely ask questions and get real answers, the mystery started to dissipate. We emphasized that no question was too basic and that these meetings were a venue to get those "I should know this but—" questions answered. It also helped that we took notes, aiming for thoroughness over perfect organization so that people could search their questions in Google Drive and find information about these under-addressed parts of our infrastructure and wider engineering history. Never underestimate the utility of giving people a place and time to ask, "Why on earth do we use that tool?" particularly if you're prepared to give a real answer.

This was before the pandemic, so while we used video conferencing to loop in other offices, it wasn't organized in a Zoom-first way and wasn't recorded. If I did it today, I'd keep and share the recordings with the notes. People commented for months after how much it helped to have that material available because it wasn't the culture to record meetings as meticulously as we did in these notes. What you record can be used later to guide your efforts in building education, including documents, how-to videos, new-engineer orientation, and how your team explains its work.

You might realize that referring to OWASP or AWS concepts just don't land with engineers at your company without additional explanation, and these meetings can tell you exactly what explanation to provide.

Honestly, along with a broad, guiding star of "don't be a jerk," these meetings are the single most rewarding strategy I've followed to turn the culture around. People might be timid at first, in which case your first and most important job is to hold the space in a friendly way. Silence is awkward, but it's required in order to make room for questions that have remained unspoken for months or years. Come armed with some jokes or stories, invite the most socially adept engineer you know, invite the thorniest engineer with the best-pointed questions, and be prepared to hold space for the first couple of meetings. However, if you do it right, people will probably be more forthcoming with inquiries than you could've hoped. When you show up open, willing, and good-hearted, most people will meet you in the same way.

Because the solution to a lot of security culture problems is transparency. It's generally understood across engineering organizations that we can't talk about everything, for reasons of legal restrictions, customer data sensitivity, or just not wanting to scare people for no reason.

Security Sharing is Caring

But if you're not held back by law, common sense, or kindness, ask yourself and your team why you aren't sharing what's going on. Every team has things they don't broadcast, but security in particular needs to share everything except what they can't. Security controls so many things: individual workstations and their software, company email, physical office spaces, handling threats from outside, and so many other practical or existential risks for the company. This can make people outside of security feel like they're at your mercy, particularly if parts of your team haven't been the kindest about it in the past.

> The more you share, the more people will trust you. This can be an everyday strategy, like talking about recent work at lunch with someone on another team, or more formal, like security leadership having a regular spot in engineering all-hands to share what's going on now and what to expect in coming months.

Teams that act like they have something to hide plant seeds in the imaginations of others that grow into tenacious distrust. Be extremely careful what you sow.

The Security-Boosting Magic of Showing Up as a Person

It's hard to do the kind of security work we're talking about without being present. Beyond the strategic one-on-ones we discussed earlier, this can also mean ensuring a security team member is always present and ready to contribute at relevant cross-team meetings. (This will get relevant again later when we discuss maintaining your shiny new culture of yes.) When you're introducing this way of working, though, you'll need to be more visible until people come to understand that your team is working differently than it used to.

This can work in a few ways. In this era and for those wise companies that will persist in being remote or remote-first in later pandemic times, ChatOps is one of your most valuable tools. I've been a Slack-based professional organism for many years, so my examples tilt heavily toward that, but these recommendations can be adapted to Teams and other chat-forward collaboration tools.

At a minimum, your team should have these avenues for communication:

- A private team channel for quick collaboration with a limited audience
- A public team or security org channel where announcements and discussion happen
- A channel dedicated to handling help requests and other questions

- A steady alias that reaches a designated member of the security team, possibly attached to an on-call rotation

- An open invitation to DM team members

Each of these should have clearly expressed and accurate expectations on how quickly people can expect a response. This can be a formal SLA but doesn't need to be, particularly if you're just getting started. These can be stashed in a channel topic or a team charter linked in the appropriate channel topic. Don't underestimate the power of the team charter. I've seen reactions from gratitude to relief when I've been on teams that created and circulated these. People really just want to know what's going on with teams they depend on, and a personal statement of your goals and responsibilities clears up a lot of ambiguity.

When staffing these channels, never underestimate the value of a well-placed emoji or gif. Some of this may seem over the top if you're not used to it. Don't do anything that feels fake or forced, but try to find a way to exist in the chat with some warmth and personality, whatever that may mean for you. Expressing your own weird, enthusiastic humanity tells people that you're more likely to see theirs too, and it doesn't require a mandatory 15 pieces of flair, I promise.

And when your team leads events or training, try to inject a human moment there too. A teammate of mine likes to ask people what show they're binging as part of our new-hire training, and it is shockingly effective, especially if you engage a little with what people say. Ask people their pandemic obsessions, their favorite thing they did last weekend, something they ate recently that they really liked, what they love about where they live, or something else that lets them bring some warmth to what can seem like a pretty rote exercise. Do a roses-and-thorns round where people can talk about something they liked recently and something that's weighing on them. Sometimes we just want to get things done, but engaging with people as people is a long-term investment that will make it easier for you to get those things done in the future.

Consider how many people have had experiences with security teams that left them feeling cold or, worse, like a walking error in need of correction, and maybe you can see why this kind of effort can pay such dividends. I know, lots of people get into tech and security in particular because they don't love people, and that's OK if you're in the right role. We have room for misanthropes if they can mind their manners most of the time. However, if your work involves people, as a lot of security work usually does, your team needs to have a strategy to cultivate the human side of things. It doesn't have to be clever; it only needs to be sincere and offered in good faith.

In my experience, the right amount of this is when it feels like a little too much, but I'm pretty introverted by nature. You may have a higher aptitude for it, which is your good luck.

Become the Company Security Mentor

Another way to grow this trust is to redefine yourself as a teaching team. I'm biased and I bet you are too, but here's the thing: security is really cool. It's fascinating, it changes all the time, and it touches everything. We don't have to work to make security interesting, but we can make it interesting enough to work for us. When I collaborate with a colleague in a strictly Security Representative context, I try to teach them something they didn't know before that can help them with their work. I also try to learn something new about their work that I didn't know, which can help me be more effective too.

Creating a Reputation as Knowledge Providers

The more we're known as providers of knowledge that can help them get ahead in their careers, the more people will want to talk to us. This can happen in new-hire orientation (and if your company doesn't include a security session in that programming, it's time to add it), team check-ins, or any interaction where you're acting as an official security person. Even if you're fairly new, you know something other people don't, and it's your job to share it with anyone who wants to learn.

It's becoming more common that front-end and back-end engineers are expected to be conversant in at least basic security principles, and if you can help someone future-proof their career by shoring up that knowledge, you won't have to ask people to talk to you. They'll find you.

Write the Docs

For the times you're not available, though, we need persistent resources that can keep people on the right path, and for this we need documentation. This can be as simple as resources in Confluence, Google Docs, or wherever your colleagues expect to find definitive information on important subjects, but the job doesn't begin and end there. Every engineering culture has different expectations about how information is conveyed. Some lean heavily on recorded meetings or tutorial videos (for which I and people like me will beseech you to have transcription on the video or below, both for accessibility reasons and because sometimes I need a single piece of information from your 25-minute intro to whatever and would prefer to Cmd+F). Others normalize reaching out to the right person and getting live support. Find out what people actually like and use, which you can determine through a mix of opening metrics or by asking people.

The trouble with this is that people will more often tell you what they think they should be doing, which sometimes overlaps only some or not at all with how they actually do their work. One way to get around this is to ask them to show you how they last solved a certain problem rather than simply narrating it. People can still obfuscate when they click their way through what they did, but it's harder, and it gives you the chance to see problems they've chosen to just deal with rather than call out. When you see these come up, these are excellent opportunities to make everyone's working life better, particularly if you find yourself in a culture where people feel like they shouldn't "complain" when they bump into something hard. Reassure them at every turn that your goal is to get things working well and easily, and if they're experiencing a problem, that means the system is glitchy, not them.

It's also worth trying to be inventive if you're working within an established culture that isn't working as it needs to be. Newsletters are having a moment again, and they can be a great way to get your team's work in front of others on a regular cadence. If you do something like this, be sure to define success before you send out the first dispatch. Your goal may be as many opens as possible omg, but it could also be the right five opens within the company. Know what your goal is, and then you'll know when you reach it.

Once you get a sense of what people expect and what they actually need to get their jobs done, you can court goodwill by shoring those things up. Find out what common problems are, and address them with resources. Ask those trusted colleagues you've been collecting to review it and ensure it's doing what it should, then refine based on their feedback.

When you're finished refining and have a new resource to share, light up all the channels of communication about it. Link it in the main engineering channel and then cross-post so much that you feel borderline obnoxious. Slack and other chat messages don't have a long lifetime, so you're contributing to backscroll to search later, which is its own kind of documentation. If something's especially important to a certain group, pin it in their channel. Post again a couple of days later. Mention it in team reports, send it directly to managers of affected teams, and link it from other docs. We didn't work this hard to have our docs get lost in some shared drive thicket of broken documentation dreams.

And after all of that, if you made something, meticulously wordsmithed it, and ran it by your trusted resources, and people still don't use it? Consider retiring it. Maybe the subject is better addressed in a more popular doc in a more concise way. We do everyone a favor when we clear out the clutter. Not every swing will be a hit, but every effort that doesn't work as planned can be kept from making the effective resources harder to find.

Make the Right Behavior Easy

The perpetual goal: make the behavior you want the easiest choice. We've talked about chat habits, documentation, and conversation, but let's discuss a critical one: the undeniable power of bribery. It's a strange and enduring fact that tech workers are often paid absurd wages but remain susceptible to some incredibly cheap bribes. Please note: I'm not saying I'm above any of this. I know this works because it works on me too.

Here are a few of the effective, inexpensive bribes that I've seen change behavior:

- Food, either delivered to an office or via credits for home delivery[2]

---

2 This even works at offices with catering. I don't know why, but I hope it never changes.

- Swag, like shirts, tumblers, or other smaller things that aren't usually available from the company
- Stickers, which are also swag but have their own unique power and thus require their own bullet
- Accolades or kudos in all-hands or public channels
- Special Zoom backgrounds, possibly personalized
- Tying desired behavior to reviews

The last one requires more bureaucratic sway, but if your company actually values encouraging security-centered behavior, it should be achievable. Positive sway on your colleagues' careers takes a little more work but is especially compelling; whenever I'm working with a new team, I take a minute to explain that one of my personal goals is to help non-security engineers know just enough security to have something new to put on their resume. I want them to help me make a more secure company today, but I want them to have more opportunities come from offering that help.

But if all else fails: work with marketing or design to make exclusive stickers for attending events, meeting goals, changes in process, and other desired behavior. They're among the most effective currency I've seen for eliciting the behavior you want.

Just Say Yes

Yes, making a culture of yes involves complicated architecture. But here's the most important part, and it can be the most difficult part to start and sustain if your team has struggled with it:

YOU HAVE TO BE OK TO APPROACH AND WORK WITH.[3]

I realize this is pretty broad; stick with me.

Think back to the visit to a culture of no and all the small ways our hypothetical dev encountered barriers to reaching out to security. We have to teach people that a conversation with security will not end with us scolding them for doing things "wrong." Are there actions we don't want a user to take? Oh, absolutely, but if they're able to take them or don't know that

---

3   Yes, I buried the lede on purpose to give you some time ease into things, dear reader.

they're a bad idea, it means we've missed a chance to add a guardrail or educate them. It's critical to be able to find and discuss these issues without looking shocked or put off. Even if our words are friendly, people will remember if we look scandalized.

And if you don't like refining guardrails or educating users with language and motivations they understand, you may be in the wrong line of work. There are darker, less-disturbed corners of security. Consider those instead.

To do this work correctly, security engineers have to hold themselves to a higher standard than regular developers and other tech workers, because we either are or are perceived to be in possession of greater judgment and the ability to leverage greater consequences on our fellow engineers. And it's true: some of our work does have higher stakes than other engineering work, but we can't let that inform how we act. Regular devs can joke among themselves about "bad" tech choices, but when people in a position of responsibility and leadership do that, particularly in front of more junior people, other engineers can get the impression that we're in the business of assessing people's choices negatively and loudly. And yes, giving each other shit is a time-honored pastime of engineers, particularly ones in the saltier corners of the industry. I urge you, though, to do it privately or at least judiciously, because you may know you're only joking, but someone overhearing you without context might not. This is the kind of thing that can keep someone from approaching you about something delicate, because they may not have the emotional stamina to absorb "joking" put-downs from a colleague.

Especially when you're actively transforming a culture, try erring on the side of *very positive*. Yes, we want you to tell us what you've observed. Yes, we know you're the authority on your area of work within this company. Yes, we cannot see everything, and we need your observations to do our work at all. Yes, you're important, and we're here to serve you.

I find working this way to be less stressful, but there are more tangible, measurable benefits too. When you get to fully understand people's work, because people trust you enough to be honest, you sometimes get to intervene before problems compound. When you get to experience your company's engineering culture more deeply, you better understand the problem space and can make suggestions and plans based on reality and not your guess about what's actually going on. We can't make good security decisions without understanding the people we're meant to be serving, and we won't get to understand them if they don't trust us.

Stride Toward a More Positive Future

Once you establish a different way of doing things, you're going to have to zealously maintain it, which means prioritizing this in hiring both individual contributors and managers. I don't believe in hiring brilliant assholes because the cost is always so much higher than any supposed benefit. Over the last few years, my approach to interviewing has come to reflect this. The best way I've found to ferret out qualities that don't support the kind of work I've been explaining is to ask questions that require vulnerability or copping to knowledge gaps. In technical questions, I try to find the edge of the candidate's knowledge in a non-adversarial way, which means framing the interview from the start as a fun conversation about shared computer interests between peers. This means that when I keep asking for further explanations and find the edge of the candidate's knowledge, I'm looking for curiosity instead of defensiveness. Another way to blunt that line of questioning is to immediately ask how they would find out the answer to the question because geeking out about research is fun and gives the candidate time to shine.

For behavioral questions, I avoid asking those pointless "tell me the worst thing about you" questions and try to ask questions in a more neutral space, which gives them a chance to explain ambiguity but also includes victories.

Here are a few questions I've come to really enjoy asking:[4]

- Tell me about a difficult conversation you've had recently with a colleague and how you resolved it
- Tell me about a technical decision you came to regret and how you fixed it
- Tell me how you settled a technical disagreement on your team

Candidates that can contribute to a culture of yes tend to like these questions, expressing freely if they think it's complex or they need a moment

---

4   Yes, you may hear these if you ever interview with me, which is fine. These are not gotchas.

to think. This works best if I've managed to convey that I'm on their side, which I always am. My job as an interviewer is to let candidates shine; otherwise, I should ask myself if I'm asking the right questions and doing this very important job correctly.

These questions also give the interviewer the chance to see if the candidate defaults to blaming people who aren't there to defend themselves. I'm looking to see if they can relate a difficult story in a relatively blameless way because that skill is endlessly useful.

Within your existing team, it's critical to keep surfacing feedback, which goes back to my earlier recommendation to have meetings with everyone. Managers generally should do weekly or biweekly one-on-ones with their direct reports, of course, but the individual contributors (ICs) should be talking a lot too. If the team isn't too big, I like weekly check-ins with my teammates; if we're over, say, five or six people, biweekly meetings work well. The goal is to have an ongoing mechanism to get individual feedback from everyone involved in the work and to ensure that nothing important goes unsaid for more than a week or two. If someone has to figure out when and how to say something important to you, the system isn't working yet.

On top of all that, I like doing retros. There's an extensive body of writing about how to retro that already exists, so I'll spare us both today. The important thing is offering a neutral place for people to say positive and negative things, where they know their feedback will be heard and considered. Retros are for surfacing issues, not for solving them. The freedom for people to express what they've observed without being tasked with fixing them too (one of the most normalized telltales of toxic work cultures I've encountered) ensures that you learn what you need to know from your teammates. It's our job to learn from outside of our team, yes, but if your teammates aren't getting the same benefit, the whole thing's going to fall apart. If you've gone a long time without doing retros, you might try doing them every other week until you work through the backlog of feedback. After that, monthly is often frequent enough, particularly if you're ready to do them more often if something large or difficult is happening within the team or company.

Most companies are too large to do retros for all of engineering, but it's of tremendous benefit for security teams to provide an organized, low-effort way for people to respond to our work. For that, I like surveys. I know not everyone finds them the most effective, but I've gotten great confirmation of efforts that are working and clear replies that indicate when something isn't there yet. Incentivize responses with a bribe or get someone a couple of levels above you in management to encourage responding with a public participation rate goal. Keep the surveys short, clear, and as consistent as you can. Quarterly is a good cadence for this, though you may find monthly more effective if you're trying to recover from considerable culture problems.

Questions for a Security Survey

You can ask things like:

- What should our team do more of?
- What should we do less of?
- How do you describe our security team to others?
  (That last one can take some real bravery,
  but I believe you have it in you!)

Remember that even when all these parts are working well, we have to keep putting effort into the culture we've created. Deliberate culture without maintenance will decay over time. Get the first set of plans that encourage transparency and trust in place, and then reevaluate them regularly—monthly is good at first, and maybe you can move to quarterly once your structure feels solid. Every new hire brings new elements to consider, so we don't get the chance to coast.

But if that was a problem for us, we wouldn't be in security at all, would we?

ABOUT BREANNE BOLAND

Breanne Boland is a product security engineer with the Security Partnerships team at
Gusto. Before moving into security, she was a
site reliability engineer and an infrastructure
engineer who did work in healthcare and
govtech. Prior to that, she was a professional
writer, and she still considers finishing the
docs the real sign that the work is done. She
writes fiction and zines, embroiders, makes
creatures out of clay, and travels when it feels
safe. She lives in Oakland and can be found at
twitter.com/breanneboland.

Weaponizing
Compliance

CHAPTER 9

Weaponizing
Compliance

by Alison "Snipe" Gianotto

Weaponizing Compliance

Alison "Snipe" Gianotto

Like many people in InfoSec, the path leading me here was untraditional. I've been a forex broker, bartender, web developer, fine artist, graphic designer, leatherworker, makeup artist, animal welfare organization founder, tiger tamer, CTO, and now IT software company founder and CEO, all as a college dropout.

Perhaps it is best to start at the beginning, since it may explain some of the reasons for choices I made later on and hopefully demonstrate the kind of creative problem solving that can really make your skills, whatever they may currently be, a real asset in cybersecurity.

This will be a story of failure and success, humiliation and triumph, injustice and retribution, and animals; who doesn't like all that?

Where I Started

Right after dropping out of college in my first semester, I took a job as a forex broker on Wall Street in Manhattan, all the while not really understanding what my job was. I was not one of the fancy, *Wolf of Wall Street* type of brokers; I was one of the young and wildly underpaid types. The *do-I-eat-tonight-or-buy-a-pack-of-smokes* kind.

It was pretty standard on Wall Street back then to start off making practically nothing and work your way up as you land bigger "whales" as clients. I didn't stay in that industry long enough to make it into the big time. I realized that the prospect of waking up every morning to cold-call some folks in Kansas and tell them about why they needed to buy 10 million yen

RIGHT NOW seemed like a horrible way to live.

Lying to innocent people for a living just wasn't for me, and in retrospect, learning that in my very early 20s was probably the most useful thing I got out of that experience. That, and a ton of social engineering experience, since what is sales other than manipulating people to believe what you want them to believe and that they are the ones with the upper hand?

"Oh, you have to wait until your wife gets home to make such a big decision? I see. Maybe I should speak directly to her since it sounds like she makes the financial decisions in your household."

Or if you thought a softer touch would work better:

"The markets are moving very fast right now because of ‹XYZ ripped from the headline that morning›. If I were your wife, I wouldn't want you to miss out on this unprecedented opportunity."

Each sales response was crafted to appeal to people's fears, biases, ignorance, or greed. I started to catch myself using some of these techniques on my friends and family, and that's when I knew it was time for me to find a new way to make a living.

While I certainly didn't know it at the time, all of this sales training was really social engineering training. This skill would come in handy later on in my life when I was hunting down a cat-killer and when I helped put NFL quarterback Michael Vick in prison. More on that in a bit.

What Came Next

After I left Wall Street, I sort of fell into programming. I already knew some basic programming from school, and while the World Wide Web was still pretty new, the source code was open and readable. I taught myself web design, Perl, and eventually PHP. I tried to apply for "real" jobs, but without a degree, it was slow going. So, I started by building my portfolio. I'd basically work for free for anyone who wanted a website if they just paid for the domain name.

I worked as a graphic designer for a company that did those free black-and-white magazines where you could list your car, home, or boat. My job was to digitally remove garbage cans, people, and pets out of the photos, all the while praying that my hard drive at work wouldn't fill up before the day's work was done. I offered the owner of the company a free website, and he told me "Nah. The internet thing is just a fad."

Eventually, I landed my first real job. It was in Atlanta, GA and it paid a stunning $30k a year. I felt like I had struck gold. I was working at a computer telephony company, and while I was hired to handle their website, I ended up doing booth design and all kinds of other things.

Next, I went on to teach graphic design and web development, then worked as a contractor for a while. After that, I was hired to do HTML but ended up handling a lot of systems work as well as some ColdFusion, PHP, ASP, Java, and Perl. I was leaning pretty heavily on IRC, an early internet chat system, since I was often in situations where I didn't always know what I was doing but had to figure it out mighty quick.

Eventually, I got a job offer from a company I had been doing contract work for as a Technical Director. So, I picked up my life in frozen NYC and moved to sunny San Diego, CA.

Spreadsheets, Social Engineering, and the Cat that Changed Everything

While I was in San Diego about 20 years ago, tragedy struck. My neighbor's cat was set on fire with a Molotov cocktail. A police investigation was started and we learned the suspect was a person of interest in a few other animal cruelty cases in the area, but nobody could find him. Weeks passed with no progress on the investigation.

Finally, I created a spreadsheet, because that's what I do when I feel like I need control over a situation. I updated the spreadsheet every time we learned something new and emailed it to both the Police and Humane Law Enforcement investigators. There were three sections: Facts, Needs Verification, and Rumors. "Facts" were things provable in a court of law since there was evidence or testimony. "Needs Verification" were things we knew to be true, but still needed evidence to prove in court (such as testimony from a witness we believed credible, but who was unwilling to testify.) "Rumors" were just that - things we had heard, but had not yet been able to prove or look into, but could be useful to the investigation.

I printed up flyers and started canvassing the neighborhood of Pacific Beach where the suspect was believed to be hiding. Pacific Beach is a bit of a party town, so my husband at the time and I stopped into the kinds of places we thought he might frequent based on what we knew about the suspect's habits and culture. Finally, we hit pay dirt. Someone at a local beach club knew one of the suspect's roommates. We scored an address under the pretext that I had left something at the suspect's house but could not remember his exact address. We went home to think through our next steps.

My husband at the time was a private investigator from Brooklyn and not afraid to tussle. However, we decided the best approach would be the softer one since we didn't know what we'd be up against. I put on my best cute-girl outfit, practiced flipping my hair back and forth as coyly as I could, and we set out for his apartment. He planned to wait around the corner in case I encountered any trouble. We hoped to confirm the suspect lived there so we could give a confirmed address to the police.

As luck would have it, we ran into the suspect's ex-girlfriend heading to his apartment. I asked if she knew him. She responded that she did, and her face contorted with contempt as she told us he had killed her kittens in a very cruel way. This was shocking but also not unexpected, since we already had several reports of animal cruelty connected to the suspect. The woman admitted she did not file a police report since she wanted to avoid any further trouble from the suspect or his friends.

I asked for her name hoping to add it to the spreadsheet, but she wouldn't give it to me. She wished me luck as she continued down the stairs. It was another data point for the "Rumors" column of my investigation spread-sheet. Not ideal, but better than nothing.

My hands were shaking as we got closer to his apartment door. Shaking like a chihuahua, I steeled myself and finally rang the doorbell. Footsteps thudded in my direction and the door swung open.

It wasn't him. I breathed a silent sigh of relief, even though I wanted proof that that's where he was staying. I asked the young man who answered the door whether or not the suspect was home. He looked at me suspiciously, initially saying he didn't know the suspect. I insisted that he did and mustered up some upset-jilted-girl emotions, and he finally told me the suspect had returned to his native country. I made sure to look sad and disappointed and thanked him for his time, giving him my phone number in case he heard from the suspect because "I thought we had a real connection."

I've never been a particularly good actor. There is a reason I was always on the set crew in high school and never on stage. I've never been very good at hiding my feelings; I'm a New Jersey Italian, after all. It's just not in our DNA. We talk with our hands, we're very loud, we have extremely strong opinions about pizza and what pasta sauce should be called, and we don't hide our emotions, for good or for bad. I was pretty proud of my performance that day, and at least we got a few more lines for the spreadsheet, even if it was not the evidence we wanted. We knew where the suspect had lived before he fled the country to avoid questioning.

Unfortunately, this left us at a bit of a dead end. We eventually learned the suspect had left threatening voicemails for a law enforcement officer. Later, we learned how the suspect managed to flee the United States. I wish this part of my story had a happy ending, but it does not. The suspect was never apprehended and likely never will be. Sometimes there isn't a happy ending, but you just keep going.

As Promised, a Bunch of Animals

My first experience fighting for animal welfare wasn't only my first foray into pretexts and social engineering, it was something that changed me. I ended up creating an animal welfare organization, called "Pet-Abuse.com." It started as a centralized database for animal cruelty information, but over time it turned into a sort of Megan's law for animal abusers. I compiled criminal reports of animal abusers and broke this information down by location and other violent and non-violent criminal activity.

Animal welfare is notoriously underfunded and tech-deprived, but we began to turn some heads. At the time, I worked a full-time programming job for a San Diego non-profit and came home to work each night for another 5-6 hours on this project. I hoped to hand it off to a larger organization with proper staffing, but it remained in my hands. My idea was to create a login for every police and Humane Law Enforcement (HLE) agency out there, so we could build a centralized database with meaningful statistics and the ability to track bigger patterns in animal cruelty previously unavailable.

How Infosec Became Very, Very Important to Me

Alison, where on earth are you going with this?? I'm getting there, I swear it. This is where my real foray into InfoSec began. To track criminal correlations, I would often run background checks on suspects. I started embedding myself on dogfighting and cockfighting forums, creating different personas with different backgrounds and typed speech patterns. I posted every so often so the account wouldn't appear new if I ever needed it and made sure my VPNs were location-accurate, since I didn't know how savvy the animal fighting forums admins were.

> **Always assume the person who runs the server knows at least as much as you do, even if it's not true.**

As always, I made a spreadsheet for all of my personas with their backstories.

As the animal welfare organization gained notoriety, I found myself starting to do forensic work on photos and videos. I worked with welfare organizations plus local and federal law enforcement agencies on the forensic information I discovered from file metadata, audio, landmarks, or characteristics of the video background settings. Eventually, I was asked to speak at some large animal welfare conferences to discuss my work with the database and with law enforcement.

I ran my organization's website basically on my own, including all sysadmin tasks. We had no money coming in other than the odd $10 donation. I had no time because I worked full-time, so I ran everything on a Cobalt RaQ. In 2002. If you have lost all respect for me now, I kinda don't blame you. It was what I could afford at the time, both in time and money.

So, here's where it gets good, and by good, I mean *absolutely positively awful.*

I spent another year chugging forward with my organization and forensic work. Then, I got invited to speak at a national humane society conference. They wanted me to talk about my organization, how animal control officers could use it, and how we were using statistical data. This conference is HUGE, and I'm already a wreck when I get off the 6-hour flight. I had so much imposter syndrome that I could barely say my own name at the speaker registration counter.

Me: *"Hi, I'm here to pick up my speaker badge. I'm Alison Gianotto, with Pet-Abuse.Com".*

Her: *"Welcome! I am SO SORRY to hear about what happened with your website."*

Me: *"... My... Um... what?"*

I immediately snatched my speaker packet and raced to find out what exactly the very nice registration lady was talking about.

To my indescribable horror, the homepage of the organization website had been hijacked with a looping video from Meatspin with the song "You spin me right round baby right round" by Dead or Alive at top volume over and over. I just stared at the homepage for at least 30 seconds, slack-jawed and not fully comprehending what I was seeing. I had to present this website in literal hours. Suffice to say, I tossed up a maintenance page and carefully skipped the live demo portion of that presentation.

I spent the next several days chatting with the guy who defaced the website through a series of text files left on the server. Naturally, I'd restore the pages, but because I couldn't see how he was getting in, I couldn't stop him from doing it again. Instead, I attempted to distract him and engage him on an emotional level. I had apparently done such a good job with the design, features, and copy of the organization website that he assumed we were vastly larger than we were. The end goal for him was to extort money from us. One of my text messages on the server sounded something like "Dude. We're an organization of three people, me and two unpaid volunteers. We pull in less than $3k a year in donations. You can't get blood from a stone. My day job that pays for this is at a non-profit. WTF."

If one had to pick a single defining moment in my life where InfoSec became very, VERY important to me, it was that moment in the speaker registration line feeling like all of the blood was draining out of my face, and yet somehow simultaneously feeling humiliated. So, thanks, random dirtbag! I'll buy you a drink next DEF CON. Look for the short chick with the purple Mohawk who still has a physical reaction to hearing Dead or Alive.

Eventually, I'd come to realize I was already "in" cybersecurity, I just didn't realize it at the time. I spent the next decade training cops how to recognize fighting dogs and birds in classified ads. I also helped district attorneys write better jury instructions to utilize existing animal welfare laws.

On Backbreaking Work to Move an Immovable Needle

One more story about the animal welfare and InfoSec conjunction, arguably the most notable one and one that has been covered heavily in media and books. Back in 2007, Michael Vick, an NFL player, was arrested for allegations of dog-fighting. He was subsequently convicted and served prison time. This case was fraught from the start for a variety of reasons, not the least of which being that dog-fighters tend to be very secretive and smarter than the average criminal.

Animal fighting is often associated with illegal gambling, food and drug violations, child labor violations, child endangerment, and many other crimes. It can be a challenge to prosecute animal fighting cases, especially in rural areas. For those of you unaware about this kind of activity, there is often a LOT of money at stake. This isn't nickel-and-dime criming; hundreds of thousands of dollars can be exchanged in these situations.

Enter those embedded profiles I mentioned. There were multiple, prominent dog-fighting forums that I had been working on for years. I wouldn't post every day, but often enough to pass for a real member. I'd complain about my "wife," ask questions that only a dogman would ask about fight preparation (also known as a "keep"), and keep my engagement up enough to seem like a valid member of the community. Funny thing is, when I first joined these websites, I didn't know how I'd use them. They were also largely running vBulletin, so I knew what information they collected by default.

I gained access to an additional website after months of social engineering. It was effectively a registry of fighting dogs and their lineage. Lineage is critically important since a dog from a known line of Champions or Grand Champions is worth more money than a dog from a lesser known blood-line or a dog with fewer wins. Gaining this access was a lengthy process that involved getting a post office box in Louisiana and having mail quietly forwarded to me in order to "prove" my identity to the website operators.

While this website made lineage information available, dog owner infor-mation was often obfuscated. Initials are used and colloquially-known kennel names without legal registration are often used instead of dog owner names. I encountered a series of puzzles to ownership at the regis-try level. Next, I pored over forums to find connections and build a narra-tive based on names, nicknames, times, dates, locations, and fight stories. I wish I had a social engineering tool like Maltego available at the time!

The investigation was challenging for many reasons, even though orga-nizations much bigger than mine had cadres of lawyers ready and were begging to help. Unfortunately, we struggled with the evidence we had. At one point during my research, I happened to find at least anecdotal evi-dence on a smaller, less well-known dogfighting website with evidence of the sale of fighting dogs by Michael Vick across state lines. This allowed us to get a federal warrant for bank records and escalated the case to a new prosecutor.

The reality is a lot less glam than what you see on crime shows. It was back-breaking work, but it moved what seemed to be an otherwise immov-able needle and we got our conviction.

Creative Problem Solving Is the Core of Hacking

At this point, you may be wondering where I'm going with this. This chap-ter was supposed to be weaponizing compliance and yet this very sen-tence is the first time I even mention the word "compliance". The reason it's taken so long to get here is because I want you to see the why before the how. Your whys and hows may end up being different, but they are all important, and everybody's journey is going to be different.

> **Creative problem solving has always been at the core of hacking, whichever way it manifests itself.**

My reason is animal welfare, which is how I accidentally landed in OSINT, social engineering, OpSec, and network security. I also learned OpSec because while running that organization. I'd get death threats all the time from convicted violent criminals, including death threats sent by fax.

Years after the Michael Vick case, I was still speaking at conferences and providing training materials to law enforcement to help them recognize the secret language used publicly by dog-fighters. I started a new job, where I was hired as a Senior Developer. Within my first two weeks, a colleague accidentally deleted a production server for a *very large customer.* I called in some favors to try and intercept the cancellation, but it was too late. There were no backups and the source code was in version control. The data was lost and I had to spend four weeks without sleep trying to recreate a website from a handful of screenshots that were a few years old. I also had to ask the customer for some of their data back. Welcome to your new job, Alison!

Being the shiny-new one at the org, I was trying to tread carefully. I've been called all kinds of things throughout my career: *overbearing, domineering, aggressive, too assertive, too ambitious,* you name it. So, I tried to be a little more careful. But, two weeks into my employment, I proposed a two-person sign-off system before we cancel any servers moving forward. I got approval and felt relieved I wouldn't have to pull psychotic hours again. Oh, if only.

Several months later, I was trying to implement some standards that I'd consider bare minimum: Concurrent Versions System (CVS) and Subversion (SVN), incremental backups, and a process to check that backups actually work. I started facing pushback from management, since they wanted me to work on client projects instead of mucking around with processes and servers.

Being the Person Who Really Cares About Security

I faced resistance for several months and began to feel hopeless. I made forward movements where I could, but every security control I tried to use was met with resistance because it was too expensive, too slow, too much overhead, or not necessary. Nobody cared.

I cared. A lot. I'd been on the wrong end of this before. I had slowly been picking up the sysadmin duties, the cloud architecture duties, and all of the other tasks like desktop IT. Then, a very large customer started to hold us to the same standards as they were holding other vendors who stored sensitive payment card data. We received a 40-page security questionnaire from the very large customer for each of our numerous short and long-term projects. No one in the organization other than me was qualified to answer. I set up the servers and I set up access; it had to be me.

I. Was. *Thrilled.*

Seriously and genuinely, I was. FINALLY, I had a shot at actually getting us where I wanted to be as an organization, with real money and consequences behind it. I could yowl all I wanted about security. But when a huge customer started demanding security to renew a contract, people listened. I had to keep asking for more time, money, and security resources, but I had a key customer relationship in my corner.

Security questionnaires can be challenging, and my first set of questionnaires had little standardization across definitions, questions, or anything else. I spent a lot of time chasing down answers. Over time, the customer's security department did standardize some of their questions. When this happened, I felt really good about our security posture and the customer considered us a trusted vendor. We had built trust. A few years later, I even traded war stories at DEF CON with a lead from the customer. He was delightful.

Whether or not they realized it, the customer allowed me to assign actual numbers, specific costs, and real profit and loss to the risk of not handling our security better during this previous role.

Using Customer Questionnaires to Strengthen Security

A customer questionnaire checkbox asked, "How often do you do security training at your organization?" At first, the answer was never. But, because this requirement was customer-driven, I was finally granted permission to do quarterly security training and new hire security onboarding. I continued these training sessions for as long as I worked in this role, including anything from a presentation, to aggressive red-team attempts, to phishing attempts and much more.

I started organizing capture the flag events (CTFs) for development teams because collaborating with devs can be hard. It can be difficult to convince a developer to change their code after a penetration test if they don't understand why it matters. When you turn it into something they can care about and help them understand why they should care, you are well on your way. Pizza and competition both help.

My now-husband was a systems and development lead at a different company at the time. His team started to see an increase in customer questionnaires and requirements. He reacted with disdain and contempt. I suggested we both tackle the DEF CON CTF together. The CTF was based on an insecure Ruby on Rails app, which was exactly the language he worked in often at the time. With just a little guidance, he started looking at server headers and realizing the security issues.

Next, my developer husband started writing a password cracker to handle the /etc/passwd. He calculated the execution time (no rainbow tables) to 17 days, which would have gotten him to twelve character passwords. I pointed him to John the Ripper and the password was cracked in 7 seconds. Just like that, you could see it click. Security made sense to him.

Weaponizing compliance allowed me to transform an organization from zero to a trusted vendor within two years. That's not nothing. You will not always make friends as a security person. But, it's worth it.

I will leave it up to the reader to decide if my perspective isn't something that works for you. My experience is pretty unique, and yours will be too.

In Conclusion

Use the tools you have. Sometimes those tools will be customer requirements, which hurts a little at the time, but will make you stronger in the end. Stand by the things you value. The entirety of your experience is what determines how well you can predict threats, mitigate them, and quickly react to the ones you missed.

ABOUT ALISON GIANOTTO

Alison "Snipe" Gianotto started and maintains an open source IT asset management application called Snipe IT and wrote a silly browser plugin called Downworthy that got a bit of press in early 2014. She also runs a funny Tumblr for DevOps, InfoSec, and developers, another for cranky haikus, LessThanThrees, and LovingLowCarb.net.

Snipe has been lucky enough to do some cool stuff in her forty-something years, more than half of which she has spent making stuff online. These include working with tigers and lions, co-authoring a few books on PHP/MySQL, studying krav maga, being featured in People Magazine, and being named a finalist to the Animal Planet Hero of the Year contest in 2006.

She is a keynote speaker at many developer conferences, a featured guest on many podcast episodes, a panelist, and often listed among the top developer, security, and CTO voices on Twitter by such publications as Business Insider, Hackbright, Venture Beat, AdAge, and CEOWorldMagazine. You can find her at twitter.com/snipeyhead

F*ck Security Maturity; Let's Talk about Security Health!

by Carlota Sage

F*ck Security Maturity; Let's Talk about Security Health!

Carlota Sage

Until I got into information security, my greatest gift to the world was getting Netflix to stop calling its Spanish members "miembros."

In 2012, I was on a (pre-video) conference call with our Latinx call centers and announced the rollout of the much-requested Spanish translations of the Netflix Help Center, only to be met by stone-cold silence. After what felt like an eternity, a voice very quietly asked, *"We don't call our subscribers 'miembros,' do we?"*

"Well, yes, that's what we call them in the interface...is it a problem?"
More silence.

I was getting an uneasy feeling about this.

Finally: *"Uh...we don't say that word on the phone."*

Confused, I asked why, but the director suggested he'd fill me later. Just as in English, it turns out that the word *miembro* could denote 'a person within a group,' or it could mean a particular appendage. And according to this director, the further south you went, the further south the meaning went.

I emailed this concern to Marketing, letting them know I was changing the word in the Help Center, and they needed to change it in the interface. A gentleman in L.A. whose parents came from Mexico City insisted this was not the case and I should not change anything. I responded that I had 110 people on the ground who would not use this word on the phone in the Help Center for fear of offending someone's *abuela*. I changed the word; I'd rather get fired for doing the right thing than keep working knowing I've chosen to do wrong.

A few months later, after a focus group or two, Marketing sent me a note giving me "permission" to make the change that I'd made at the very beginning.

What Does This Story Have to Do With InfoSec?

Even when we're experts in a discipline like Marketing or Security, it doesn't make us the expert in our customers' needs. NIST, CMMC, and other maturity models were made for security practitioners and not for the executives, business leaders, or employees they serve. Even when speaking the same language, we're not speaking their language with all of its cultural and historial nuances.

More importantly, just as Netflix needed to stop calling their Latinx subscribers *miembros*, we need to stop saying "security maturity" to our business leaders. "Maturity" means that you continuously get better or more sophisticated, and that's simply not the case with cybersecurity. It's much easier to lose traction with your security program than grow it. We need to talk about healthy and unhealthy security habits with our business peers. Let's stop talking about security maturity and start talking about security health.

What's Wrong With Talking About Maturity?

Simply put, it's jargon. What's worse is that we throw the NIST Maturity Model at folks while we're talking jargon at them. Don't get me wrong; the NIST Maturity Model is great if you're a security person. But for a non-security professional, the model assumes you know enough about security to interpret it. It assumes the viewer understands the relationship between information security and risk management. The arrows denote movement between tiers but assume the security professional knows what contributes to that movement. The model presumes an experienced practitioner or someone who has spent a few hours pouring over NIST documentation to understand how it works.

NIST Security Maturity Model (Prisma)[1]

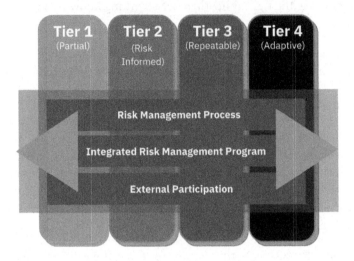

The CMMC and NIST Risk Management Hierarchy suffer the same weakness. You need to have a good knowledge of security for these models to be useful. Even with documentation, these models are about the security practitioner's implementation of security processes rather than communicating security to the business. These models are necessary but not very helpful for a CISO, vCISO, or someone trying to start a security program to bridge the communication gap with organizational leadership.

I searched the Internet for other maturity models. I found some decent ones by consulting groups, but frankly, I often found the language they used insulting or fueling "FUD" (fear, uncertainty, doubt). There is a rampant problem within our industry of security experts talking down to anyone who isn't a fellow security expert or using fear to sell security products and services. I realized I could solve two problems with one model. I could make a model meaningful to business professionals while giving a great example of how to talk about security without using a condescending tone or resorting to FUD.

---

1   Program Review for Information Security Assurance (PRISMA). NIST CSRC. (2016, December 6). csrc.nist.gov/Projects/Program-Review-for-Information-Security-Assistance/Security-Maturity-Levels

What Key Concepts Do We Need to Communicate About Cybersecurity?

There are several essential components to communicate to an executive team and board to ensure initial and ongoing support for a security program.

1. Security has an organizing principle.
Even if your organization doesn't have a security or compliance team, someone is probably practicing good security hygiene in their little corner. Some teams have implemented security basics in response to regulatory and compliance requirements. But the best way to approach security is as an entire organization, which requires organization!

2. An organization's awareness of security impacts security health.
The organization's security depth is directly proportional to the number of people who understand security basics and practice them. Awareness requires a shared understanding of security throughout the organization, from employees to the executive team and board of directors.

3. An organization's culture impacts your security health.
Highly siloed organizations or teams with poor communication have a more difficult path to security healthiness. A security program may highlight cultural weaknesses.

4. How you use technology is more important than what you use.
You could spend all the money in the world on technology and tooling, but achieving security healthiness happens when you use technology in a way that best supports your organization's business objectives.

5. Security requires leadership to stay healthy.
The executive team has to be fully committed to securing your organization to be successful. More importantly, they need meaningful insights and metrics that help them understand how security reduces the organization's overall business risk. They need to know when to invest more or change how they invest in the security program.

6. Security requires constant vigilance to stay healthy.
Security is not a "climb to the top of the mountain" activity, where once you've reached the peak, you're done! No, security is a "steer the ship

through the rocks to keep the boat from running aground" activity. There is almost never a "set it and forget it" task or technology in security.

With these things in mind, I drafted the first security maturity health model in early 2020. It lives in a GitHub repo under Creative Commons, so anyone could use it.

Security Health Model			
< Less Healthy		**More Healthy >**	
	Likely Drivers	Likely Drivers	Likely Drivers
	Grassroots or Ad Hoc	**Team- or Compliance-Driven**	**Risk-Informed or Risk-Based**
Organizing Principal	Individuals take responsibility for security in their areas, but may lack necessary resources, such as tools and training	Security measures driven by a specific team; by State, Federal or International regulations; and/or industry expectations	Security is an organization-wide risk management program, a coordinated effort of people, processes and technology
Organizational Awareness	No unified insight into nor understanding of security across teams, execs and board; lack of security awareness across organization as a whole	Executive insight primarily into compliance end-state at irregular or lengthy (monthly, quarterly or yearly) intervals, or only when requested. Board, Organization as a whole unlikely to have any insight unless there's an issue.	Executives and Board of Directors have regular briefings on security incidents and needs. Security integrated into program and/or project management frameworks.
Culture	Little collaboration between technical and business or non-technical groups; technical groups may be siloed, competitive or even antagonistic	Partnership with business and non-technical teams generally weak beyond addressing specific requests or the need for compliance	Disparate technical teams are highly collaborative. Security is brought in early & partners with the business throughout project lifecycles. All personnel (not just security team) understand their role in securing the organization

		Security Health Model (continued)	
	< Less Healthy	**More Healthy >**	
	Likely Drivers	Likely Drivers	Likely Drivers
Likely Drivers	**Grassroots or Ad Hoc**	**Team- or Compliance-Driven**	**Risk-Informed or Risk-Based**
Technology	Basic technology such as firewalls and antivirus software may be place; more advanced technology may be available but not leveraged to best potential	Heavy emphasis on controls and technology, likely without an understanding of or consideration for business risk or operations	Advanced tools, monitoring, and metrics are in place. Communication strategies, change control, and other processes in place to reduce impact on business. Expectation to scale and automate as needed to address changing risks.
Leadership Model	No central Security leadership, or Security reports into IT	Security leadership reports into the IT, Legal or Compliance team, often with no direct communication path to CEO or Board of Directors.	Security leadership reports directly to (or is) C-Suite and has direct access to the Board of Directors. Security has a budget is considered an operating cost, not overhead

It's not a "simple" model, but it is a meaningful one. It hits all six critical facets I wanted to in a single table. I included enough verbiage to make each state meaningful to someone with zero understanding of cybersecurity – and without anyone having to read a book on it (unless they really want to).

In addition to hitting the six key talking points, I felt the model embodied security health concepts in an eye-catching way that helps a business person rapidly move through it.

Driving Factors

Despite the reliance on verbiage of the organizational security health model, some key concepts help move executive teams through the model.

Grassroots or Ad Hoc

In the "Ad Hoc" concept, any approach to security is on an individual or team basis, or security is seen as a problem that can be solved with technology alone. There is no organization-wide approach to or understanding of security and no centralized ownership of the security strategy.

Team- or Compliance-Driven

In the Compliance-Driven concept, government regulations, industry standards or customer expectations drive an organization towards security. Security awareness and collaboration coalesces around compliances needs, shifting security to being a "compliance problem." Technology emphasis shifts to compliance controls, potentially endangering any focus on business risk.

Risk-Informed or Risk-Based

In the Risk Management-Driven concept, security becomes a vehicle for managing business risk across the organization. There is a shared understanding of security both across the organization and at the leadership/Board level. Security is viewed as an integral part of any business endeavor, with technology implemented in alignment with business objectives. Security strategy is centralized and has a direct communication line with the Board of Directors.

Most importantly, the model talks about "Security Health" rather than Maturity...

Less Healthy vs. More Healthy

I found it was difficult to paint a quick picture or make a quick analogy using the "less mature vs. more mature" or "immature vs. mature" verbiage. Instead, I chose "less healthy vs. more healthy;" in discussions, it's easier to compare the maturity scale to grabbing a candy bar, a granola bar, or a chicken salad for lunch. You're fulfilling the core objective of getting calories into your system, no matter which one you get. It paints a swift image that making less healthy security choices, like only ever eating candy bars, leads to increasingly less positive outcomes over time.

Use the Security Health Model as a guide for meaningful discussions with your executive team and Board of Directors. Start with the embodied concepts to paint the bigger picture, then fill in details with the six key talking points to help leadership understand where the organization as a whole is now and where they need it to be. Use the simplified version to keep maturity concepts fresh as you give the executive team and Board updates.

Turning the Security Health Model into a Health Checkup

Security is a classic case of the chicken and the egg:

How do I justify the cost of security tooling when I don't have a security program? How do I measure my security program if I don't have security tooling?

I felt like the Security Health Model could help solve this conundrum, but I didn't want to just slap a scale on it. However, after looking at other business and security models from common frameworks and consulting groups, slapping a scale on it was the most obvious evolution. If your scale is meaningful, it's operational. By having a scale, you can better communicate where you are and where you need to be, then use it to drive improvements in security operations, even if they create a net spend.

Since there were three major themes in the Security Health Model, the simplest thing to do was start with a three-point scale. I distilled the Health Model to its three key stages.

With these three stages highlighted, the scale starts to take shape:

1. Little or no consideration of information security.
2. Information security has an organization-wide structure, documentation and project management.
3. Security is considered a critical business and sales tool. Practices are repeatable, scalable and optimizable.

You can absolutely use the simple three point scale, but a five point scale gives more nuance by defining the "between" states, allowing an organization to better see its progression. The difference between a 1 and a 2, or between a 2 and a 3, on a three point scale is a big leap for a smaller organization. The difference between a 1 and a 3, or a 3 and a 5, on a five point scale better delineates a path by defining the middle ground between them.

1. Little or no consideration of information security.
2. Information security efforts lack structure and organization. Even if processes are well defined, they are generally poorly documented. Successful efforts are localized and unlikely to be repeatable or scalable.
3. Information security has basic structure, documentation and project management; there is organization-wide oversight/insight even if scalability is an issue. Security likely be driven by compliance/regulation rather than an understanding of risk management.
4. Processes are well-defined, well-documented, repeatable and scalable, incorporating data analytics for insights. Information security is a risk management tool rather than a compliance tool.
5. Information Security program or team has the experience and technology needed to provide near real-time insights

to the executive team and business units. The focus is on process optimization for the entire organization, not just security.

Now that the scale was set, I had to figure out how to use it.

What Are We Measuring?

In Technical Support Operations, I coached a lot of support engineers on how to troubleshoot and helped technical writers with creating trouble-shooting guides. In troubleshooting a problem, whether it's hardware or software, it's helpful to break the system down into components. Problems can happen within a component—where two or more components inter-act—or at the interface to the user.

That's why it's helpful to think of an organization as a system, with secu-rity as one component. We need to understand what can go wrong with the pieces internal to security (i.e., the security component), the interac-tions of the security component with other business components, and how security is presented or interacts with the company's customers.

With this structure in mind, the health model measures the organization as a system, including its cross-functional relationships, cybersecurity operations, and external relationships.

Measuring Security in an Organization	
Cross-functional Relationships	
Business Alignment	What Security needs to know about the Business
Awareness & Training	What the Business needs to know about Security
Compliance & Audit	What Business and Security need to know about Regulations
Communication & Change Management	How Security supports and interacts with the Business
Cybersecurity Operations	
Program Management	How Security functions
Asset and Vendor Management	What Security needs to secure
Detection	How Security monitors assets and environments

Emerging Threats & Vulnerability Mgmt	What Security needs to know about external risk
Incident Response	How Security responds to immediate threats
Communication Strategy	How Security communicates what's happening
External Relationships	
Partner Relationships	How Security interacts with external Partners
Customer Relationships	How Security interacts with external Customers
Public Relations & Crisis Communications	How Security presents itself to the public at large

Where Are We Measuring?

For larger or mature organizations, align these metrics to existing business units: Finance, IT, Marketing, Sales, Customer Service, etc. For smaller organizations or organizations without a traditionally defined structure, align to Operations and Product Lines.

An example of an initial Security Health Check is excerpted below. This example company is measuring the security of its internal operations, along with two different products.

Example of Security Health Check at Time = 0 Months			
	IT or Internal Ops	Product 1	Product 2
Cross-functional Relationships			
Business Alignment	2	2	2
Awareness & Training	1	1	1
Compliance & Audit	2	2	1
Communication & Change Management	1	1	1

How Are We Measuring?

I like to start these as team discussions to bring a balance between those who gloss over things and those that focus on the negative. Later, they're easily updated as a part of your internal review or audit.

Use these questions to help you guide these discussions.

Questions to Consider when Assessing Security Health

Cross-functional Relationships

Business Alignment	Do employees know what to do or who to contact if they have security questions or concerns? Do employees understand the data they handle and their responsibility for handling it securely?
Awareness & Training	Have employees completed the organization's baseline security training this year? Has leadership worked with the security team to identify additional training needs for their group?
Compliance & Audit	Is leadership aware of industry or government regulations that impact both the company and their group in particular? Is the group prepared for an audit tomorrow, and if not, how long do they feel it would take to prepare?
Communication & Change Management	Does the group include security as a consideration/ communication need in project and change management procedures?

Cybersecurity Operations

Program Management	Is there easy access to security information from the systems most commonly used by this group? Is security information managed and shared in a way that this group feels informed?
Asset and Vendor Management	Are physical and digital assets for this group included and regularly updated in asset inventory? Is security reviewed as a part of vendor or third-party review and engagement?
Detection	Are the assets and systems most used by this group included in any detection platform used by the security/technical team?
Threat & Vulnerability Management	Is this group's attack surface larger than or a significant portion of the organization's attack surface; if so, is there increased visibility into those areas? Is this group's resources appropriately prioritized for systems patching and vulnerability management.

Incident Response	Is this group's needs included in the corporate incident response plan?
Communication Strategy	Is this group included in security communication policies/plans or any security RACI matrices?
External Relationships	
Partner Relationships	Does the security or leadership team have contact information for those responsible for security and privacy at partner organizations? Does the security or leadership team have regular (quarterly or yearly) reviews of partner security practices?
Customer Relationships	Is there an escalation path from front-line customer support and social media personnel to security? Is the security and privacy information on the corporate or product website easy for customers to access and understand? [B:B] Does the security or leadership team have regular (quarterly or yearly) communication and reviews with customers?
Public Relations & Crisis Communications	Is there an easy way for good samaritans to report issues found with your website or product? Does your organization have or participate in a bug bounty program? Are crisis communications and plans well documented and easily found by employees?

The Health Model in Action

Let's assess one of these questions for the health model using our five-point scale from above.

"Do employees know what to do or who to contact if they have security questions or concerns?" If the answer is:

- "How do I know if my question is related to security?" = 1
- "Yes, I pop into Slack and ping IT," = 2
- Follow-up question = "What does IT do next?"
  - If IT has a process for handling this, great! They're still at least a 2.
  - If IT has an accurately documented process, even better! They're now a 3.
  - If IT has an accurately documented process AND that process can still function if your company suddenly doubled, this is best!! This is a 4!

It's important to note that a "3" is the baseline – I tell new clients (who are usually all 1s or 1s & 2s when they come to us) that "3" is where I want them to be after six months.

You'll often find that someone, perhaps even an entire team, is behaving in a security-conscious way. But if that process isn't documented, that team is not achieving even the baseline of 3. All they have to do to reach the baseline is write down the existing process. That's it! So while time-consuming, it can be very easy for that team to reach a baseline of 3, which positions them well for a SOC 2 audit.

> **IMPORTANT:**
> I don't expect any sub-500 person company to be a 4 or 5 – this requires a significant investment in security tooling that non-enterprise organizations usually can't afford. The initial goal is to get an organization to a baseline of 3.

How Often Are We Measuring?

My team at Fractional CISO creates an initial security health model as a part of the gap analysis with a new customer, then after six to eight months together, so they can see their improvement. After that, yearly for very mature/stable organizations or biannually for growing organizations. The SHM will help ensure that healthy security practices are maintained as an organization grows.

What Does Improvement Look Like?

Below, you'll see that the organization we looked at earlier has made some improvements after six months of work!

Example of Security Health Check at Time = 6 Months			
	IT or Internal Ops	Product 1	Product 2
Cross-functional Relationships			
Business Alignment	3	3	2
Awareness & Training	3	3	3
Compliance & Audit	3	3	2
Communication & Change Management	3	2	2

So there. Fuck Security Maturity. Long live Security Health!

ABOUT CARLOTA SAGE

Carlota is a vCISO Principal at Fractional CISO. She spent much of her technical career driving the development of technical and customer knowledge bases, including the NETGEAR Support website and Netflix Help Center.

Carlota discovered her love for cybersecurity when she took over FireEye's customer-facing communities in 2014. Over the next three years, she helped hundreds of security teams solve hardware, networking, product and security issues while completing her MS in Information and Knowledge Strategy from Columbia University.

Since joining the Fractional CISO team in 2021, Carlota has brought her history in knowledge strategy, collaboration and culture to securing small and mid-sized businesses. Carlota also serves on the Board of Directors for The Diana Initiative, a group committed to fostering diversity in cybersecurity.

You can download Excel files with Carlota's models and other handy tools under the Creative Commons license from her Github: github.com/carlota/showmethemoney

Carlota hopes you customize these resources to your needs and use them to improve your organization's understanding of security health!

Repositioning
Cybersecurity

CHAPTER 11

Repositioning Cybersecurity

by Lisa Hall

Repositioning Cybersecurity

Lisa Hall

Introduction

After months of saving, you've gone out and purchased the car of your dreams. Oh, it is all you've dreamt of–new car smell, amazing speakers, turbo launch, all the bells and whistles. You love this car.

Six months later, it's Saturday morning, and you have about a million errands to run. You hop in your fancy new mode of transportation, turn the key, and bam–there it is, shining in all its glory–that damn check engine light.

Car repair is the last thing you want to be doing. Where will you find the time? Will you need a rental? Does the dealership have a car service? How long will this take? Who's going to pick up the dog from daycare? Can this wait? Is driving the car with the check engine light on dangerous? If so, **how** dangerous is it **really**?

All of these questions address risk. Like traditional cybersecurity risk assessments, you are trying to gather as much information as possible to identify your "actual" risk. What is the likelihood of it happening, and if so, what is the potential impact? For example, what if the tire tread is low? The risk there could be a possible accident that might harm you or others. Driving down the block to the shop on a sunny day is a very different risk scenario than driving that same car for a week, during the rainy season, on an hour-long freeway commute to the office. The longer you wait to get new tires, the greater chance you will be in a dangerous situation.

I bet no one gets overly excited when they see a check engine light come on, not even our mechanic. Generic alerts are vague signals of 'something' wrong without indicating actual risk. It takes a specialist, usually a computer, to diagnose a potential issue, but even that generally needs to be validated and then fixed by a human (mechanic).

The antiquated view of security teams is that we are the check engine light and the car mechanic giving out bad news. Everyone dreads seeing us pop up unexpectedly with urgent requests that have little context but cost a lot of money–right? Risk can be tricky to explain and is sometimes not communicated very well. Let's challenge the old view of security as bearers of bad news, a blocker, Big Brother, or a money pit.

Security teams must reinvent themselves as business enablers, partners, and even revenue-generators. That's right, revenue-generating! We want to be the team you check in with before the product is live, the team you call when you want to understand risk and trade-offs. We are not a team of blockers; we are enablers.

Show Me The Money: Security As Revenue Generating

The old view of security teams is they are non-revenue generating and expensive. Talent and tooling are expensive, and having an incident or breach can be expensive. When we identify problems, our solutions are expensive. In contrast, the modern security team plays a significant role in building customer trust and sales enablement. We build product security, enhancements, building security into processes to improve the business while reducing risk and challenging the antiquated security culture of "no."

Customer Trust and Sales Enablement

People understand the importance of data security, even if they don't know all of its nuances. Today, even a less tech-savvy customer will ask about security when evaluating new products or solutions. A good security team arms the business with the information to effectively communicate how data is managed and protected. The old school thought of closed-door security practices or security through obscurity is gone. Hell, SOC 2 reports are table stakes these days, and often a potential customer will have enough chops to ask more detailed security questions than what appears in a single audit report. With security frequently in the news and as a part of our daily lives, the audience for security has expanded exponentially.

Modern security teams build customer trust and enable sales. We play a particular and vital role in forming relationships with customers and securing trust. A smooth security review process could mean a signed deal and an ongoing trusted partnership. It's like going to a great mechanic. Once you find a good one—you keep them. Customers commonly ask for security questionnaires to be completed or even a phone call to verify security before signing on. When the security team responds with standard, vetted answers demonstrating security's value, the time to signature can be dramatically reduced.

It's like shopping for a new car and asking about the safety features. If my car dealer has a pamphlet of features, if they have studies that show crash test results, if they can speak about the car's safety, I trust the car will be safe. If, on the other hand, my salesperson says over the phone, "this car is super safe," but I show up at the dealership and the car doesn't have seatbelts, I have some serious questions. Our customers count on this same level of transparency regarding security.

Product Security and Enhancements

Security teams also play a role in customer-facing product security. This can include product feature enhancements or security design reviews for internal designs. Security teams invent new ways to be secure. We file patents. We invent technologies. Extending the mechanic analogy, this security team not only fixes the check engine light; we are the mechanics that understand and love our specialization so much that we invent new and interesting features.

My brother has a car shop, and throughout the majority of his day, he is fixing cars or managing car repairs. But he also does side work where he designs, patents, and builds parts for motorcycles. We do that very same thing in the security space. We are builders as much as we are breakers. You have to take the car apart to understand how it works. Once you know how it works, you can be more efficient with modifications, repairs, and upgrades. A good security practitioner understands the business and the product to provide the best guidance on how to secure it.

Building Security into Processes to Challenge the Security Culture of No

People tend to cringe dealing with the security team, just like people cringe dealing with a car mechanic. You usually only see us when there is a problem, and we use a lot of internal jargon no one understands. Once we get under the hood, there are ten more things you should fix, right? And by the way, everything is of equal importance and risk; they all must be done NOW.

With the right approach, security can make business more efficient while making the company more secure. Take, for example, patch management. No one likes proactive maintenance. If you have a security team who understands how to grow *how the business builds*, they can make the process more efficient and secure. For example, creating secure, ephemeral baseline images that allow development teams to move fast, be safe, and remove the pain of the standard maintenance process.

If we partner with development teams early in the life cycle process, we can help define tools and processes to make it easy to code securely. Instead of saying, "no, you can't do that," we work together to find creative solutions. A solution like writing secure code development in the IDE instead of shipping it off for review afterward results in happy developers, fewer on-call interruptions, and less maintenance for subsequent fixes. It's like having the safety group work with the car designers as they create the plan. The building process (and the car) is more efficient if we think about safety early, instead of finding out we should staple in seat belts after the first crash test.

Communicating 'Actual' Risk to Better Partner With the Business

Part of providing value as a security org is to understand risk and have the ability to communicate that risk to business partners and collectively take action on that risk. Working together adds value to an organization and allows businesses to make informed, cost-effective decisions. We can be selective in creating mutually beneficial plans to protect where the actual risks lie in the process. I won't take my car to a body shop for an engine problem or try to sell you snow tires if you live in Miami. Similarly, I won't suggest my company invest in state-of-the-art surveillance equipment for the office if our employees are remote and data is hosted in the cloud. Or why I won't spin up a red team engagement if my organization is still figuring out vulnerability management and incident response holistically.

Using this same car/mechanic analogy, let's look at the four risk treatment scenarios we see in security: acceptance, avoidance, mitigation, and transfer, and how they each can be used to better partner with the business.

Acceptance

Your car needs a new transmission, and the mechanic gives you a costly repair estimate. By continuing to drive the car, it will only get worse and might end up with you on the side of the road calling for a tow. But you don't have the money or the time for such a repair. You chose to continue to drive the car as-is. In business, it is impossible to mitigate every risk, especially as new risks arise. We must assess which risks are most important, plan ahead, and accept some risks. The above example accepts risk based on a lack of time and resources. A common scenario in business is accepting the risk of running out-of-date software based on the time and resources it might take to update.

Avoidance

Let's say I am car shopping and I find a car, but they need to sell it TODAY, and there's no time to have a mechanic look at the car. Because they are in a time squeeze, they are offering a great deal, but there's a risk of not knowing if there is anything wrong with the car. I decide not to purchase the car and avoid the risk. Avoiding risk can be beneficial but may lead to missed opportunities. In business, avoiding too much risk can lead to a lack of innovation or competitive advantage. If we don't take any risks, we get in our own way or move too slowly.

Mitigation

Mitigation is the process of remediating the risk. If my car has a mechanical issue, I take it in and fix it. There is a trade-off between resources and rewards; I am taking my time and money to fix the car in exchange for reliability. In business, this trade-off is similar- costing the business time and money to mitigate risk. The goal is to balance priorities and the resources invested in reducing the risk.

Transfer

Transferring risk means I am passing that risk on to a third party. For our car scenario, that would be a warranty or insurance. We often do this in business by putting the risk on third parties. If a third party takes on the risk, we can still face repercussions if they have an issue. If I buy cheap brakes for my car manufacturing business, and those brakes fail, no one will care where I bought the brakes. They care that the brakes failed, and they cannot trust the car. Conversely, if I am not an expert in a specific area, I am better off transferring risk by outsourcing to someone with expert knowledge. Credit card processing is a good example. Many companies don't specialize in processing credit cards or PCI, so it is generally less risky to use a third party who specializes in that to reduce risk to the business.

Conclusion

Security teams excel when they understand risk and how it impacts business situations. Each company's risk profile is different. In an ideal world, the value of security controls should be proportionate to the burden. In this reinvented world view, the value of security reduces the burden. We must challenge the assumption that security are blockers and struggle with adding value. Security teams are reinventing themselves as business enablers and partners. We are teams of creative problem solvers, driving the new face of security.

ABOUT LISA HALL

Lisa Hall is Chief Information Security Officer at Color.

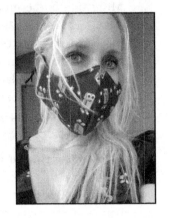

With over 15 years experience in the information security field, she is focused on building security programs from the ground up, strategic planning, risk management, and driving process adoption company-wide.

Lisa believes security should make it easy to do the right thing. Lisa has previously held Information Security roles at PagerDuty, Twilio, Glassdoor, and EY.

CHAPTER 12

Open Source Lessons on Smashing Barriers to Contribution

by Rin Oliver

Open Source Lessons on Smashing Barriers to Contribution

Rin Oliver

As an engineer with deep open source roots, I approach cybersecurity from the perspective of a 'builder'. But before I worked in cloud-native and DevSecOps, I had an extremely strange and winding path to tech. My first exposure to basic coding was in my early 20s, when I used HTML and CSS to write about World of WarCraft. I eventually finished my BA and spent some years doing technical writing and cloud native journalism before finding a place in open source software (OSS). While I currently work in closed-source (proprietary) technologies, open source was a full-time focus and career for a big portion of my journey.

I did not know that programming was a career in my early 20s. I am a multiply neurodivergent person with dyscalculia, dyspraxia, ADHD, and autism. I arrived at tech because I wanted to show people I was more than 'alternative education classes' or occupational therapy appointments. I realized I was different from others at a young age and I often have to work much harder than others to become good at things. This tenacity influenced my entire journey and helped me succeed when I first started working on a major open source software (OSS) project. Documentation and code were not easy for me at first. I did not know how to use Git when I started to maintain version control. I broke more than a few pipelines learning how to squash and commit, or how to merge my contributions.

I had never heard of CI/CD.[1] But, I worked extremely hard since I had something to prove and I prevailed.

Open source projects are a critically important pathway to careers in cybersecurity and engineering, particularly for people from underrepresented backgrounds since it gives us enough hands-on experience to eventually break into paid work. OSS projects consist of self-organizing global teams who work asynchronously. Cybersecurity and DevSecOps teams at organizations can learn a lot about being more inclusive from open source communities, including how to better include neurodivergent individuals such as myself. I share my story to empower others, in hopes that everyone finds a technical community or team where they are comfortable contributing.

Overview

This chapter is about what the cybersecurity industry can learn from open source software, or OSS, communities about smashing barriers to contribution for people from underrepresented backgrounds.

Small changes can have a big impact, and one of my specializations is inclusive, accessible documentation. Technical docs matter and they are also an area where everyone from DevSecOps directors to junior engineers can pitch in to help neurodivergent individuals thrive.

We need full participation among individuals from diverse backgrounds to solve tomorrow's greatest cybersecurity challenges, including individuals with Autism, ADHD, Tourette's, dyspraxia, dyscalculia, specific speech conditions, and sensory processing conditions. There is growing recognition that neurodivergent individuals bring huge advantages to cybersecurity and DevSecOps teams, since neurodivergent individuals often bring advantages such as non-linear problem solving and hyperfocus.

---

1 Continuous integration and deployment (CI/CD) is a DevOps method that relies on automation to deliver frequent app updates by streaming testing, delivery, and deployment.

I share my story to empower others, in hopes that everyone finds a technical community or adopts new practices. Inclusion is mandatory.

Smashing Barriers For Neurodivergent Contributors

"Neurodiversity is the diversity of human minds, the infinite variation in neurocognitive functioning within our species," writes Dr. Nick Walker.[2] Many neurodivergent individuals have excellent technical capabilities before they become formal contributors to an engineering team or open source project, after spending their childhood and adolescence using technology to connect with others around shared interests.

Diversity makes us stronger. Creating environments where neurodivergent people can be successful can provide organizations with access to excellent engineers. According to well-known advocate Temple Grandin, neurodivergent people can bring unique strengths to tasks requiring strong attention to detail, especially minute details that can seem unimportant to neurotypical individuals.[3] Grandin worries that there aren't enough neurodivergent people in critical jobs to drive safety and precision.

Creating more inclusive engineering practices is a shared responsibility that spans effective leadership, culture, and communications. One mandatory way to help individuals from underrepresented backgrounds succeed in global technical teams is to write stronger and more inclusive technical documentation, also known as developer docs, contributed guidelines, or simply docs. Many neurodivergent people prefer clear instructions and can struggle in an environment where there is little guidance on how to get started. Well-maintained docs may have particular benefit for underrepresented backgrounds, but they also benefit everyone.

---

2   Walker, N. The Writings of Dr. Nick Walker. NEUROQUEER. neuroqueer.com
3   Curry, S. (2019, May 13). Neurodiversity: A competitive advantage in cybersecurity. Forbes. www.forbes.com/sites/samcurry/2019/05/13/neurodiversity-a-competitive-advantage-in-cybersecurity/

Many open source communities are ahead-of-the-curve when it comes to creating inclusive, high-quality documentation for a pretty simple reason: they've relied on asynchronous, global collaboration for years. OSS specialists excelled at remote work long before the COVID-19 pandemic hit and have always consisted of people from different cultures, backgrounds, demographics, and timezones. In some cases, organizations can learn a lot from open source, particularly when it comes to creating inclusive documentation. OSS docs are designed for a self-service contributor experience and they are also written in a way that includes neurodivergent people, is understandable by non-Native language speakers, and is accessible to individuals using assistive technologies.

High-quality technical documentation helps engineers write better code and make decisions that improve the customer experience. Continuous effort to make your documentation inclusive and accessible matters.

Everyone Can Smash Barriers With Better Docs

The best contributor guidelines for builders are not only about code. They are clear guidelines that welcome a new contributor to an organization and explain how code is planned, used, and maintained. High-quality developer guidelines are mandatory in OSS communities since these projects rely on volunteers. A similar standard should be mandatory in organizational environments, since it can help people from all backgrounds feel empowered to add value.

Please note that I am not claiming open source projects all have perfect contributor guidelines, because that simply is not true. Docs are hard and almost everyone struggles with it. Developer surveys show that the top pet peeve for OSS contributors is incomplete or confusing documentation. In the best case scenario, outdated docs lead to frustrated developers or bugs. At worst, docs can make contributors feel like they are not able to contribute and add to feelings of imposter syndrome.

The Most Common Signs of Ineffective Docs

1. Incomplete
2. Outdated
3. Specifications Without an Explanation
4. No Clear Instructions
5. Missing Update Guidance or Schedules
6. A Lack of Style Guidelines

There are a lot of reasons to write better documentation beyond inclusion - bad docs have a very real and negative impact on code quality and company revenue. While few communities or projects have perfect docs, we can still learn from self-organizing and global OSS teams to improve our own contributor experiences.

Write For New Contributors

All engineers reference documentation from time to time if there's value in it. Consider it a win if seasoned engineers use your contributor docs to resolve uncommon questions since it means your decision-making frameworks are valuable for edge cases.

At the same time, these senior builders are not the primary audience for your docs. Write your docs for new contributors. It is critically-important to ensure your docs are clear and comprehensive enough to serve newbies, since it moves the needle on a better contributor experience for everyone.

Update Early and Often

Not every project update requires an update to your documentation. But, most organizations do not struggle with updating documentation too frequently. It is far more common for docs to fall behind process and procedure. If you expect contributors to change behavior, you must update your docs.

Assign Direct Responsibility

Every project needs to have a Directly Responsible Individual (DRI) who is available to answer questions about projects or documentation. This person should be extremely familiar with the docs, the stack, and very comfortable serving as a resource for new hires. Ideally, the DRI will improve the docs based on real-time learning during their daily interactions to make sure your docs become more useful and inclusive over time.

In addition to a DRI, every organization needs to assign responsibility to a number of maintainers who can actively drive updates to an assigned section of the docs. Everyone can and should contribute to your docs, but it should also be a core job responsibility for some designated maintainers.

Be Extremely Thorough

Step-by-step instructions are important to any global team, particularly teams that include neurodivergent people. Many neurodivergent people have experienced a lifetime of difficulty following instructions from neurotypical people. Instructions can be challenging for neurodivergent people for a myriad of reasons, including attention and comprehension. It is not always apparent to a neurodivergent individual if instructions are mandatory or important, especially if the instructions are vague.

Beverly Vicker of the Indiana Resource Center for Autism has a set of requirements for instructions that make sense to many neurodivergent people:[4]

- Clear instructions that are not too complicated to understand and remember
- Directions that are presented in a sufficiently accessible way to comprehend
- Recognizing the words, meaning, and syntax of instructions
- Knowing which action to take based on instructions

Step-by-step instructions in your technical docs should not be ambiguous

---

4   Vicker, B. Comprehension of the message: Important considerations for following directions. Indiana Resource Center for Autism. www.iidc.indiana.edu/irca/articles/comprehension-of-the-message-important-considerations-for-following-directions.html

or written in complicated language. Include a lot of detail, images, and video. Clarity helps neurodivergent individuals succeed as well as many others, perhaps especially newbies and individuals who are not native language speakers.

Creating a numbered list with step-by-step instructions is important for all key technical processes. It is critical to create numbered lists with step-by-step guides if you rely on asynchronous collaboration. It is much easier to help a new contributor troubleshoot if they can reveal exactly where they ran into a problem, such as "I got stuck on step seven in the environment setup instructions."

Rely Heavily on a Glossary

It is very difficult to avoid the use of jargon since there are countless project and product-specific terms in the world of cloud native technologies and OSS. It is more inclusive to completely avoid the use of jargon and proprietary terms, but it's rarely possible to do this in technical docs.

If you can't avoid jargon, have a glossary available with complete definitions of the terms used in your doc. Assign responsibility for a glossary owner and make it clear that the glossary is accepting contributions to capture definitions from many contributors.

Work very, very hard to surface your glossary to builders as they navigate the docs. Link to a glossary definition every, single time you use a term that is unfamiliar to a total beginner. Every time, without exception. Clear definitions are important to the experience of neurodivergent contributors and they really smash barriers for everyone.

Balance Wit with Inclusivity

There is a lot of debate about how much warmth and unique tone should be included in engineering docs. Technical documentation is notoriously dry and boring, so many brands and OSS projects choose to infuse wit and humor into their contributor guidelines. It is fine to make jokes, but it is also important to consider whether your humor is accessible to everyone.

Many neurodivergent people have difficulty grasping jokes with sarcasm or dual meanings. Behavioral analyst Ali Arena believes that sarcasm is hard for many neurodivergent people to understand because they interpret statements very literally.[5] Neurodivergent people are not the only ones who can struggle with docs that have too many jokes. Pop culture references do not always translate across individuals from different cultural backgrounds or lived experiences.

Your docs should not be too dry. They should be warm, welcoming, and filled with personality. At the same time, you should avoid humor or references that are exclusive towards some.

Use Positive Language in Your Documentation

New contributors often feel worried about their skills and abilities, perhaps especially neurodivergent people and individuals from underrepresented backgrounds. Your documentation can play a role in helping contributors feel like they belong. Write your guidelines in a positive, inclusive tone.

Always avoid talking down to your users, even in subtle ways. It is best practice to avoid using the words "simple" or "easy" in step-by-step instructions or any other part of your docs. Remember, "easy" is highly subjective. An "easy" process might seem really confusing to a brand-new contributor, leading them to further doubt their ability.

Thank people for their contributions in your documentation and be encouraging about code that is submitted for review. Taking a compassionate and appreciative tone in your contributor docs to help all newbies feel a lot less overwhelmed.

Set Clear Expectations For a Pull Request

Diverse, global teams write better code. It also takes a village to write great and inclusive documentation. Individuals from non-technical backgrounds might feel comfortable submitting a documentation pull request (update to the docs) before they submit code and that's just fine. Docs are a shared responsibility and people with a diverse set of lived experiences can add new viewpoints.

---

5   Clark, J. (2020, October 30). Getting to the basics of humor for people on the autism spectrum. WHYY. whyy.org/segments/getting-to-the-basics-of-humor-for-people-on-the-autism-spectrum/

Your documentation should make it clear what is expected from a pull request, regardless of whether a contributor is pushing code or documentation updates. Use templates as much as possible to help new contributors adhere to style guidelines.

Other Ways to Be Inclusive in Technical Documentation

1. Create Style Guides

Style guides are usually extremely important to maintain consistency of tone and style throughout your docs. This is particularly important if you have a lot of docs or a lot of doc owners. It can be difficult for neurodivergent individuals to navigate a sudden change in tone or style when they are figuring out a new project. A style guide also encourages neurodivergent individuals and newbies to contribute since it sets clear parameters on what is expected.

2. Maintain Outlines, Layouts, and a Table of Contents

It almost goes without saying that docs need a table of contents to provide a positive user experience. But, it is important to make sure the structure is clear and consistent. Be strict about consistent header formatting to improve the navigation experience. Use numbered lists to write instructions for processes such as install or set up.

3. Be Accessible

Set clear guidelines for accessibility to ensure your documentation is accessible to everyone, including individuals with disabilities. Add alt text to all images to be inclusive towards people using screen readers. Add subtitles to any video instructions that are embedded in the technical docs and make sure any audio/visual content includes a high-quality transcript.

4. Always Define Scope

Docs are a never-ending effort, which is why it's crucial to define scope for any docs project regardless of whether you are doing a first-time overhaul or adding a new section. Do your best to determine how long the project will take and who is responsible for contributing.

Define requirements for collaborating across other teams, so all contributors understand if they are expected to interview customer success, site reliability engineering (SRE) or other teams.

A lesser-known (but crucial) best practice is to put updates and maintenance requirements into scope so it is extremely clear who is responsible for the docs after a new section goes live. This is rarely practiced, but very helpful. Defining responsibilities for the docs lifecycle can prevent a lot of quality and continuity issues!

5. Avoid Scope Creep

It is very common for technical documentation to be out-of-date. If documentation is actively updated, it is also extremely common for scope creep to occur and create problems. Scope creep is a particular risk if a documentation project involves cross-functional collaboration or input from subject matter experts (SME).

6. Make it Unpainful to Draft Documentation

The environments used to draft documentation can vary enormously between organizations and tech stacks, so there are no absolutes on what constitutes painless documentation drafting. It depends on your Acceptable Use Policy, the Git vendor, and factors such as homegrown systems.

While your mileage can (and should) vary on optimizing documentation drafting experience, put in work to make it painless for contributors by minimizing version control issues or laggy Git interfaces. Ensure that documentation can be drafted collaboratively to build confidence among newbies and neurodivergent contributors.

If revising or publishing docs is cumbersome and error-prone, look into new tools that are specifically designed for collaborative drafting and publishing. It doesn't have to be painful to write or update documentation and contributors are much happier to pitch in if you have the right tools.

Creating a Neurodivergent-Inclusive Culture

I've seen a lot of companies start to build out Neurodiversity Employee Resource Groups (ERGs), and while I've never had the chance to experience one myself, they seem really awesome. I'm a fan of this. I think that there's definitely something to be said for a community where you don't have to mask your neurodivergent traits.

In the tech industry, ERGs are often touted as a resource, a bonus of joining a new team, and are sometimes used as a hiring tactic. I've had a few interviews with certain tech organizations who have made it a point to highlight to me that they have a gender diversity ERG, and a neurodiversity ERG. While that's a start, I'm always the person to ask what they're also doing to retain the neurodivergent and employees from underrepresented gender identities.

It's not enough to hire people with the promise of an ERG as a bandaid to real change. When those employees get there, what will they encounter? How will they be supported long term? Make sure that you've got a plan in place to support people after the rose-colored glasses come off if your role involves employee retention or experience. I believe individuals in any role can contribute to a better experience for neurodivergent employees since many of us can write better docs, advocate for smarter hiring practices, or improve the neurodivergent contributor experience in other ways.

Remember, Your Worst Day Is Only 24 Hours Long

All of us experience setbacks in our personal and professional lives. I have experienced countless lows in my life, including everything from discouraging job searches to a hurricane that hit my home within days of starting a new job. I have also been extremely persistent to build my skill set as a DevSecOps engineer and pursue new opportunities while also allowing myself to pursue non-work interests such as the candle business I share with my wife Elizabeth. Today, I do meaningful work that pays fairly, I am a member of many communities, and I have used my experiences to educate and encourage others.

During a recent conference keynote, I reminded the audience that your worst day is only 24 hours long. I wish I remembered that advice when I faced setbacks earlier in my career and knew that if I kept persisting on building skills and community, I would one day be a successful cybersecurity professional who frequently speaks at conferences about DevSecOps, community, personal development, and many other topics. Your worst day will not last forever, and persistence can result in change even though the results are not always immediate.

In the end, I think that's what security is all about. Understanding that difficult days are never permanent and moving forward with a hopeful attitude. While security work can feel impossible and we all make mistakes, chances are you will recover and prevail as an individual or team. If we all work together and encourage others, we can achieve just about anything.

ABOUT RIN OLIVER

Rin is a software engineer at US Bank and a former employee at Camunda, Esper.io, and Gitlab. They are a neurodivergent, nonbinary technical community builder, DevSecOps engineer, and OSS contributor experience advocate. They enjoy discussing all things open source, with a particular focus on diversity in tech, improving hiring pipelines in OSS for those that are neurodivergent, and removing accessibility barriers to learning programming.

Rin is also a member of Kubernetes, a contributor to Spinnaker, and involved in the special interest group (SIG) for the Kubernetes contributor experience. Rin is on the board of Directors for The Diana Initiative, and a frequent speaker and keynote speaker at industry conferences such as SANS Institute, KubeCon, MozFest, CNCF, and countless others.

Rin lives in Shreveport, Louisiana with their wife and pets. When not immersed in all things OSS and cloud-native, they can be found making candles, cooking, and gaming.

CHAPTER 13

Project Overhaul: Creating a More Dynamic, Diverse, Credentialed Workforce

by Joyous Huggins

Project Overhaul: Creating a More Dynamic, Diverse, Credentialed Workforce

Joyous Huggins

I stood before them with messy twists, parted to the right side. A Marvel vs. Capcom graphic tee peered between the opening of a ten-year-old Mario zip-up hoodie. The over-the-air headphones rested gently on the base of my neck, softly humming my Lo-fi playlist. There is an enthusiastic conversation about *Attack on Titan* and *Seven Deadly Sins*. Fluent in action anime, I provide critical analysis of story arcs and character development. Eyes shut, arms crossed, I politely close my thoughts with, "I mean, that's just my opinion. You guys ready to start class?"

"There is no way you are a grownup."

Often, my students question my age. Sometimes I wish I wasn't fully grown, but I definitely am.

"I am 100 percent a grownup." I pause. "I have full bills and responsibilities. I'm a whole grownup."

They look at me with perplexity and say, *"How?... From foster kid to -this?"*

"I always believed in myself. And, I didn't let other people's choice to believe in me determine where I went in life."

Dropping my arms, I let out a slow, tired, exasperated sigh and shrug.

"Adulting is hard."

I hope they take my words to heart.

I was born into a life of service. I am a confidence coach, a comedian, and a caretaker to my family. My passion for service led me to teach middle and high school students cybersecurity through my business, Defender Academy. I am a US military veteran, and I work full-time as a senior-level civilian for the Department of the Navy.

At my core, I swear by the power of intent - constant introspection, purposeful communication with others, and objective ideas. All students are capable. Boring classroom computer science and security lectures need to be completely overhauled with more project-based learning. By rethinking our approach to fundamental cybersecurity, we can close the skill gap and create opportunities.

How it Started

I grew up in the "World's Largest Village." Skokie, Illinois, was just as exciting as the next Chicago suburb. I ran around having adventures with a bunch of ragamuffin friends. If you have ever seen *Stranger Things*, you understand precisely the type of diverse, fun friend circle I had.

My grandmother worked at a Midwest-based technology company that manufactured hardware and embedded software systems. Later, this company began selling appliances, eventually branching into manufacturing smart connected Internet of Things (IoT) devices. Whenever my grandmother brought defective products home, I would start tinkering. Out of boredom, when she was away, I would tear these devices apart and struggle to repair them before she returned. I spent so many heart-pounding hours trying to undo my experiments. *It was exhilarating.* Street markets didn't care if the store thought they were 'defective.' Any piece of technology she brought into our home was considered expensive.

As a kid, you don't know the value of costly things, but you do know when your curiosity goes too far, and you had better cover your tracks.

My friends and I were interested in technology. Our interest occasionally broke plenty of hardware and developed some super basic programs. One day, we decided to splice into an ethernet cable. It was either a CAT5 or CAT5e. We took out the ol' Gateway laptop (Josh's dad did notice its absence) and started pulling a lot of digital information off this cable and playing with the numbers. We had no idea what we were doing, but watching the numbers change across the screen was fun. Later, we found out the cable belonged to Harris Bank, known today as Chase Bank. The streams of numbers on the net were us transferring money between random accounts. And, as suspected, we got in trouble for it.

My technology misadventures were pretty cool and fun, even if it wasn't always the smart thing to do. When I think back to where my love for cybersecurity began, I remember the fun I had with my goofballs, breaking devices, and splicing cables.

My upbringing was rough, but I got to have fun and be curious. Often I look back and think how fortunate I was to have very supportive foster parents. Never once did any of my parents limit my potential. Every time, regardless of the trouble, they encouraged it. My love for understanding how things work eventually became this natural curiosity and passion for all things cybersecurity.

How it Went

I went to college at 17 to pursue my dream of becoming a math teacher in urban education. I loved math, but I never really lost my interest in cybersecurity. After three years in college, I switched my major from math to computer science. Then life happened. My youngest brother was staying with some relatives in the south, and unfortunately, he was removed and placed in foster care. We had other siblings, but our connection was different. I was all he had left and needed to step up. It is nearly impossible for trauma-infused full-time college students to provide stability to trauma-infused kids. And so, I did what I had to; I did what I thought was best. I dropped out of school and joined the military.

I often say that military service was the best-worst decision I ever made. I did not enjoy my time in the service. But, I met many amazing people, learned a lot about myself, and found the direction I so desperately needed. The service shaped a lot of my character and influenced who I am today. My military jobs involved scrubbing fo'c'sles, sewing search and rescue (SAR) equipment, reviewing policies and performance, and most importantly, working with information technology and cybersecurity. The cyber gigs exposed me to security concepts, but it was entirely up to me to apply these skills and eventually turn this knowledge into career opportunities.

No matter how much I wanted to separate, the military had its benefits. At every opportunity, I kept pursuing my passion for cybersecurity by doing a lot of side projects. I did plenty of work for free to refine my skills and better understand the types of roles I wanted to pursue as a civilian. I would often take my resume and compare it to job descriptions. Ambitious about adding new skills, I checked a box as soon as possible and moved on to the next side project or learning experience. Game-changer. The secret sauce to professional development and career progression is to find your dream job, see how it is being marketed, and perfect what you are missing.

How it's Going

After the military, I quickly realized that I had a passion for helping to establish continuity in the government sector. Many projects can get started in defense, and the government often needs civilian contractors with clearances or military backgrounds to finish these projects. With the US Navy, I have taken on increasingly strategic roles that span people, processes, and technology. I enjoy what I do, and I'm at a place to make a change. It can only get better from here.

By Way of Confidence

My career journey was not always easy. People had their opinions and would set their expectations of me. I suppose that's just people, though. I experienced a lot of discrimination throughout my career. There was always something: they didn't like the way I dressed, my satire, or my general existence. These were the same people who would second-guess my ability for whatever reason. Fortunately, I was here to save them from their monotonous work environment.

Being second-guessed fuels me. It is the sole reason why I am so passionate about serving my community through cybersecurity education. My students need to see me. They need to see themselves in cybersecurity. They deserve to know someone who believes in their abilities.

The Real Impostor

Impostor syndrome is tricky. It is a cunning little fox. My fox created a tiny fox hole at the base of my professional insecurities. People who worked with me, like me or not, never questioned the quality of my work. To be honest, I just needed a representative in my space to help me navigate my career.

It may sound crazy, but I was discouraged by social pressures and a lack of representation. Disrespectful leadership and peers began to weigh on me. I had to become my own advocate. Eventually, I started setting traps for that fox. Self-advocacy is established when you are tired of being hurt, embarrassed, or ridiculed, and I got tired. Burnt out, I took some time off and looked at my life in milestones.

The first milestone started with emails. I went to my early college career and looked at some emails I wrote to professors. I was so wordy and long-winded. Shortly after, I looked at emails to companies where I did projects. My emails were shorter and less verbose. Now, I barely have four sentences. It sounds elementary, but from revisiting those emails, I changed. I started to trust myself; I either have a question, or I don't. I either have the information you're looking for, or I don't.

Somewhere, my communication began to evolve. Somehow, I began to value my time. From my emails, I looked at my projects. The growth in formatting, the pointed questions to PM for clarity, the organization of thoughts...I was empowered. After building a couple of cybersecurity training curricula for a company, I realized that I did not need imposter syndrome in my life. There was no shame in the fact I was figuring out much of my work as I went since everyone else was doing the same and figuring it out along with me.

The Shift from Shame

I often tell my students and peers that there is no need to feel wrong about your journey. **Be shameless.** Grow from the things that do and do not work for you. It is okay to figure things out as you grow through your career. That ideology was the paradigm shift for me. I stopped believing that I needed to be a complete expert. Framing my experiences in the context of what was required for a successful work project, became easy. I began understanding and breathing life into the value I brought to a project or client.

Learning how to speak about myself and my work gave me confidence and helped me overcome imposter syndrome. It also helped me progress in my career and even outperform some doubters. I started thinking about my journey as a competition with myself and my own goals. I competed against projects and raced to add new skills. As soon as I discovered this confidence, much of the noise died down and I could focus on success.

Rethinking Cybersecurity Training

The cybersecurity skills gap is hardly a secret. There are 65 percent fewer qualified professionals than needed to fill current cybersecurity job openings.[1] Such an enormous skills gap shows that it is time to rethink how to train tomorrow's talent. We are overdue for meaningful conversations about creating a more diverse and dynamic workforce. We need to evaluate which cybersecurity jobs are professional and which are vocational jobs for highly-skilled trade professionals. While there are no simple answers, the industry must consider vocational pathways to cybersecurity careers.

The Reality

Many of the thousands of unfilled cybersecurity jobs do not require a college degree. Many cybersecurity careers rely on skills like keystroke memorization and very little development of custom programming language unless you're in a developer role. If you're running tools or exploits from scripts, you don't need the skill set to build infrastructure, and many of the day-to-day requirements for cybersecurity have minimal technical

---

1   (ISC)2. 2021 Cybersecurity Workforce Study. isc2.org/Research/Workforce-Study.

requirements. Instead, they require a solid grounding in fundamental concepts developed via vocational training or apprenticeship programs. More than likely, Human Resources did not consult with the experts to draft up those ridiculous position descriptions.

There are many powerful models for vocational training from the trades. Take, for example, the pathway for an individual to become a licensed electrician in the US. The path starts with an apprenticeship program. Apprentice electricians are paid a fair, entry-level wage for their time in the classroom. Usually, apprentices attend 144 hours of classroom training (4 weeks) in highly-relevant topics like electrical theory and building codes.

After finishing classroom training, apprentice electricians usually spend between 4,000 and 6,000 hours doing hands-on electrical work under the supervision of a journeyperson while receiving regular pay raises and access to more challenging work assignments. After about two years of paid work experience, an electrician can become a master or journeyman of their trade by passing a licensing exam.

A similar approach to apprenticeships has the potential to close the skill and opportunity gap in cybersecurity. It's time to consider ways to give students access to hands-on participation within days - not months or years - of starting training and how to pay apprentices a living wage for their cybersecurity training.

The Unspeakable

We need to seriously reconsider our bias toward individuals with a college degree as an industry. Someone who has pursued a degree in cyber is typically looking to do more managerial or program management work. There are some hidden politics that no one wants to talk about or touch, but the reality is getting a degree sets an income bracket more than it establishes your skillset, technical or not. In 2022, this mainly affects demographics such as People of Color (POC), women, and persons with disabilities. *insert eye roll emoji*

A degree does little to prepare many cybersecurity professionals for their future careers. Instead, cybersecurity fundamentals are often learned outside of the classroom, through home labs or group projects. The need for persistence and curiosity is why kids from urban backgrounds can excel in cyber. Entry-level technical cybersecurity professionals need fundamentals, practical skills, and the endurance to see something through.

The brightest cybersecurity minds I've encountered while teaching can often struggle in a traditional classroom but shine in groups or classes infused with project-based learning.

Considering new pathways to cybersecurity training can help us create a more dynamic and diverse workforce for tomorrow, and provide opportunities for kids who struggle to focus in a traditional classroom setting.

Fundamentals of Cybersecurity Skills

To make cybersecurity careers more accessible to my students at Defender Academy, I stripped technical security work to the fundamentals. What is cybersecurity without specialization? I considered how other fields approach fundamental education using the medical field as my guide. All future doctors need to learn about the cardiovascular and respiratory systems, regardless of how they plan to specialize. I used that same fundamentals-focused approach to identify the fundamentals in cybersecurity.

The basics of cybersecurity are surprisingly simple. A foundation in networking concepts, program management, and customer service, are the prerequisites to specializing in cyber. While there is a tendency to over-complicate cybersecurity skills, students do not need to develop a specialization before they learn the basics.

1. Fundamentals of Networking

In its most basic form, network computing is how computers or nodes work together over a network. Students do not need to memorize the OSI layers. Instead, students need to understand the concepts and technologies of network computing. They need hands-on exposure to comprehend that all computing systems have a brain (or a server), an operator (a hub), and a client that interacts with them directly.

The fundamentals of networking can scale to virtually any computing scenario. The idea of a brain, an operator, and a client applies to future specialization in industrial control systems (ICS), AppSec, or cloud computing.

Example: Project-Based Learning for Networking

One simple, project-based approach to networking concepts is building a computer. In addition to building a computer, the students should explain which components create tunnels for networking. Ask questions such as What is the internet? And, which of these pieces get you to the internet?

Often, students engage more readily with networking concepts when I draw from familiar and cutting-edge technology like IoT devices. I will bring in a device that students are familiar with, like a smart home assistant. Then I ask if students have ever seen a device like this before. The students usually have some familiarity and a personal story about their experience with the device.

"Cool." I say, "So, how does this talk to your mom's phone? Because your mom can turn it on and off, right?"

Students will generally respond with "Uh, it is controlled by an app."

"Okay, so, what is the app controlling?..."

Familiar examples like smart home assistants allow us to work backward by walking through networking concepts.

Devices and toys help students gain excitement about networking because... well, computers are boring. Computers are super boring. Different hardware is often a more exciting way to teach the same networking fundamentals. There is no need to stick with computers when our world has so many other devices to explore.

Kids struggle to sit through lectures on computers. But, they can sit through a group project that involves a smartphone and touching. Lots of touching. They develop a passion for technology through facilitated group exercises, like taking a cell phone apart and learning about the pieces and how it talks to the internet. These types of group exercises emphasize curiosity, discussion, and research. They have now taught themselves more about cell towers, radio frequencies, and any additional information about their device through interactive dialogue. With interactivity and real-world hardware that students care about, you can solidify the fundamentals of networking.

2. Program Management

In any cybersecurity role, technical or not, you may find yourself at a dead stop and need to figure out what to do next. Program or project management is the ability to identify a process and improve it. A foundation in program management can allow students to navigate many workplace situations by creating project plans, identifying blockers, and creating SMART goals.

Every student should know enough about program or project management to succeed in a project-based work setting. This applies to any cybersecurity role regardless of how they choose to specialize. Basic program management skills can include how to make lists and boards, how to follow ideas, and how to ask the right questions when collaborating.

Example: Project-Based Learning for Program Management

Program management fundamentals can be as simple as group-based discussions about the steps needed to accomplish a goal. We often start with something simple and familiar. I'll ask the group, "So, how do you tie your shoes?"

One student said, "You get your shoelace, and you make a bunny loop, and then you make the other bunny loop, and then you pull the bunny loop, and then you're done."

"No," said another student quickly. "You're missing too many steps because you didn't make your shoes tighter."

"Yup," I said. "We need to make the shoelaces tight. But, why does the shoe need to fit tightly?"

A student piped up immediately, "Oh, well, we need to make the shoe tight because we don't want the shoe falling off. It defeats the purpose of us tying the shoe if it isn't tight enough."

Students don't need to deploy a giant piece of software to understand the fundamental steps to manage a project. Instead, their first exposure to program management can be as simple as walking through something they already know how to do, step-by-step. With project-based learning in a group setting, students start catching things they would never have thought of on their own. They learn the value of process-based thinking and how to work collaboratively.

3. Customer Service

Every industry has some hospitality elements and everybody in cybersecurity has a customer. Sometimes, I refer to this fundamental as "how to people" - working with others and forming productive workplace relationships. This essential is need-to-know information before any role in cybersecurity. Take, for example, SOC analysts. A SOC analyst's customers are their peers and their leadership. They need to speak to their peers for review and confirmation, and they need to be able to articulate and prioritize the incident when reporting to leadership correctly. Without these customers, it is challenging to kick-start mitigation procedures.

Future cybersecurity professionals need to learn how to speak to a customer. They need to know how to ask the right questions to gather a customer's project requirements. If someone lacks customer service skills, it doesn't matter if they know the fundamentals of networking and program management; no one will want to hear what they say.

Example: Project-Based Learning for Customer Service

Customer service fundamentals can also be taught simply by asking students about familiar situations. For example, I will ask students if they have ever asked their Mom for something.

"Yeah, I ask my Mom for something all the time," they might say. "She acted crazy the whole day."

Then I ask, "Do you ever consider your Mom a customer, or an investor? "

I hear, "What do you mean, Miss Huggins?" Or, "what do you mean, Miss Joy?" ("Miss" anything makes me uncomfortable.)

"For example, if you wanted to go and hang out at the mall," I ask the students, "what's the first thing you are going to do for your customer?"

"I'm going to ask her first," someone said.

"I ain't asking her for nothing" replied another student. "I'm making sure my house is straight, and I got my homework done."

"That's right," I said. "You're making sure you have all your ducks in a row before you introduce your case or your product to your customer. Because you're selling the idea of going to the mall, right?"

Students invariably respond with something like, "Yo, Miss Huggins, that's crazy.", but I can see the pieces coming together in their head. Evaluating everyday people in their lives and analyzing how they interact creates a healthy foundation for customer service in future careers. The idea is to package your product and get to "yes." You already know what your customer wants from you; use that to your benefit.

The Future is Now

My students are the future of cyber, and THAT is what motivates me to keep going and do better. I understand that I add a different element to the industry. I'm a little rough around the edges, full of spontaneity and fun, and not what you see when you think of cybersecurity. To me, that is part of the problem. Students need role models who look like them and have had similar life experiences to envision themselves in a cybersecurity career. Representation matters.

I believe that cybersecurity's most significant and brightest minds are sitting right in front of us. Creating a more dynamic, diverse, and credentialed industry requires us to train our community early and often with project-based learning, infusing productive seeds, and teaching pathways for incredible minds who may struggle in a classroom. By rethinking the fundamentals of skills training and how students can prepare themselves for the workforce, we can recruit and train younger, harder, and faster.

If we wait for secondary education to utilize immersive, real-life, project-based learning, we will forever be at a deficit of essential professionals. You don't have to commit yourself to teaching middle and high schoolers; you can volunteer with local organizations and work to introduce different pathways to careers within your workforce. Tomorrow's cybersecurity problems will need everyone's participation to be solved. Creating a healthier and more inclusive future for the cybersecurity industry is everyone's responsibility.

ABOUT JOYOUS HUGGINS

Joy Huggins is a foster kid born into a life of service. From Girl Scout to veteran to community volunteer, she has dedicated her talents to her local community. Today, she lives in Baltimore, Maryland, where she works in a high-level Civilian Contractor role for the United States Department of the Navy.

In the spirit of sharing her knowledge, Joy founded Defender Academy, a training institution for middle and high school students to learn cybersecurity fundamentals. She is also the founder of Hack Joyously, a confidence coaching program for women and minorities that encourages a resilient and confident cyber superstar!

Joy is passionate about educating the next generation of cybersecurity professionals to help close the workforce gap. She believes that new approaches to fundamental skills development can create a more dynamic, credentialed, and diverse security workforce for the future.

CHAPTER 14

Breaking into Cybersecurity

by Yvie Djieya

Breaking into Cybersecurity

Yvie Djieya

I look up at the clock as the sun peeks through the window in my living room. It's 9 a.m., and another day has begun before I was done for the night. I get myself organized for the day by clearing off my desk of textbooks and reading from last night's study session. This week, I happen to be on call and going through new-hire checklists and help desk requests. As our company's first line of defense, the security team focuses on protecting our employees, data, and customers. While I could sit here and tell you about my current role as a Cybersecurity Assurance and Risk Analyst, let me first share more about my story.

I'm exactly where I want to be in life right now. I'm a cybersecurity analyst by day, and I'm a college student by night. Like many in our field, I did not follow a straight path to a career in cybersecurity. Two things you should know, I view learning as a lifelong entrepreneur's job, and baking is my saving grace and strategy for avoiding burnout.

Growing up, I was amazed by how much I enjoyed using technology, playing games, or chatting with friends online. I never envisioned actively pursuing a career in the tech field when I was younger. As a child, I dreamt of life as a psychologist, which received the stamp of approval from my father.

My creative side blossomed as I headed into high school, as did my love for fashion and the arts. I took every opportunity to head to New York City, absorbing its diversity and dynamism as I paraded the streets with my Rihanna-inspired pixie cut, designer bag, and thrifted outfits. If I close my eyes, I can practically hear the sounds of the bustling city filled with inspiration, life, and color. And the endless eye candy was a bonus.

I wish I could say that the story ended there with me finding my passion and purpose, but it didn't. Somehow, somewhere down the line, I lost myself. Life got the best of me. It stripped me of my joy. While I can't remember the exact moment, the feelings, still raw to the touch, sit a little deeper below my dark skin's surface now. Life robbed me of my identity and confidence. The free-spirited and ambitious girl everyone knew cowered away in fear, and it wouldn't be until much later in life that I understood anxiety was at the root of it all.

Anxiety can be fear, dread, or uneasiness all rolled into one. I wish I knew then what I know now; impostor syndrome is real and that I didn't need to doubt my abilities or feel like a fraud. Now I realize this is a part of being human.

My young adult years included periods of confusion and conflicting opinions of who others thought I should become. Sometimes you need a north star to guide you in the right direction towards your purpose. A friend's plea to attend a tech bootcamp with them sparked my budding interest in cybersecurity, which is now, surprisingly, helping me rediscover myself and find my voice.

My Journey to a Career in Cybersecurity

I immigrated to the United States from Cameroon when I was six. While I had already completed kindergarten in Cameroon, my primary school decided I needed to start over because I didn't speak English well. My father pleaded for the school to reconsider, arguing that I was a quick learner, but they refused to budge. My older brother and kindergarten teacher worked tirelessly, teaching me how to speak, read, and write in English. My father assigned me a new book to read every week once I had mastered the language. Their dedication was rewarded when I was promoted to the first grade halfway through the school year.

My family's dedication to academic excellence paid off as I continued through school. I had the option of graduating high school a year early, but I chose to graduate with my class. In my senior year, I worked full-time and took two advanced placement courses. I developed a love for fashion and the arts, and I was split between studying psychology or fashion in college. I went with the latter and enrolled in art school to pursue a bachelor's in

Fashion Merchandising and Marketing. The school was expensive, and it took a scholarship, financial aid, and working two jobs to pay for tuition and books.

A typical day for my first two semesters was spent waking up in the mornings at 5 a.m., catching a metro train to Virginia for classes, then taking a train to DC to work my full-time retail job before returning home. To avoid burning the midnight oil, I completed the majority of my homework in between classes. I worked part-time as a hostess at a restaurant on weekends and covered shifts on the weekdays as they came up if my schedule permitted.

I was offered an opportunity to work at the headquarters of a high-end fashion brand in New York, but I declined the offer. I entertained the idea at first, but a heart-to-heart conversation with a supervisor changed my mind. While she was excited for me and thought I would succeed, she didn't want the "ugly side" of the high fashion industry to dissolve away my kind-hearted nature. She didn't want me to lose myself, but the truth was I was already losing myself. Her words echoed through my mind incessantly because I knew this career wasn't for me.

I did not return for the second year of art school. Instead, I transferred my credits to a local community college and switched my major to Communications focusing on Broadcast Media Production. My dad tried to convince me to switch to nursing, but that wasn't happening. So, I settled with him to attend a CNA (certified nursing assistant) program in order to make "decent" money to help pay for school. After three months out in the field, I got pulled into the office and assigned to work in a mental health clinic. The clinical experience validated my earlier decision in high school; a career in psychology was not for me.

During the summer of my last semester, I did a part-time internship at an international multimedia broadcasting company. Unlike other interns who were stuck with a mountain of paperwork, my department allowed me to go out on the field, operate technology, conduct interviews, create content for shows, and assist with directing radio and TV programs. I loved the fast-paced and creative environment but couldn't see myself working in the field long-term. Nonetheless, I transferred to a four-year university and continued my studies in Communications.

Now my story begins to take a turn for the better. A dear friend reached out to me midway through my junior year, inviting me to join her in registering for a cybersecurity bootcamp. She had just given birth to her first child and was barely making ends meet with her job. She was at a crossroads in life and didn't want to embark on this journey alone. Most of our friends used hashtags like #womenintech and #blackgirlsintech to update their social media profiles. Someone recommended the bootcamp to her, saying that they were able to find a job earning three times their previous salary after three months. I wasn't interested, but she managed to drag me to the first day of training and persuade the teacher to let me sit in.

I sat in the back of the cybersecurity bootcamp classroom, yet I was fully engaged and felt inspired for the first time in a long time. Nobody was more surprised than I was. That same day, I turned in my application and half of the deposit. I even switched my major to cybersecurity management and policy a few weeks later. Sometimes inspiration comes from the most unexpected experiences.

My Experience at Cybersecurity Bootcamp

Now, let's dive into the cybersecurity bootcamp. The class participants included young adults in undergrad and grad school looking for supplemental income, working adults primarily from the healthcare field looking to transition careers, and a few people who had recently moved to the U.S. from another country.

The bootcamp lasted four months and consisted of three-hour-long classes on Tuesday and Thursday evenings and Saturday mornings. We didn't get much help writing resumes or finding jobs, but we did spend a great deal of time practicing mock interviews. The interviews were conducted by alumni who provided feedback on how to best answer questions.

Upon graduation, we were added to an alumni support group and advised to pursue a CompTIA Security+ certification to help us break into the field. I failed my first attempt but passed on my second. The thought of having to pay $370 to retake the test hurt me more than being a few points shy of a passing score!

It took a year for me to land a job in cybersecurity. One bootcamp graduate received a job offer two weeks after graduating from the program, a majority hit the jackpot of offers within six months, and some took over a year to land their first tech job.

Breaking into Cybersecurity

While tech jobs are in high demand, they can be hard to land. Employers often create cybersecurity job descriptions with elite requirements. Some junior roles require you to have at least six years of hands-on experience plus advanced certifications. I find this absolutely absurd.

Many factors, including your work experience, level of education, location, professional network, and the state of the economy, can influence how long it takes to secure a new job. After receiving your education, training, or certifications, the real work of landing your ideal cybersecurity gig begins.

> **My Advice: Be patient!**
> **Set reasonable expectations, and be willing to wait.**

Job Search Methods

Networking is the fastest way to get a job in technology. Reach out to your professional network and friends to let them know that you're looking for a new job. Connect with recruiters and hiring managers on LinkedIn. When you get through to real people, your application is more likely to be read.

To meet new people and grow your network, I recommend attending networking events, conferences, and workshops. The Department of Homeland Security's first Cybersecurity Awareness Day was the first tech networking event I attended. I also attended an AfroTech Conference. I am sharing a sample set of discussion questions and reflection guidelines for networking events that are inspired by a handout from Cybersecurity Awareness Day in hopes that others can optimize networking experiences.

> **Cyber Networking Activity Prompts and Takeaways**

Sample Networking Questions to Ask Industry Professionals

1. What motivated you to pursue a career in cybersecurity?
2. What path did you take to get to your current job?
3. What does a typical day at work look like for you?
4. What skills and abilities do you find most important in your job?
5. What do you like the most about your job?
6. If you could do it over, would you still take the same path?
7. If you could change one thing about your job, what would it be?
8. What advice would you give to a student who is considering a job in cybersecurity?

Key Takeaway Activities for Networking

- After the cyber networking event, take a moment to reflect on your conversations.
- Notate items to follow up on or that you want to remember.
- What personal and career attributes did the cybersecurity professionals possess that you currently have or wish to develop and strengthen?

Both events gave me the opportunity to step outside of my comfort zone, meet new people, learn about the latest tech innovations and the different paths people took to break into the field.

> **My Advice: Follow up and stay connected while your new contact is warm.**

If you've applied to 30 jobs and haven't received a single interview request, it's possible that your resume needs to be rewritten or reformatted. Most companies use an applicant tracking system to help them filter through resumes.

Here are some tips to consider when constructing your resume:
- Use a chronological or hybrid format
- Tailor your resume to a specific job description by incorporating keywords
- Use both the long-form and acronym versions of keywords. [e.g.. intrusion detection system (IDS)]
- Avoid using tables because it can make your resume unreadable
- Use common section headlines like 'Summary' 'Objective' 'Education'

I also created a cover letter template for applications, which I was able to customize for applications fairly efficiently. The student cover letter template I used during my job search is shared below, in hopes it provides inspiration or value to others:

Dear Hiring Manager:

I am a senior at _____ studying Cybersecurity Management and Policy. I am writing to apply for the _____ position at _____ posted on _____. I'm excited about the field of information technology and would welcome the opportunity to bring my strong analytical skills, attention to detail, and cybersecurity experience to your growing team.

As a cybersecurity student at _____, I've gained a broad knowledge and understanding of security risk assessment, planning, and mitigation strategies. The courses I have completed have given me a solid foundation in the Risk Management Framework process and NIST Compliance. I have a proven ability to learn challenging concepts quickly and have developed competencies in the following areas:

- Skill A
- Skill B
- Skill C

Additionally, I have over 4 years of experience in health administration. My background in health administration has afforded me a well-rounded skill set, including project management, client relationship management, team collaboration, and problem-solving abilities.

I'm excited at the prospect of bringing the skills I've developed through these experiences to the _____ role at _____. I very much hope that you will look favorably upon my application and recognize my enthusiasm and future potential. My enclosed resume will provide you with greater details of my background and what I can offer.

Thank you for your time and consideration. I hope to hear from you soon.

Sincerely,

_____

Commit at least one hour each day to apply for jobs on various job search websites. The more jobs you apply for, the greater your chance of getting an interview. It's a numbers game. To find your ideal job, you must invest the time and energy into your job search. I primarily used Indeed, LinkedIn, and Dice during my job hunt. AngelList is a good place to start if you want to work at a startup. If your goal is to get a job in the government sector, I recommend USAjobs.

Try to obtain one industry certification to boost your resume's credibility, especially if you lack any hands-on experience. It will make you more marketable and strengthen your knowledge and understanding of foundational security concepts. The CompTIA Security+ certification has no prerequisites and is often required for most entry-level positions.

Be flexible. I started applying for internships and part-time jobs. Rather than landing a dream job, I focused on gaining hands-on experience. I was able to land a summer internship, and having that experience on my resume increased the number of interview requests I received.

Take Time to Prepare and Practice for Interviews. Preparation is Key!

Sometimes, like the Bennett Olsons and Chris Harkins of the world, you have to get creative and post your resume on a billboard. For my job search, I was willing to make cold calls and walk into businesses to introduce myself and inquire about job openings. It didn't come to that, but the fact that I entertained the idea for the first time, despite the fact that I'm an introvert, spoke volumes about how badly I wanted to break into the field!

> **My Advice: Send a follow-up email within 24 hours after an interview.**

A simple follow-up email expressing her interest in the role and restating why she would be a good fit for the position secured one of my friends her dream job. Below is a real-world example of an email I sent while interviewing for my current role.

Hello Kenneth,

Thank you so much for taking the time to interview me yesterday. I really enjoyed learning more about the Cybersecurity Assurance and Risk Analyst position at JupiterOne, and how the team is expanding.

It sounds like an exciting opportunity and is one that aligns with my interests and skills. I'm confident that I can take what I've learned as a security analyst intern and step into your role and be successful. I believe that my hard-working skills, keen attention to detail, and passionate nature, coupled with my ability as a quick learner will be of immediate value to your company. I have the ability to evolve within a job, meet deadlines for multiple projects, and build positive relationships with work colleagues and clients.

I admire the mission that drives your company and would be thrilled to join a team of innovative and passionate individuals.

I look forward to hearing from you about the next steps, and please don't hesitate to contact me if you need any additional information.

Thank you again.

Sincerely,
Yvie Djieya

You've Landed a Cyber Job. So, What Now?

Breathe

If your role is fairly technical, you'll be swimming in a sea of confusion for a while, but things will begin to make sense with time. Take it from me; I've spent several days in your shoes. Friends have told me it took them nearly eight months to grasp their role.

I was both excited and nervous on my first day on the job. I went into full panic mode when I was asked to write a blog article on my second day of the job. The panic attacks continued for the next four weeks, and I also suffered from severe imposter syndrome. I couldn't get my mind off my anxiety long enough to concentrate, let alone focus on stringing words together in a cohesive sentence.

I'm not one of those people who talk to themselves in the mirror, but there I was, every morning, afternoon, and sometimes evening, telling myself to get it together. To ease my anxiety and confront the imposter syndrome head-on, I reviewed old school notes and assigned readings and started taking programming courses on Skillshare and Udemy to fill my skills gap.

Don't Be Afraid to Ask Questions!

We all have different learning styles. Personally, I prefer to look for answers on my own before seeking help. If your job is fully remote, ask if you can record your training sessions. Make it a habit to learn something new pertaining to your role every day. It's not enough to just learn a process—understand why and how things work the way they do.

Give Yourself Grace to Learn, Grow, and Adapt

The industry is constantly evolving and new challenges arise requiring you to develop new skills or present opportunities to step outside of your comfort zone.

I've been blessed to work for companies with great work cultures. I've also been the first or only woman of color at the majority of those companies. I was one of only two black women in my high school class for two years in high school. Because of this, I didn't shy away from seeking employment at companies where I might have been under-represented. Instead, I saw it as an opportunity to create space for minorities.

When I was in the room, certain conversations were navigated with caution, and people's uneasiness sometimes made me chuckle inside. To drive effective change in the workplace, I believe that discussions around race, ethnicity, and diversity require candor rather than diplomacy.

Show Up for Yourself Every Day of Your Journey

"For everything there is a season, a time for every activity under heaven...A time to plant and a time to harvest...A time to tear down and a time to build up. A time to cry and a time to laugh. A time to grieve and a time to dance. A time to scatter stones and a time to gather stones. A time to embrace and a time to turn away. A time to search and a time to quit searching. A time to keep and a time to throw away. A time to tear and a time to mend. A time to be quiet and a time to speak."
- Ecclesiastes 3:1-8[1]

As you embark on your journey, don't be discouraged. I felt stuck for a long time in my life and found comfort in the Bible passage of Ecclesiastes 3:1-8. Remember, what worked for someone else might not necessarily work for you. We've been conditioned to believe that there is only one way to attain success in life. How often have you planned something only to not have it go as expected?

My Advice: Don't be afraid to pave your own path.

I'd like to leave you with this quote: "There are people less qualified than you doing the things you want to do, simply because they decide to believe in themselves."

I challenge you to show up for yourself every day regardless of how difficult and cumbersome life seems. It is worth fighting for the best version of yourself.

---

1   New Living Translation English Bible. (1996). Tynsdale House Publishers.

Here is my favorite tart recipe that helped me through my cybersecurity journey.

Fruit Tart Recipe

Crust

1 ½ cups of all-purpose flour

1 ½ sticks of unsalted butter, softened

½ cup of powdered sugar

¼ teaspoon of lemon zest

Filling

1 pack (8 oz) of cream cheese, softened

½ cup of cane sugar

1 teaspoon vanilla extract

Topping

Strawberries, kiwi, blackberries, raspberries, blueberries

Glaze

¼ cup of apricot jam

2 teaspoons of water

Directions

Crust: Mix flour, butter, powdered sugar, and lemon zest in a food processor until it starts to form a ball. Cover the dough in plastic wrap and refrigerate for at least 30 minutes (until firm) or place in the freezer for 15 minutes.

Preheat the oven to 350 degrees. Spread dough onto the bottom and sides of a 9-inch removable bottom tart pan. Bake for 12-15 minutes (until golden brown). Cool completely.

Filling: Mix cream cheese, sugar, and vanilla extract in a bowl.

Assembly: Spread the filling over the tart and top with fruits.
Mix apricot jam and water in a bowl and heat in the microwave for 30 seconds.
Use a pastry brush to spread apricot glaze over the tart.

ABOUT YVIE DJIEYA

As a student and full-time cybersecurity analyst, Yvie views learning as a lifelong entrepreneur's job. She proactively pursues security upskilling in security operations & GRC compliance through Udemy and Skillshare courses. Yvie pivoted from communications to cybersecurity after a cybersecurity bootcamp.

Yvie is a member of the Phi Theta Kappa Honors Society. She regularly volunteers at homeless shelters and group homes. This year, she is pursuing missionary work in South Africa.

CHAPTER 15

A Little Less Yasss Queen, A Lot More Action!

by Angela Marafino

A Little Less Yasss Queen, A Lot More Action!

Angela Marafino

When I was a child, there were no limits to the games, stories, or characters my friends and I would make up on any given day. From superheroes to cartoon characters (like the Teenage Mutant Ninja Turtles) to famous sports figures and "grown-ups" with various jobs. There isn't one instance I can recall when anyone told us that we could never actually be that bad-ass turtle, professional baseball player, or banker (I really loved Monopoly)! Obviously, Leonardo and his crew weren't real, and major league baseball is comprised of only men. It never crossed my mind that a similar place didn't exist for me in the future of what would become my adult career.

As I went through middle school and high school, I was always encouraged to do what I wanted regarding extracurricular activities and academics. If anyone ever told me I couldn't do something, it was likely a boy, and I was highly likely to respond, "Oh, really? Wanna bet?" followed by me proving —or at least attempting to prove— them wrong. I was somewhat rebellious, confident, and fearless throughout this time in my life. Typically, I would be the first to try something new or weird, and I was always up for taking on a dare or even a DOUBLE DOG DARE! Oh my!

Of course, this didn't last forever. I struggled to choose a finite career path in college and felt a bit lost after losing the comfort of a support system of childhood friends and teammates. It was just me now. Even after two bachelor's degrees, several random jobs, and moving around the country to different states, it would take me many years to rebuild the levels of courage and confidence in myself as I had up until age 18 or so. The primary catalyst for this would be throwing myself into an industry that I had no idea would garner as much passion in me as it did.

Cybersecurity 101

Many of you reading this will already know, but just in case you aren't aware: cybersecurity is a booming focus area of the technology industry right now! Booming as in, career changers and job seekers are very popular and in-demand. Booming also as in cybercriminals and attackers making bank off of the lack of cybersecurity-focused roles at all levels, teams focused on cybersecurity, and precautions taken by organizations and individuals to protect themselves from these threats. You might be saying, "this has BEEN a problem!" You're absolutely right. However, as of this writing, it is an increasingly pressing topic and is being discussed publicly more than ever in mainstream news and media outlets. Now is the opportune time to break into cybersecurity. I happened to stumble across this industry through an article in an in-flight magazine while relocating to a new state. Once again, I was attempting to reinvent myself with a "fresh start" somewhere new (this wasn't the first or last time I would do this, but it would turn out to be one of the most important).

When I say I stumbled across an article and into cybersecurity, I mean it! As I was flipping through the pages on the way to the crossword at the back, I found a technology section covering "CYBERSECURITY" as a hot new industry. The article referenced the hundreds of thousands of job openings in this field (late 2017, currently predicted to pass 3 million by the year 2025).[1] It discussed how almost every company would need to hire cybersecurity experts regardless of their industry and described the attributes necessary to succeed in this field. I fit the criteria with my love for solving problems, curiosity, and eagerness to learn. So mathematically and logically, it made perfect sense to pursue this career path, and I did so almost immediately.

---

1 Morgan, S. (2021, November 11). Cybersecurity Jobs Report: 3.5 million Openings in 2025. Cybercrime Magazine. cybersecurityventures.com/jobs/

Remember those two bachelor's degrees I mentioned earlier? They were in Fine Arts and Legal Studies. After deciding against going to law school or graduate school for art, I was now on the hunt for how to break into the tech industry. Other than a friend or two who worked as developers, I had no idea what "working in tech" meant or how I would get into this industry. My family has owned computers since the early 1990s, and I always loved going into all of the settings and changing everything and then changing it back. My dad never enjoyed that I did that, but I sure loved learning about what each setting did! The next step would be for me to find something as exciting to me now as that was when I was younger.

Commence Drinking From a Fire Hose

After getting settled in my new home, I researched everything about cybersecurity and the educational programs available aside from traditional college degrees. I couldn't stand the thought of getting a third undergraduate degree and I didn't want to spend years getting into a new line of work. At this point, I began working days and attending a cybersecurity bootcamp remotely on weeknights. This six-month training program taught the fundamentals of computer networking and information security concepts, along with hands-on labs and frequently sought-after skills. The situation was perfect for me as a 30-something career changer looking to finally begin a meaningful career path. All of this was exciting as I was learning more and more every day, getting closer to a career that would excite me in an industry in dire need of more candidates. But here's a secret: all the skills and concepts wouldn't have meant all that much if I didn't have a great instructor and mentor to guide me.

This professor was an experienced leader and highly-regarded cybersecurity professional. I greatly valued all of the time and information he shared with our class. The best piece of advice he emphasized time and time again was the importance of networking with other cybersecurity professionals of all levels and backgrounds. I believe I was the only person in that class to take his advice at the time and put myself out there by going to professional meetings, such as those hosted by the local Information Systems Security Association (ISSA) chapter. These are intended for more of a c-suite executive audience than students, but I went anyway! It was the beginning of what could be called a brief obsession to network with industry leaders and other students in technology to make as many connections as I possibly could.

Many presentations went over my head during those first few meetings I attended as a student, but I eventually caught on to the technical jargon. However, what did stick with me was the lack of women and other underrepresented individuals in attendance during those meetings. While the topics addressed in the presentations I heard were all product, process, or technique-based, this quickly changed as I became more deeply involved in the cybersecurity community. I began attending other local tech interest group meetings to help myself grow my career and help others break into the industry. Some groups were mainly developers, some for beginners, and others focused on women only. I joined the hacker space in my city, located in a warehouse/garage filled with new and old gadgets and techies whose interests were all across the board. I also got involved in a women's group that focused its efforts on helping other women break into and thrive in cybersecurity.

Learning more about the specific struggles women and underrepresented individuals face in the tech industry made it even more important to give back the mentorship and guidance given to me. No one ever told me I couldn't make it in tech or cybersecurity, even though I had no previous experience in these fields. However, it quickly became apparent to me that this wasn't the case for many others. Other students and career changers were told it would be too difficult or competitive. Unfortunately, they also told themselves they weren't good enough and didn't belong. Despite passing interviews and being hired as cybersecurity professionals, they feared the hiring was a mistake, and eventually, they would be discovered as an imposter. What's worse, others told them they probably had imposter syndrome in an attempt to validate their feelings.

Imposter Syndrome Has Entered the Chat

Imposter syndrome has been one of the most talked-about topics in meetings and conferences over the past three years. Most presentations on the topic are aimed at women and often present ideas of "battling" or "fixing" someone's imposter syndrome. Imposter syndrome is "a psychological pattern in which an individual doubts their skills, talents, or accomplishments and has a persistent internalized fear of being exposed as a 'fraud'.[2] Despite external evidence of their competence, those experiencing this phenomenon remain convinced that they are frauds and do not deserve all they have achieved." A quick search of the phrase "imposter syndrome" pulls up about 6,720,000 results! Unfortunately, this is a popular topic on people's minds right now. As a side note, my preferred search for "Imposter syndrome is bullshit" only returned about seven relevant search results out of the millions, including the phrase itself :-(

The phrase was initially called "Imposter Phenomenon." A Google Trends search comparing the two naming conventions shows a spike in the term "syndrome" replacing "phenomenon" beginning around 2015 and then jumping drastically over the past three years.

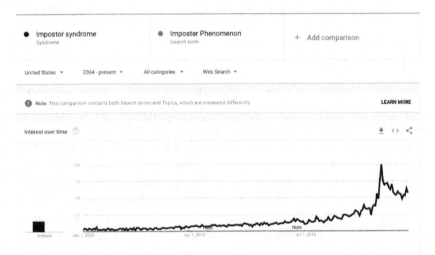

There is no clear answer why "syndrome" is used now instead. Still, it has skyrocketed into a hot topic in everyday conversation within the cybersecurity industry.

Suddenly, it seemed like everyone on social media and in my network was opening up about having imposter syndrome to each other, and I

2   Langford, J., & Clance, P. R. (1993). The imposter phenomenon: Recent research findings regarding dynamics, personality and family patterns and their implications for treatment. Psychotherapy: Theory, Research, Practice, Training, 30(3), 495–501. doi. org/10.1037/0033-3204.30.3.495

couldn't relate. As someone who poured everything they had into changing careers, I knew I belonged in this industry, and no one could tell me otherwise. I never felt like an imposter, but I knew other people who did. Not because I never doubted myself, but because I knew I belonged, and that self-doubt was a natural piece to the human psyche puzzle that everyone feels at some point in their life. I made it into the tech industry with no background in a relevant field, but with six months of training and a fierce passion for changing my life with these new skills I had learned.

Now everyone around me confessed that none of them thought they belonged (including previous managers, peers with computer science degrees, senior-level engineers, etc.). Those who stated they never felt imposter syndrome faced push-back and criticism, so I never spoke up when it was mentioned around me. Instead, I listened and vented to my friends and family about my frustration that the feelings I had weren't a syndrome, they weren't something that could be diagnosed, and they weren't feelings that I needed anyone to help me with. I either needed to step up and get my shit together if I wasn't prepared for a task, or I needed to be in an environment where I could thrive if the one I was in was preventing me from doing so. This was in 2020.

I'm Not the Only One

Harvard Business Review published an article in February 2021 by Ruchika Tulshyan and Jodi-Ann Burey titled "Stop Telling Women They Have Imposter Syndrome" which addresses the fact that despite the number of people experiencing imposter syndrome, "What's less explored is why imposter syndrome exists in the first place and what role workplace systems play in fostering and exacerbating it in women." Additionally, "as we know it today, imposter syndrome blames individuals, without accounting for the historical and cultural contexts that are foundational to how it manifests in both women of color and white women. Imposter syndrome directs our view towards fixing women at work instead of fixing the places where women work."[3] Coming across this article was the first time I had heard anyone address imposter syndrome in a way other than "Yasss

---

3   Tulshyan, R., & Burey, J.A. (2021, February 11). Stop telling women they have imposter syndrome. Harvard Business Review. hbr.org/2021/02/stop-telling-women-they-have-imposter-syndrome

queen, me too!" After I shared this article on social media, I received more responses than almost any of my other posts from people (mostly other women) that reached out saying this more accurately aligned with their views; they just didn't know how to put it into words. I felt the same way.

Finally, there was publicly-stated opposition to using the phrase "imposter syndrome" to address the bigger issue. People everywhere self-diagnose and impose on others the theory that "oh, it's okay, everyone has imposter syndrome, and here's how you can fix it." Addressing it as a syndrome is damaging in itself. The term "syndrome" is synonymous with the concept that someone has a condition or disorder that makes them less capable and needs individual treatment. This is a HUGE burden to put on someone, not to mention that imposter syndrome is not a medically diagnosable condition!

At least the phrase "imposter phenomenon" lent itself to a broader concept of an event or an experience faced at a particular time, rather than an individual experience requiring treatment. As Burey and Tulshyan mention in their article, "imposter syndrome as a concept fails to capture daily battles with microaggressions, expectations, and assumptions formed by stereotypes and racism and puts the onus on women to deal with the effects. For women of color, self-doubt and the feeling of not belonging in corporate workplaces can be even more pronounced." [3]

Now What?

How can we stop fueling this fire and change the conversation here? Burey and Tulshyan have an answer to that question as well. "The answer to overcoming imposter syndrome is not to fix individuals but to create an environment that fosters a variety of leadership styles and in which diverse racial, ethnic, and gender identities are seen as just as professional as the current model, which is typically Eurocentric, masculine, and heteronormative." "Leaders must create a culture for women and people of color that addresses systemic bias and racism. Only by doing so can we reduce the experiences that culminate in so-called imposter syndrome among employees from marginalized communities. Perhaps we can stop misdiagnosing women with 'imposter syndrome' once and for all."

A few months later, in July 2021, Jodi-Ann Burey and Ruchika Tulshyan had a follow-up article published in the Harvard Business Review titled, *End Imposter Syndrome in Your Workplace*.[4] This follow-up article is full of suggestions to help managers take action and effectively end imposter syndrome for those working on their teams. A few of my favorites include: change the language employees use to describe how they feel, be honest about how bias impacts others, and, last but not least, quit gaslighting and listen! Here are the direct quotes you need in your life right this instant:

- "While supporting your team members individually is important, take a both/and approach to meeting their unique needs while also making the organizational shifts required to address imposter syndrome at its true source."

- "Understanding the unique challenges faced by people who are different from them builds the managers' capacity to fully grow in their roles. Managers cannot be considered effective if they can only manage employees who are like them."

- "Gaslighting, a type of psychological manipulation that causes one to question their own reality, can take many forms in the workplace. When it comes to women of all races and people of color of all genders, acknowledging imposter syndrome without naming its context within systems of racism and bias is arguably a form of gaslighting."

Brene Brown interviewed Burey and Tulshyan about their two articles on imposter syndrome and how to address it head-on.[5] Two of my favorite takeaways from this episode on the Dare to Lead podcast were: "White folks and leaders need to look at themselves and ask, 'What am I doing to make these people feel as though they can't bring their authentic selves to work.'"; and "You're either uncomfortable, or you're doing it performantly." In the article, *End Imposter Syndrome in Your Workplace*, the authors mention that women discussed having managers who reinforced belief in their abilities and showed direct support by using phrases such as "I know you can lead...I've seen you succeed before, and I believe in you." These affirmations could help them overcome feelings of self-doubt.

---

4   Tulshyan, R., & Burey, J. A. (2021, July 14). End Imposter Syndrome in your workplace. Harvard Business Review. hbr.org/2021/07/end-imposter-syndrome-in-your-workplace

5   Brown, B. (Host). (2021, October 11). Imposter Syndrome with Jodi-Ann Burey & Ruchika Tulshyan. Dare to Lead Podcast. brenebrown.com/podcast/imposter-syndrome/.

"Managers best supported women by genuinely listening to their experiences of gender and/or racial bias, and expressing the view that it was the organization's responsibility to fix it." A key piece to solving this puzzle is to ask more questions! What are you feeling? Why do you feel the way you do? How long have you felt this way, and was there a catalyst to cause you to have these feelings? Since we are speaking in the context of workplace "imposter syndrome," what aren't you getting from your company, manager, team, etc., that you need to excel?

Talk it Out

To be clear, I do think that the willingness to be open and share struggles, such as feelings of imposter syndrome, is beneficial. Perhaps the term "imposter syndrome" is the corporate version of the 50 Shades of Grey series – the books and movies may have been a terrible representation of consent and personal agency within relationships, yet they were a catalyst for a generation of women to open up about desire in a way they hadn't felt able to before. The term impostor syndrome, while flawed, has given people a socially acceptable way to describe the ways they have felt doubt or marginalization in the workplace. Sharing these experiences and feelings is a healthy expression and can help identify issues within a work environment that may be contributing to an employee's feelings of self-doubt. Regardless, we need to stop focusing on the individual as the reason they feel a lack of confidence or unpreparedness and start looking deeper at their environment, access to resources, and those they often interact with in the workplace.

Let's stop assuming that because someone voices opinions about self-doubt, being nervous in a new role or environment, or are questioning their own skills, they must have imposter syndrome and then go on to affirm their feelings with "it's okay, me too" or "it's okay, everyone has it" (no, not everyone does and likely not for the exact same reasons). This type of feedback loop does not provide any constructive actions to take at the managerial or the individual level to help a person understand their situation in greater detail and determine who or what is failing them.

I wouldn't assume that every person with insomnia, attention-deficit disorder, and migraines is named Angela. So why would every person who expresses any amount of self-doubt, second-guesses themselves, or doesn't feel prepared at some point in time automatically be labeled as having imposter syndrome? Let's ask deeper questions, do the digging, and start making the changes necessary to address these issues and the unique situations that come along with each of them.

ABOUT ANGELA MARAFINO

Based out of Seattle, Angela is currently a Program Manager focused on Security & Compliance products at Microsoft. As a woman who graduated college with two degrees unrelated to information security, she is extremely passionate about diversity and inclusion and making lasting connections with others in and out of technology.

Outside of work, she runs the Hacker Book Club on Discord, hosts two podcasts under the ITSP Magazine Channel, mentors others interested in cybersecurity, and spends time with her family, friends, and pets in the Pacific Northwest!

CHAPTER 16

Do I Fit?

by Coleen Shane

CHAPTER 16

Do I Fit?

Coleen Shane

Questioning our fit is something many of us have experienced. Doubting whether you fit into an industry, a role, or a community can happen for many reasons, including setbacks, inexperience, or a frustrating job search.

I believe there is room in the cybersecurity industry for all of us, perhaps especially those of us who have felt like a misfit at some point in our lives. I have reached a point where I love myself and feel comfortable being my authentic self within communities of cybersecurity professionals.

Experience has shown me the incredible value of cybersecurity communities that connect in digital and physical spaces and how groups of like-minded individuals can spark change by having meaningful conversations. I have also learned that networking yields incredible returns over time and how a network can help you find a balanced fit.

Overview

This chapter shares my experience navigating digital and physical communities in InfoSec over the past few years and what I learned along the way. I hope it offers value to readers at all stages of their career since community and networking can be essential tools for overcoming obstacles, up-leveling your career, and sparking important industry change.

Networking does not always yield immediate returns, but it's an essential pursuit. My community has been a defining part of my journey during my engineering career, a divorce, a difficult job search, and my transition. In particular, I will cover:

Navigating the Cybersecurity Community to Find Your Fit

The first time I ever questioned if I fit in the cybersecurity industry was August 2019 during DEF CON 27. I had spent nearly a decade of my career in cybersecurity, IT, and network engineering, but 2019 was my first trip to Las Vegas for Hacker Summer Camp, a collection of annual conferences including DEF CON, Queercon, BSides Las Vegas, and Black Hat USA.

My journey to find my place in cybersecurity communities really started several months before these conferences when I joined Twitter. I was looking for growth and new opportunities in both my personal and professional life, so I decided to start creating a digital community using Twitter. InfoSec Twitter is definitely a thing, and I began to make connections. Many people in my budding community were heading to Las Vegas for DEF CON and Queercon, so I decided to go, too.

I really had no idea what to expect from my first trip to Hacker Summer Camp. I thought I'd meet cool hacker people and get to do cool hacker things. Somehow, I expected I'd just run into all the people I knew from InfoSec Twitter at the Vegas conferences. I signed up to volunteer during my trip to give back to the cybersecurity community and meet more like-minded people.

Turns out, I was completely unprepared for the realities of Vegas cybersecurity conferences. InfoSec Twitter can be loud but it's nothing like the overwhelming experience on the ground at DEF CON or other shows. I was surprised to discover some event venues were so crowded that it was difficult to navigate some hallways. The first hotel room I booked was not physically secure, so I booked a different room at the Venetian. My plans to volunteer fell through when I learned they did not need my help. As a woman, I was significantly outnumbered by men at the conference, and the behavior of some men made me worried for my safety.

I looked for people I knew at the conference, but it was far too crowded to successfully connect with folks I recognized. I was too afraid to log into my Twitter account the entire week since Hacker Summer Camp is a notorious hotbed for security threats. It was a mistake to completely avoid social media, especially since I could have logged into my Twitter safely each night from my hotel room. I didn't know it at the time, but safely accessing social media is a powerful tool for cybersecurity conferences. It is where all the best unofficial conference activities are advertised, like parties where you can mingle and make connections.

Safety Tips for Hacker Summer Camps

DEF CON and Black Hat are notoriously hostile networks with many cybersecurity risks to conference attendees. DEF CON even has a Wall of Sheep village, featuring a massive screen display of usernames and partly-obscured passwords stolen from conference attendees who failed to protect their credentials.

I was aware of these security risks heading in, so I avoided logging into Twitter for most of my first week. While I do NOT recommend that you lose contact with your friends and community by being overly cautious like I did, I do recommend that others are careful.

The following ten safety tips are a bare minimum:

1. Update all device operating systems, apps, and anti-virus before you arrive.
2. Avoid conference WiFi, free USBs, and ATMs.
3. Bring device privacy screens.
4. Protect your credit cards with a RFID sleeve or foil.
5. Close all device ports by turning off Bluetooth and NFC and clearing your WiFI settings.
6. Be aware of your surroundings and do not leave your items unattended.
7. Scan your devices for malware.
8. Use multi-factor authentication on all accounts.
9. Use a virtual private network (VPN).

10. Don't bring unnecessary electronics or cards anywhere.

To be as safe as possible, do not take any devices outside your hotel room. Carry only a burner phone and a notebook. Always pay with cash or prepaid debit cards.

How I Finally Got the Vegas InfoSec Experience I'd Been Waiting For

I fired up my Twitter account from my hotel on the last day of the conference and was honest about my experience the prior week. Most DEF CON attendees had already left Vegas, but I planned to stay to spend a day by the pool. I got an immediate response on Twitter. Some other attendees reached out and said they had similar experiences. Conference organizers responded and said they would work to create more inclusive and safe experiences. I attended a women's brunch and spent some time with a few cool women in cybersecurity, including one who became a close friend. This type of meaningful conversation and connection was what I hoped to find in Vegas, and finally experiencing it was wonderful.

Overall, my first Vegas conference experience was incredibly positive. I learned a lot. But had I not sent that tweet detailing my experience, I wouldn't have met some important people in my network. If I had not expressed my thoughts on safety and inclusivity to conference organizers, I would not have sparked dialogue about creating con experiences that work better for everyone.

I also learned that the best conference experiences blend digital and face-to-face communication and involve a fair amount of planning. Your conference experiences are likely to be better if you assemble a crew before arrival and make plans to attend sessions and events together. At minimum, having one person is important. Having someone to check in with periodically can make the experience much better.

Making the Most of Your First Cybersecurity Conferences

I cannot recommend attending cybersecurity conferences strongly enough. It is a solid way to make connections in the industry. I also would like to pass along some great advice which was given to me after my DEF CON 27 experience.

- Find your people, locally or online, and get a group together and make plans to do some activities together at the con.

- Start with smaller conferences, like regional, or local. A quick search, or social media post asking about these should quickly turn up some results.

- Remember that huge conferences are, well, huge conferences, and no one has the same agenda or itinerary. You will need to plan a bit in order to be successful.

Navigating Systemic Bias

It is no secret that cybersecurity and other tech industries have a diversity problem. I have personally faced bias during my career, and I observe systemic bias from a unique viewpoint. I am a 47-year-old trans woman who officially began her transition in 2015-2016, after seven years in this industry. I once benefited from white male privilege. After legally changing my name from male to female, I noticed I was treated very differently by prospective employers. I received significantly fewer phone calls after applying for new jobs.

I lost a prior job in February 2020, just before the COVID-19 pandemic hit, and I struggled to find another role. I did what anyone would do, I started applying to anything and everything I would qualify for. I have a relatively diverse set of IT and security skills, including a lot of hands-on engineering, system administration, and network administration. It should have been relatively easy for me to find something to pay the bills. COVID made my job search more challenging. I also experienced obstacles applying for engineering roles after legally changing my name from Colin to Coleen in 2019.

I continued to apply. What else could I do? I searched job boards, joined lists, and shared job posts that weren't the right fit for me on Twitter to benefit other job seekers. Eventually, I decided to start applying as C.M. Shane. I scrubbed my LinkedIn, changed my LinkedIn display name to C.M. Shane, and changed my avatar to a very gender neutral headshot. I left my LinkedIn settings this way until I eventually found a job.

Systemic bias against women occurs across countless industries and it can start early. Countless women have been labeled "not technical enough" and their contributions to any field are ignored or discounted. Systemic bias can start early - my daughter was informed by a high school instructor that she would struggle with CAD software since "she was an artist and not into mathematics." It was so upsetting to see a child's spirits crushed like that. Those words affected her, despite our encouragement. Fortunately, she found a much better and more supportive CAD instructor in college who restored her confidence. If your role includes teaching or training, it is critically important to make sure you are not dismissive towards people's technical potential, particularly if they are women or people from underrepresented backgrounds.

Women are a minority in the cybersecurity industry, and this shapes our experiences in our career. Gender is a factor during job hunts, at conferences, and on social media. The fact we are underrepresented does not mean men are more adept at technology than women. I personally know some extremely technical women and non-binary individuals who run circles around non-technical men, so beliefs that women are less technical are clearly outdated and should be recognized as such. We all have a shared responsibility to dismantle systemic biases against women. It is time to update how we train, recruit, interview, hire, promote, and compensate women and non-binary individuals.

Dealing with Imposter Syndrome

Questioning if you fit can coincide with feelings of imposter syndrome at any time during your career. I even experienced feelings of imposter syndrome earlier today, after being informed a worksite was having connectivity issues after adding a second WAN interface for network reliability. It turned out I had misread a configuration setting within the network management software.

A small mistake caused feelings of imposter syndrome to resurface, even though I logically know everyone makes mistakes. In my case, I am less familiar with the particular network vendor being used, despite tons of experience with countless other vendors. I know imposter syndrome is ridiculous and that it does not serve me to believe I need to be an expert in everything. Collectively, the cybersecurity industry needs to relinquish our fear of not knowing everything because no one person can be an expert on everything. Unreasonable expectations toward ourselves, and sometimes others, can be deeply ingrained behaviors but we need to do our best to let them go.

This small mistake caused my feelings of imposter syndrome to resurface, even though everyone makes occasional mistakes. I have less familiarity with this particular networking vendor, especially compared to countless others networking technologies I have worked with for years. However, I also recognize these feelings as ridiculous. Collectively, we need to relinquish our fear of not knowing everything in cybersecurity. No one is an expert on everything or every vendor. Unreasonable expectations are deeply ingrained behaviors, but we need to do our best to let them go.

When Imposter Syndrome Makes You Question "Do I Fit"?

Keep in mind that everyone on this planet has felt this way at some point in their careers, perhaps many times. Recognizing that imposter syndrome is a shared experience can help us feel less isolated during moments of self-doubt.

Education, training, and practice all lead to experience, which builds confidence like no other. Luckily these days, it's relatively easy to find online training and virtual practice modules for just about anything; for everything else, there is YouTube! This last bit may seem like a joke but watching online videos has helped me with many of life's technical challenges.

Last, and I cannot recommend this one enough, networking. Network with other like-minded individuals in your field to collaborate and learn from one another. Twitter has been extremely helpful in my career as it has allowed me to connect with many people with similar interests and challenges. It has also introduced me to many important people in the field who have been helpful in locating available career opportunities.

Networking & Community

During my recent job search, I doubled down on my networking efforts since we are often told that networking is the best way to find a job. My primary avenue for networking was InfoSec Twitter, especially Twitter spaces dedicated to cybersecurity job seekers. I found it very helpful and encouraging to participate in these spaces since I was in a position to help others as well as myself. I learned that returns on networking are not immediate, and the best time to start building your network is before it's necessary.

My networking efforts did pay off, even if the result was not instantaneous. I saw a slow but steady increase in the number of interviews on my calendar. Every job interview you attend teaches me something, and I learned a lot about my strengths as a candidate. I learned how important it is to maintain the trust of people in your network, especially if they give you an interview referral. Perhaps most importantly, I learned the best approach to networking during a job search is to be honest with yourself and others.

Navigating Cybersecurity Interviews

Interview loops for cybersecurity roles typically involve at least one panel, which are appointed to rate a candidate's suitability for a role and organization. Technical panels are notoriously challenging, and they are often composed of a demographically homogeneous group of interviewers. Without creating diverse panels, there is little benefit in panels for women and minority candidates such as myself. People from similar backgrounds cannot provide a well-rounded set of candidate feedback, especially if the interviewers are given a strict script of interview questions to ask.

Almost everyone in cybersecurity has stumbled in a panel interview at least once. I stumbled often, since I did not always grasp the nomenclature used by interviewers. I would kick myself hours later when I figured out what was being asked by interviewers. The experience of stumbling during an interview can be difficult and make candidates feel like they have reached the end of the road for a position, especially when you are interviewing for highly competitive roles at prestigious organizations.

Both job candidates and hiring managers should recognize the barriers to success for cybersecurity job seekers. If you have the privilege and influence to hire, evaluate if your job descriptions and interview loops are creating candidates. The cybersecurity industry is notorious for unrealistic job postings and unreasonable expectations for candidates. We have all seen memes about job postings that require 20 years of experience with a new technology. Many of us have also personally encountered entry-level job postings that require professional-level certifications, such as the CISSP.

Try to avoid falling prey to imposter syndrome after an unsuccessful panel interview, even though it is easy to become discouraged. It is not easy to stay positive, especially since I have firsthand found myself questioning my abilities after a string of negative interview experiences. I have been passed over for roles that I am well-qualified for.

My network was encouraging me during my job search. I advise others who are feeling discouraged in their careers to find supportive people in the cybersecurity community however they can. I relied on InfoSec Twitter, but you may find another community that you prefer. Also, I believe it is important to strive for balance during a job search or a setback. Pursue a few non-professional interests and work to be your authentic self in your communities. I was eventually bold enough to acknowledge that I am more than just a technology worker online, which is exactly what led to #InfoSecBikini.

The Story of #InfoSecBikini

Networking and social media are powerful tools to connect with other people who have similar interests, both in and outside of cyber. I have met people through the cybersecurity community who share non-work interests with me, including electronics, LEGO®, rusty abandoned buildings, and skateboards. Technology pays the bills, but it's important to find balance between cybersecurity and your other interests. I am glad that I allowed myself to pursue these interests and connect with others about personal interests during my job search. A little chaos in our community can be fun since my entire professional existence is spent putting things into order.

Many cybersecurity professionals, particularly those who are active on Twitter, are familiar with #InfoSecBikini. It was a summer 2021 event that is probably best described as a viral conversation about gender and bias in cybersecurity. It is also a story about me wearing a bikini and becoming a hot topic.

It all started one Sunday when I was headed to the beach in my bikini and felt kind of cute. So, I posted a picture on my Twitter account. I'd only been out as a trans woman for a few years and I was just becoming comfortable with showing my body. I had a great day at the beach. The next day, I woke up and opened Twitter to discover someone asked, "why are women in InfoSec always posting underwear pictures? That's an unfollow." I quickly replied, "It's a bikini and I am a human being who is interested in more than just InfoSec. Adiós."

Before I knew it, this exchange sparked a lot of dialogue. Many cybersecurity professionals came to my defense, tweeting that it was rude for a stranger to drop an unwarranted comment on my beach tweet. Someone started the #InfoSecBikini hashtag and it quickly took off. I don't know who started it, but I would love to give them credit if I ever find out. Before I knew it, everyone in the industry started posting pictures in bikinis - men, women, pets, stuffed animals, and more. While I appreciated the show of support, the #InfoSecBikini hashtag also sparked input from a lot of detractors who felt the whole conversation was inappropriate.

The dialogue was a brief, viral moment in our industry, but it was more than just swimwear. It was a big and important conversation that highlighted a double standard in the industry. Many of us felt that men in cybersecurity are encouraged to have hobbies and non-work interests and praised for these efforts. Women in cybersecurity, on the other hand, are often discouraged from being anything more than technologists.

Swimwear is just swimwear, but in the summer of 2021 bikinis were a symbol of systemic bias. I am still appreciative toward all the men in cybersecurity who donned bikinis in support of equity.

#InfoSecBikini happened around the same time as another major online dialogue about gender equity in technology, the #devspelades movement.

That was a significant online conversation about a Brazilian woman engineer who, like me, had a bigger identity than her day job duties as a developer. These two equity movements found each other, joined forces, and gained momentum. There was a lot of crossover and it was awesome to see people of all genders participating in a global protest of double standards and sexism in technology.

The Aftermath of InfoSecBikini

#InfoSecBikini faded quickly, much like any other viral phenomenon, but it had a lasting impact on my individual brand and cybersecurity network. I received many invitations to events at DEF CON 29 and a complimentary pass to Black Hat. People frequently recognized me, some of whom were brave enough to come up and say hello. I appreciate those willing to connect at conferences when they recognize virtual friends. These supporters really made me feel like I fit in the industry.

Many people at DEF CON who recognized me from #InfoSecBikini told me "right on." Others wanted to chat or take a photo with me. One person even cried after meeting me at the conference since they had experienced a career filled with challenge and bias. It gave me a lot of confidence that my experiences in cybersecurity were not entirely unique and that others appreciated my fight for a more equitable industry. I felt renewed. And, I totally felt like I really did fit into the cyber community and I felt that way for the entire week!

Finding Internal and External Balance

Many of us have questioned whether we fit into many different communities, not just cybersecurity. As a transgender woman, I would be severely remiss if I did not mention issues with fitting into the trans community or judgments about whether someone is "trans enough." I have faced scrutiny because I have a deep voice and laryngeal prominence. I take issue with judgments on whether someone else fits, particularly when it is based on appearance, body, or medical factors. I love myself now more than at any other point in my life, and I don't see any surgery improving this whatsoever.

I don't think I have ever been a perfect fit in any community in my life and I know that experience is not entirely unique. I am finally coming to terms with being an outlier, and in fact, I am coming to enjoy it. While I cannot claim to be in harmony with my surroundings and communities at any given moment, I have found a way to be in balance with my environment and the communities of people who surround me.

My decision to quit drinking helped me find balance within myself, which made finding balance with communities easier. I like to think I bring balance to social media and other cybersecurity communities by consciously giving back to my network and ignoring other people's insecurities. Finding my own sense of balance and identity as a person and professional means I can still create a little chaos from time to time. Still, my shenanigans are always mischievous and never malicious. While I cannot tell you to view yourself as a perpetual misfit, it is the mindset that worked for me. I advise others to find or make their own place and then defend it and protect it, so that it can grow and become a safe place for others.

From "Do I Fit?" to "Where Do I Fit?"

Perhaps "Do I Fit" is the wrong question, maybe we should be asking "Where Do I Fit?" If you cannot find an answer to this question, then do what I do. Make a place from what you can find.

Looking for friends and allies is critical to survival in any environment, so a little flexibility and willingness to relent to others on occasion are essential skills to develop, but do not be subservient to anyone, because that's not a very happy life to lead. It can be challenging to find balance, connection, and community, especially for someone who is very shy and introverted. Still, it is well worth the effort for your career and personal life.

ABOUT COLEEN MICHAEL SHANE

Coleen is a Senior Network Security engineer for a medium sized business with locations throughout the U.S. Coleen has been in the field since 2008, while working on her AAS in Computer Security and Networking. She also has a B.S. in Information Security with a minor in Networking, and many, many industry certifications. Coleen has worked in this capacity for the government and private sectors in industries ranging from health-care, testing, and retail. She has two adult children who both live nearby in San Diego.

Coleen is an outspoken supporter of Women's and Trans rights and supports many phil-anthropic causes from feeding children to equal opportunity and education. Being so outspoken, she has also caused a small bit of controversy within the Information Security Industry with her antics and her bikini. Coleen loves to hike, drive really fast, explore abandoned places, and stir things up in her spare time.

CHAPTER 17

Ageism is Your Achilles Heel

by Rachel Harpley

Ageism is Your Achilles Heel

Rachel Harpley

Introduction

Job growth in the cybersecurity industry continues to increase, and with it the need for trained professionals. The headlines have highlighted the need for millions of professionals to join the industry for many years. Rapid job growth has created a skills gap which leaves most cybersecurity teams short-staffed and companies vulnerable to attacks. In addition to this shortage of skilled professionals, the volume of cyber attacks have drastically increased with the availability of Ransomware-as-a-Service (RaaS) in which ransomware creators and operators license their malicious code to affiliates, making complex attacks more accessible to low-level bad actors.

This chapter seeks to identify how traditional workforce development strategies and ageism have delayed our ability to close the skills gap, while limiting the rate at which the industry can hire. The primary goal of this content is to present solutions which could rapidly solve the skills gap, whether for one team or the industry as a whole. This chapter may refer to the information technology landscape as a whole, but the focus of this piece is cybersecurity. At times, the term security may be used synonymously with cybersecurity, IT security and information security unless otherwise noted. The inclusion of various source materials in this piece is not intended as an endorsement of their authors or their other works.

To be clear, age is only one way to categorize people into social classes and this article is not an attempt to claim that age is in any way the most profound identifier for a person. Hopefully we may use ageism as a way to examine our assumptions and prejudices - a gateway to greater change, equity and inclusion. Age is, however, a category of personhood that we are all likely to experience, and for workers of 40 years and over, it is also one of the employment categories protected by the U.S. Equal Employment Opportunity Commission (EEOC). The EEOC is an oversight commission empowered to levy fines against employers, sometimes as high as $500,000 per instance.

IBM & "Dinobabies" - A Case Study on Ageism

In February of 2022, the New York Times published an article presenting a pattern of ageism discrimination by IBM's leadership.[1] This news covered the filing of a class action lawsuit against IBM by Ms. Liss-Riordan, known for cases against Amazon, American Airlines, FedEx, Lyft, Square, Uber and numerous food delivery companies relying on the gig economy. The filing was in conjunction with the release of a "trove of previously sealed documents" that has now been made public by a Federal District Court.

In this news report, it is the colorful language of an IBM executive that is nearly a meme of itself. According to the article, an email from a top executive discussed a plan to "accelerate change by inviting the 'dinobabies' to leave" in reference to older workers, so that IBM could make them an "extinct species." That's powerful imagery, and for many of us, it's poignant.

Detailed in this report by Noam Scheiber is IBM's pattern and stance on older workers. Within the article, an IBM spokesperson shared that the median age of IBM's US workforce was 48 years old from 2010 to 2020. That means IBM's workforce is primarily Gen X. Supporting that claim within these newly unsealed documents, there is a memo from a top executive who shared that IBM's "millennial population trails competitors," detailing that "Accenture is 72% millennial we are at 42% with a wide range and many units falling well below that average." For context, Millennials are often considered 26 to 42 years old. The term Elder Millennial is used to

---

1   Scheiber, N. (2022, February 12). *Making 'Dinobabies' extinct: IBM's push for a younger work force.* The New York Times. www.nytimes.com/2022/02/12/business/economy/ibm-age-discrimination. html

speak of the oldest in this group, and they qualify for age-based protections under EEOC, while the youngest Millennials are in their mid-20s.

That executive had a way with words, and in comment to this New York Times article an IBM representative came back with a few too. Their spokesperson claims that "IBM never engaged in systemic age discrimination" yet the article identifies several ways that IBM systematically targeted older workers. Some of these policies were built to encourage older workers to leave, like shift changes and forced relocation, or to lay off older workers while writing policies to prevent the layoff of younger workers. The article also mentions a 2020 report from the EEOC summarizing their investigation which revealed IBM leadership was actively directing managers to take aggressive actions to reduce the headcount of older workers.

What was the culture that led up to this? Ginny Rometty accepted the promotion to CEO in 2012, stepping into this leadership role a year after IBM's annual revenue peaked at an all-time high in 2011 and retiring in 2020 when annual revenue had decreased year-over-year since its peak.[2] Of course, in 2011, no one could know that was the peak, yet clearly something about IBM's strategies was negatively affecting revenue and it seems leadership was convinced it was their aging employees.

In researching this story to include it here, I found an editorial in USA Today written by IBM CEO Ginny Rometty in 2016 titled "We need to fill 'new collar' jobs that employers demand." IBM's revenue had dropped by $27 billion annually at this point, and the article reads like a press release declaring IBM's call-to-action strategy.[3] In the article, CEO Rometty shares that IBM intends "to hire about 25,000 professionals in the next four years in the United States, 6,000 of those in 2017." Rometty goes on to say that "IBM will also invest $1 billion in training and development of our U.S. employees in the next four years." Curious about the specifics of this investment in their US-based employees I read on, but only found mention of investments in young people with additional technical six-year high school programs.

2 Alsop, T. (2022, April 8). *IBM Revenue 1999-2020*. www.statista.com/statistics/265003/ibms-revenue-since-1999/
3 Rometty, G. (2016, December 13). *We need to fill 'new collar' jobs that employers demand: IBM's Rometty*. USA Today. www.usatoday.com/story/tech/columnist/2016/12/13/we-need-fill-new-collar-jobs-employers-demand-ibms-rometty/95382248/

No mention of new skills training for their existing workers.

With further digging, I found an MIT Task Force on Work of the Future from 2020 titled "The Learning System at IBM: A Case Study" and at first, I was excited.[4] It calls the IBM learning program "state-of-the-art" but that program seems specific to badges associated with learning accomplishments. This is nothing more than gamification which has been part of educational systems since at least the 1980s. Additionally, this MIT paper is about a training program for salespeople selling technology; it is not for technical skills development.

IBM's rampant culture of ageism is not unique in tech as can be seen in a 2016 article from USA Today stating that "since 2012, 90 age-related complaints have been filed against a dozen top tech companies in Silicon Valley, according to the California Department of Fair Employment and Housing (DFEH)[...] Cisco Systems is named in 11 filings, followed by Apple (9), Google (8), and Oracle (7) and Genentech (7). Yahoo, Intel, LinkedIn, Facebook, Tesla Motors and Twitter were also named."[5] Ageism is an issue pervasive across large technology organizations and industries.

The Challenge - A Definition of Insanity

The need for skilled cybersecurity workers has continued to rise exponentially for the last decade. During this time, most employers and workforce development programs focused on building a talent pipeline via traditional means, such as college-degree programs and other technology trade programs in high schools. This investment in future generations has value, but only strategic long-term returns. It will not solve the cybersecurity skills gap on its own. The need is too great, and the need is too immediate.

Admittedly, it was those early headlines about job growth that caught my attention and contributed to my choice to pursue this industry. Curious

---

4   The Learning System at IBM: A case study. MIT Work of the Future. (2020, December 15). workofthefuture.mit.edu/research-post/the-learning-system-at-ibm-a-case-study/
5   Swartz, J. (2016, December 2). 90 age-discrimination complaints reflect growing issue for Tech. USA Today. www.usatoday.com/story/tech/news/2016/11/22/90-age-discrimination-suits-reflect-growing-issue-tech/93110594/

when this demand surge became an industry discussion I turned to (ISC)2, an international, nonprofit membership association that provides training, certifications, and research on the industry.[6] Their first Global Workforce Study was in 2004 in which they briefly mention a growth of headcount in this field (referring to current professionals), but it appears that the first mention of "Demand for Professionals" was in their 2011 report, coincidentally, the same year of IBM's highest reported revenue, potentially signally an overall boom in technology for business.

The next Global Workforce Study from (ISC)2 was in 2013 with several other special reports including a Skill Gap Analysis. This study projected that the security workforce would grow at a compound annual growth rate of 11.3% globally between 2013 to 2017, calling for an additional 2 million new workers during that time. As of February 2022, the U.S. Bureau of Labor Statistics (BLS) Occupational Outlook Handbook on Information Security Analysts says "employment of information security analysts is projected to grow 33% from 2020 to 2030, much faster than the average for all occupations."[7]

IBM was following traditional models of workforce development; it was doing the same old thing and expecting different results. Creating a six-year high school program for tech jobs is a repeat of trades schools like plumbing and electrical. That's not to say there isn't a need for those schools as a long-term strategy, but these schools cannot produce new professionals at a speed needed to meet the current talent shortage. Failing to include mature workers in workforce development puts these efforts behind. Instead organizations that harness innovative career pathways will create for themselves a significant hiring advantage in one of the most competitive recruiting markets of our lifetimes.

With a 33% job growth projected by the BLS, it's clear that the industry needs this additional headcount today rather than years from now. And that was clear by 2013 with the results of a Global Workforce Study by (ISC)2. Yet tech industry leaders focused on building programs for teenagers. In the specific example from IBM in 2016, investing in 6-year tech

---

6   (ISC)2.Cybersecurity Workforce Research Archive. www.isc2.org/Research
7   U.S. Bureau of Labor Statistics. (2022, April 18). Information security analysts : Occupational Outlook Handbook. U.S. Bureau of Labor Statistics. www.bls.gov/ooh/computer-and-information-technology/information-security-analysts.htm

trade schools means those students would not be ready to join the workplace until this year 2022, the year of this publication. Yet the skills gap remains wide and teams remain short staffed. IBM is just one example of major tech enterprises across the United States seeking younger workers, while failing to invest in Boomers, Gen X and even older Millennials. In addition to the lack of investment in training these adult workers, executives ignored the cries of overworked and understaffed teams of experienced employees. Cybersecurity can be a high stress career; burnout is unfortunately too common. So, while we cannot train new professionals fast enough, we are also losing highly skilled talent too often.

A term more common than "dinobabies" is "digital native" coined by Marc Prensky in 2001 to describe the generation of people who grew up in the era of pervasive technology, including computers, the internet and mobile phones.[8] Prensky also defines "digital immigrants" (those who have had to adapt to the pervasiveness of technology) and "digital refugees" (those whose jobs, livelihoods, and lives have been disrupted by the rapid advance of technology).[9] In this way, Prensky seeks to identify the differences between generations.

There has been much discussion around the idea of digital natives, and the perception that growing up around technology makes a person inherently more technologically adept. But do fish know more about water than humans do? Humans have developed the ability to collect, store, and analyze data in a way that no other species has accomplished. We have libraries and databases, involved parents and teachers. Wisdom, and inherently passing down information, is our greatest asset as a species and yet we actively dismantle that strength with ageism in technology.

In a June 2017 article titled "The myths of the digital native and the multitasker," Kirchschner and Bruyckere present "scientific evidence showing that there is no such thing as a digital native who is information-skilled

---

8   Prensky, M. (2001, September 1). Digital Natives, digital immigrants part 1. On the Horizon. emerald.com/insight/content/doi/10.1108/10748120110424816/full/html
9   Prensky, M. (2001, November 1). Digital Natives, Digital Immigrants Part 2: Do they really think differently? On the Horizon. www.emerald.com/insight/content/doi/10.1108/10748120110424843/full/html

simply because (s)he has never known a world that was not digital."[10] Just as the fish isn't more knowledgeable about water than a human, children aren't inherently more capable of performing technical tasks because growing up they may have had a tablet or computer. Later that year, Prensky shifted his comments on generational stereotypes in a Huffington Post interview, encouraging us to "see beyond old" as we decipher our digital culture.[11]

Even though younger generations do not inherently know more about technology than the older generations that built it, there is something to the idea that there is a difference between youth and maturity. I was discussing this article with my aunt, who is now twice retired after having a second career as a research librarian. She mentioned having recently read about a concept of two types of intelligences: fluid and crystallized. These concepts were first defined by Harvard professor Raymond Cattell and later cemented as part of the Cattell-Horn-Carroll theory of cognitive abilities. Through clinical research, these two types of intelligence were defined and explored.

According to the Cattell-Horn-Carroll theory, we display "fluid intelligence" in our youth, which is said to be the ability to analyze novel problems in pursuit of new solutions. While fluid intelligence is believed to peak in adulthood, it doesn't disappear completely. Meanwhile, "crystallized intelligence" builds upon our life experience as you gain it. Our "crystalized intelligence" is the ability to apply existing skills and knowledge to create solutions. It grows as we age, meaning for mature workers, work history is a strength that young workers haven't yet developed. This model also implies the value in hiring both young and mature professionals. Doing so offers your organization better diversity of thought in service of more dynamic problem solving.

The goals of all of these concepts is to measure or quantify someone's capacity in specific areas. There is more than one way to define intelligence, as we've seen with the concept of the Intelligence Quotient (IQ), the Emotional Quotient (EQ), and now Adaptability Quotient (AQ). In 2019 as

---

10 Kirschner, P. A., & De Bruyckere, P. (2017). The myths of the digital native and the Multitasker. Teaching and Teacher Education, 67, 135-142. doi.org/10.1016/j.tate.2017.06.001
11 Brenoff, A. (2017, August 24). There's no such thing as 'digital natives'. HuffPost. www.huffpost. com/entry/digital-natives-dont-actually-exist_n_599c985de4b0a296083a9e8a

part of its annual survey of skills in demand, LinkedIn announced that Adaptability made the top five requested soft skills.[12] These days the tech industry talks about the Adaptability Quotient (AQ) as the next frontier in intelligence measurements. It was Charles Darwin who defined the importance of adaptability, stating: "It is not the strongest of the species that survives, nor the most intelligent, it is the one that is the most adaptable to change."[13]

It seems IBM leadership might score low on an AQ test, for failing to adequately adapt to the changing workforce landscape. They knew they needed to change, yet IBM replicated old workforce development models in the face of novelty. IBM's traditional plan to train young people didn't provide the organization with the technical talent it needed in an effective time frame. But as I said, they weren't alone in their approach. IBM only serves as a case study of our systemic challenge of ageism.

In 2016, I was honored to contribute to the National Initiative for Cybersecurity Education (NICE) funding program labeled the Regional Alliances and Multistakeholder Partnerships to Stimulate (RAMPS) Cybersecurity Education and Workforce Development.[14] NICE RAMPS granted regional funding to a handful of groups across the U.S. "to build multistakeholder (sic) workforce partnerships of employers, schools and institutions of higher education, and other community organizations." Of the five grants awarded, only the Southwest Region was an acting consortium of public, private, non-profit, and education providers. The other four were run by higher education, which is in part because NICE is in service of education-based initiatives, but this is also due to the cybersecurity ecosystem within Arizona. At the time, Arizona already had several existing efforts developed over the previous years, and the goal of the consortium was to unify these efforts and improve our collective efforts.

12 Anderson, B. M. (2020, January 9). The most in-demand hard and soft skills of 2020. LinkedIn. www.linkedin.com/business/talent/blog/talent-strategy/linkedin-most-in-demand-hard-and-soft-skills

13 Darwin, C. (1859, October 1). Darwin Online. darwin-online.org.uk/content/frameset?itemID=F373&viewtype=text&pageseq=1

14 Regional Alliances and Multistakeholder Partnerships to Stimulate Cybersecurity Education and Workforce Development. NICE. www.nist.gov/itl/applied-cybersecurity/nice/regional-alliances-and-multistakeholder-partnerships-stimulate-ramps

As the Executive Director of the consortium would say, "a rising tide raises all boats."

During this regular engagement with business and education providers discussing the cybersecurity skills gap, my impression was that the primary focus of workforce development was training solutions for high school and college-age students. As someone who had changed careers myself, I found it remarkable that reskilling and upskilling seemed regulated to the unemployment office. In 2016 the existing scholarships, internships and externships all appeared to be focused on young people. In the past, even security conferences and certification companies focused on the youth when awarding scholarships for attendance, training or certifications. While I have continued to give my time to workforce development initiatives, I have always been perplexed by the limited focus on reskilling and upskilling. It is only within the last couple of years that security conferences and professional associations have dropped age requirements for some of their scholarships. This is a welcome change.

When I was very new to technical recruiting, I often had longer conversations with tenured tech professionals. I can speculate a few reasons why but what's relevant here from these exchanges, is that I was able to quickly learn from their experiences and insights. One of the trends that became apparent: IT Managers and IT Directors expressed to me a sense that they had hit the ceiling of their career. While they advanced their careers by becoming operational leaders, their employer (and the market) decided that they had become "too distant" from the technology. These experienced technologists were being told they had not kept up. And then as I began to learn about cybersecurity, I was regularly told that the basics of security are built on a foundational knowledge of IT infrastructure. The way data moves across the internet hasn't fundamentally changed. The fundamentals of network traffic and infrastructure remain the same. It was clear to me that these tenured IT professionals were prime for upskilling into cybersecurity.

On the other side of the age spectrum, I would repeatedly hear how current college graduates, even from cybersecurity programs, lacked fundamental knowledge of business operations, having learned only abstract theory. These young adults lack real-world business experience. Higher education cannot fully prepare students for the reality of business operations, that's why there is a reliance on internships and externships. Careers in cyberse-curity are about securing the business, meaning cybersecurity profession-als must have both technical and operational skills to perform effectively. For example, the context of a finance department, how it operates and what kind of sensitive data it uses.

The reality of information technology is that it wouldn't exist without the work of the adults that came before us. Specifically within cybersecurity, experience and wisdom are essential to a worker's successful response to new threats and incidents. Combining the dynamics of network infra-structure and a knowledge of the vast array of threats, with the com-plexity of business operations – cybersecurity is a critical service to the business and cannot be effectively performed without knowledge of all of the above. Without the wisdom and experience of accomplished security professionals, this industry will continue to flounder.

The "Entry-Level" Misnomer

It is also important for us to address an industry challenge such as defin-ing basic terms like "entry-level" and "junior" when describing jobs and people. Both terms are often associated with "young professionals" but shouldn't be considered exclusive to young people. Also, these terms are often used interchangeably when these terms are not the same. An entry-level job should have no hard requirements for experience, and for exam-ple, a job is not entry-level if it requires years of experience. If any years of experience, formal training, or certification are required, that job is likely a junior-level job or higher.

This distinction between "entry-level" and "junior" is also relevant to our discussion on mature professionals looking to move into cybersecurity. Traditionally these are often called career changers but it implies that these workers are starting over, when instead they're building on what they already know, which is experience employers need to capitalize upon. These professionals are building on their existing knowledge, skills, and abilities in order to launch in a new direction. Because of transferable skills, many professionals could already be considered junior skill level in the cybersecurity industry.

For professionals with a background in IT, I saw that the ramp to effectiveness in cybersecurity roles could be achieved in 6 to 12 months with some combination of either self-taught learning or instruction and then some on-the-job training. This is how I saw these professionals, not just as career changers but career pivoters. By building on their existing expertise, they could pivot into these cybersecurity careers and launch quickly to become effective contributors. This is an advantage that our industry has not yet capitalized upon. Career pivoters can quickly close the skills gap.

A teenager attending a 6-year technical high school program may need a total of 7 to 8 years to be an effective cybersecurity professional, from start to finish. A college student may need 6-years to be fully effective, with the traditional 4-year program plus 1 to 2 years of on-the-job training. It is career pivoters who offer industry the fastest ramp to effectiveness, possibly as short as 1 year or less.

The First-Job Hurdle

And yet remarkably, despite the complaints of understaffed and over-worked cybersecurity teams, the first job is often the hardest to find for new cybersecurity professionals of every age, because of the focus on hiring experienced professionals. For college students there is a career-entrance pipeline via internships, as many employers look for interns they can then hire full-time. But unfortunately, no standard pipeline exists for career pivoters. These adult professionals have their work cut out for them.

To show this transition timeline for experienced professionals, I will share three stories from career pivoters I met in my work. These professionals, and tens of thousands more, informed my professional opinion that adult workers from a variety of professional backgrounds are junior level in cybersecurity and should not be considered entry-level like a young student without work experience.

In our first example, we'll call him George, this mature professional had over 15 years' experience in software development before being laid off. He then used that time for small side projects, but primarily he focused on immersing himself in Application Security (AppSec) through local security events and online groups including OWASP. Yet his transition into cybersecurity wasn't complete until securing his first AppSec role which

Timeline to Effectiveness in Cybersecurity Careers

This visual represents the estimated timeframe for a worker to complete training and reach effectiveness as a contributor in cybersecurity role, from the perspective of the employers.

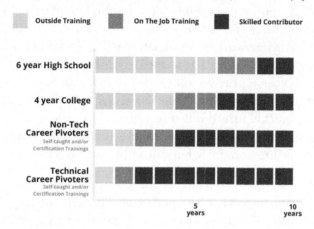

Exhibit A: Ageism is Your Achilles Heel   Copyright 2022

took nearly 2 years despite having both technical and operational leadership experience. Once in the security field, George quickly progressed into leadership roles and is now a Chief Information Security Officer (CISO). In every leadership role since joining the security industry, George has worked to develop entry-level positions for new people to build their careers. He has become the change he wanted to see.

Let's also consider Hannah, who obtained her bachelor's degree in animation, she found that her passion wasn't providing the quality of life she sought. Serendipitously, she has a friend in cybersecurity and they encouraged her to research these careers. Hannah then drove into studying the foundations of cybersecurity and learning technical tools. She was able to use this new knowledge to mitigate risks at her non-cyber employer at the time, before moving into security full-time with a major financial enterprise. While there, she advanced to a senior role within 3 years, a much shorter ramp than someone without professional work experience. And ultimately, in under 5 years, Hannah successfully grew her career into a role as a security advisor for a high profile security vendor. While Hannah's background didn't begin in information technology like George, her rapid advancement in cybersecurity is comparable to our other examples.

In our last example, we will look at Matthew's career progression. Matthew began his career serving in intelligence operations in the Air Force and the NSA. He is a polyglot accomplished in multiple spoken and technology languages, with his first career out of the military as a web developer and then a systems/network engineer, later he became a professor of linguistics. Ultimately, he decided he wanted to return his focus to threat intelligence and cybersecurity, but the transition took 2 years of job hunting and the first job he landed was as a technical writer for security compliance, which he quickly turned into a security analyst role, and in just over 2 years he secured a role as an Information Security Officer (ISO). The fastest ramp of our three examples, but still within the 1 to 3 year average.

Each of these experienced professionals struggled to find that first role in cybersecurity, despite having a professional background directly relevant to the industry. When it takes one to three years for experienced professionals to enter the cybersecurity industry, the industry as a whole suffers. And when the industry suffers, employers suffer, and when employers suffer, professionals suffer by carrying the weight of understaffed teams for longer than necessary.

What we are talking about is making a change to cultural systems in which we are entrenched. This type of change requires action and investment from both people and organizations. If we leave systemic change as the sole responsibility of the individual, then the system will not change significantly. Organizations that continue to rely solely on traditional workforce development initiatives will continue to lag behind. However, if more organizations invest in building new cybersecurity talent, the entire industry benefits. This rising tide will raise all of our boats. Conversely, if we continue to do what we always have done, we will get the same results.

The Solution - Oldies but Goodies

Perhaps my vision of these systemic challenges is unique because of how I was raised. I was blessed to grow up under the influence of four grandparents, all of them remarkable people. Relevant to this discussion is my dad's dad. Grandpa was born in 1910 as the youngest son of a large immigrant family, a sharecropper's son in rural Michigan. Despite the Great Depression, he found opportunity in metro Detroit's automotive industry. I heard often the story of his hire, during a time when there were not very many jobs to be had, and every day men would line up around the block for one job. Each of them showed up in a clean, white work shirt to make a good impression but on this particular day, my grandma sent him in a red shirt. He was the only red shirt in line, and he was the only man hired that day. After working his way up to a supervisor role, Grandpa retired at 65 years old with his pension, and they moved to Florida.

My first memory of a personal computer was in Grandpa's office. It was the early 1980s and I was of preschool age. Grandpa was showing his home computer to my dad, and when he saw that I was interested, he showed me the connected, folding papers with images from his dot matrix printer. I remember him saying that he had received the images, flowers and animals and the like, from people around the country. Even as a child I knew it took my family a couple of days to drive from Michigan to Florida, and yet somehow, he was getting these pictures from all over, in just hours.

In his 70s, my grandpa helped my dad write a computer program that advanced my dad's business from a few contracts into a successful business operating in several counties. In reminiscing about my grandpa with my sister, she reminded me that he also wrote a computer program for me, apparently it used fireflies which I regrettably don't recall. My grandparent's success fueled my parents' success, both of them first generation college graduates, degreed in the hard sciences. Both of my parents were continual learners just like Grandpa, adapting and harnessing new technology as it became available.

I didn't grow up with the message that older adults couldn't tackle new technology, in fact my elders proved the opposite.

My grandpa grew up dirt poor without a telephone before household telephones were common in rural places, and in his early 70s he taught himself how to use a personal computer and write computer programs. My family always joked that his success was rooted in that red shirt years ago, but success doesn't exist in a vacuum. He was a member of The Greatest Generation and the boom of the U.S. during that time. Age is not the primary factor determining someone's success with new technology.

Just like some Boomers, there are people of Gen X and Gen Z that struggle with technology, or rely on it "to just work" rather than learning the technology to make it work for them.

It was my grandpa's pension that afforded him the resources to learn how to use a personal computer in his 70s. The primary factor influencing someone's ability to learn new technology is whether they were afforded the resources to upskill on the new technology. Those resources could be time, money, or availability of instruction. Most adults have a shortage of one or more, their time and money are often needed for their children. Adult professionals often have more responsibilities than workers in their teens and early twenties, and it can be even more challenging for adult professionals to carve out the time or money to invest in the process of changing their career, but these challenges can be addressed.

By 2024, 32.9% of workers will be 55 years or older, according to the U.S. BLS in 2017.[15] Given the stark need for cybersecurity professionals the costs of ignoring this talent pool are likely higher than the cost of the solution.

Available Resources

The common rebuttal to hiring someone new to cybersecurity is that the organization needs experienced, tenured cybersecurity professionals to build and advance the organization's cybersecurity posture. It is often claimed that only the mature cybersecurity programs can manage entry-level and junior professionals, because they need to be guided. First, this implies that only an experienced professional can provide value while a junior professional will be more of an expense than a benefit to the organization. This claim is fascinatingly the opposite of our ageism problem. Second, this claim ignores that we can and do hire adults; adults who could use industry standards and frameworks as guides regardless of their experience level. It appears that this rebuttal could support the solutions discussed here.

The good news is that there are now developed standards and frameworks available from trusted providers, often at no charge. These resources

---

15 Toossi, M., & Torpey, E. (2017, May). Older workers: Labor force trends and career options : Career outlook. www.bls.gov/careeroutlook/2017/article/older-workers.htm

support those wishing to build cybersecurity teams, regardless of whether their organization has existing security professionals. With these resources organizations may assess the maturity of their internal cybersecurity program, and make a plan to empower and advance their teams. Additionally, these resources can be harnessed by less experienced professionals as guidebooks to building their careers.

Before we discuss resources more in-depth, let's address the acronym soup that is modern industry, both information technology and government initiatives. These are the federal leaders in the United States contributing to cybersecurity workforce development initiatives.

- National Institute of Standards & Technology (NIST)
- National Initiative of Cybersecurity Education (NICE)
- U.S. Department of Homeland Security (DHS)
- Cybersecurity and Infrastructure Security Agency (CISA)
- National Initiative for Cybersecurity Careers and Studies (NICCS)

Each of these organizations has built several resources as detailed guides for employers and professionals to advance this industry and their careers. In addition, several professional associations provide large global studies and professional resources, as well as training and certifications.

- International Information System Security Certification Consortium (ISC2)
- Information Systems Audit and Control Association (ISACA)
- Information Systems Security Association (ISSA)
- Cloud Security Alliance (CSA)
- Computing Technology Industry Association (CompTIA)

There is also the federally funded not-for-profit MITRE Corporation which produced the MITRE ATT&CK and D3FEND frameworks. Some of these resources will be discussed here, and the reader is encouraged to explore all these more.

Around 2014, NIST produced the Cybersecurity Framework through a collaboration between industry and government. This Framework identifies functions which organize the basics of cybersecurity activities at their highest level as: Identify, Protect, Detect, Respond, and Recover.

The NICE Cybersecurity Framework is property of the
National Initiative of Cybersecurity Education.

Though the Cybersecurity Framework is not intended as a one-size-fits-all approach to managing cybersecurity for all organizations, it is ultimately aimed at reducing and better managing risks, and is designed to provide a common language for all organizations regardless of sector or size. The goal of this Cybersecurity Framework is to empower organizations to determine activities that are important to operations, then these organizations can prioritize and plan investments to maximize impact.

As a further and more detailed iteration, the NIST "Special Publication 800-181 NICE Cybersecurity Workforce Framework" in 2017 outlines seven categories, each with expounded and thorough documentation that can assist leaders in identifying the necessary duties, job titles and corresponding the knowledge, skills, and abilities.[16] This sets the foundation for employers to use the NICCS & DHS "Workforce Development Toolkit" to

---

16 Petersen, R., Santos, D., Wetzel, K. A., Smith, M. C., & Witte, G. (2020, November). Workforce Framework for Cybersecurity (NICE Framework) . nvlpubs.nist.gov/nistpubs/SpecialPublications/ NIST.SP.800-181r1.pdf

customize these plans to the specifics of any business.[17] Some organizations are ready for and need this level of detail.

For those teams that need less detail or prefer a tool that is more visual, there is the "Cyber Career Pathways Tool" from CISA's NICCS group, which provides an online interactive overview of common roles within these categories and how those roles intersect, as well as training resources aligned with each.[18] It's not as detailed as the Workforce Development Toolkit, but many see it as a more accessible reference. Among visual tools, there is also CyberSeek.org which provides two interactive resources; the 'Career Pathway' which is an interactive resource exploring careers, and the 'Heatmap' which provides aggregated data on US markets for how many jobs and professionals are out there, along with what skill sets and certifications are available and in-demand.[19]

For smaller organizations, there is good news for these teams too. The National Cybersecurity Alliance offers free resources, collectively called "CyberSecure My Business," built to assist businesses in becoming safer and more secure online with a streamlined and simplified approach to building a security program based on NIST's Cybersecurity Framework 1.0.[20] This set of resources offer a variety of interactive tools and events to support leaders from a variety of backgrounds, in their efforts to advance their organization's security posture.

All together, this collection of resources provides organizations with industry standard operating procedures and ways to define and streamline their teams and careers in this industry, all to advance and grow the talent pool within cybersecurity. From here, organizations and professionals need to operationalize these resources, whether part of a collaborative workforce development initiative or within a single security team in their workplace.

---

17 Cybersecurity Workforce Development Toolkit. National Initiative for Cybersecurity Careers and Studies. niccs.cisa.gov/workforce-development/cybersecurity-workforce-development-toolkit
18 Cyber Career Pathways Tool. National Initiative for Cybersecurity Careers and Studies. niccs.cisa.gov/workforce-development/cyber-career-pathways
19 National Initiative for Cybersecurity Education (NICE). CyberSeek. www.cyberseek.org
20 CyberSecure My Business™. National Cybersecurity Alliance. (2022, February 1). staysafeonline.org/cybersecure-business/

Continuous Training as an Industry Standard

The continuous evolution of the threat landscape is just one of the reasons that cybersecurity professionals need to stay up-to-date on training. This means that continuing education is a crucial resource for cybersecurity teams, regardless of their experience level. Every cybersecurity team needs a dedicated budget for continuous learning. Just as athletes train regularly, so must your cybersecurity team. This investment returns value in two ways: your team is prepared with the latest knowledge, and investing in your team improves morale and recruiting efforts. Failing to invest in your cybersecurity team means having to backfill when your team resigns, choosing instead to work for leadership who will invest in cybersecurity resources & their professional development.

Once a budget includes funds dedicated to training, there is an even greater advantage to hiring entry-level and junior candidates. Here we will consider the potential savings available when comparing the compensation costs of various skill levels of talent. And the specific advantage of hiring career pivoters with professional work experience and demonstrated interest in pivoting their career into cybersecurity.

According to the US BLS in 2020, the nationwide average compensation for an Information Security Analyst with 5 years or less experience is $103,590 per year. Let's consider a few points of context here. This datum is about "analysts" rather than "engineers," the latter often receiving higher compensation. Also, this datum is a national average, pooling rural and metropolitan areas. Lastly, this datum was taken before the surge of demand with Ransomware-as-a-Service, The Great Resignation, and a pandemic. Salaries for experienced cybersecurity professionals have gone up since this report. And as discussed earlier, organizations often seek to hire experienced professionals with 5 to 10+ years of experience while paying $130,000 to $190,000 (or more) and still struggling to find those experienced professionals.

With the frameworks and industry resources such as those listed above, a professional pivoting their career into cybersecurity (the junior with other professional skills) could be hired at around $65,000 to 85,000 and then provided some formal training for a total top-end investment around $95,000. This is an annual savings of at least $10,000 to $60,000 a year per employee, in comparison to focusing on hiring senior talent.

Another common rebuttal here is a concern about whether a junior employee will be loyal after this investment, and without their loyalty the investment is lost. Remember that annual training needs to be standard in the budget, even for experienced talent, although the type of training investments may change based on experience levels. Also, there is no loyalty guarantee with experienced talent. An (ISC)2 study in 2018 found that 84% of cybersecurity workers are open to new employment opportunities, including 14% who are actively looking for a change (again this was before The Great Resignation). Additionally, according to a 2021 ISACA Global Workforce Study, the majority of organizations find it takes 3 to 6 months (or more) to hire experienced cybersecurity professionals. [21]

Hiring junior talent, specifically the career pivoters, takes less time and saves money every year you run the program. This investment saves the company money overall in both compensation costs and in time by shortening the time-to-hire, and all while building the pool of talent in the industry. Even if that role is vacated and needs to be hired for again, the company has still saved money and created a competitive advantage for itself by building a reputation of investing in team members. And the company will save again, when hiring another junior career pivoter.

One common concern for career changers is compensation. Often someone "starting over" in a new career is expected to experience a reduction in compensation. This is because compensation is often aligned with years of experience, however supply and demand is another factor determining compensation as well. Cybersecurity careers often offer a higher compensation than even information technology careers. Most of the IT Managers and IT Directors with whom I spoke were making about $85,000 to $100,000 annually, which is comparable to the BLS data for a security analyst with 5 or less years of experience. Yet these IT career pivoters bring more transferable skills making them more valuable to organizations. Upskilling professionals into cybersecurity makes sense, for employers and professionals.

While in some small organizations this could be done with one security hire to an IT team, for large organizations with a cybersecurity team or

21 Van Camp, E., & Kessinger, K. (2021, May 4). New ISACA Study Finds Cybersecurity Workforce Minimally Impacted by Pandemic, but Still Grappling with Persistent Hiring Challenges. ISACA. www.isaca.org/why-isaca/about-us/newsroom/press-releases/2021/new-isaca-study-finds-cybersecurity-workforce-minimally-impacted-by-pandemic-but-still-grappling

department, the challenge is often finding the time to mentor and provide on the job training. It's common for teams to be stretched thin with more projects than contributors and time. A solution for these teams could be creating a role with a 5/20 plan. For example, of the five categories (Identify, Protect, Detect, Respond, and Recover) a 20% project could be identified for each and assigned to a new hire who is an entry-level or junior professional. Each of these 20% projects would then have a mentor or mentors instead of the responsibility of the entire mentorship landing on one person, whether teammate or leader. With a 5/20 plan, the work of mentoring and on-the-job training is dispersed. Additionally, this new hire builds risk resilience into the cybersecurity team. In the case of attrition, there is already someone in place and informed on the role who can provide coverage and possibly a backfill, even if this is only for the time it takes to hire.

Keep in mind how you advertise for these entry-level and junior roles matters as much as the programs you build for the roles. You want to make sure that your job descriptions (and job postings) are not detracting from your efforts. To write better job descriptions for entry-level and junior professionals, examine the minimum and preferred qualifications. If it is an entry-level job, the minimum qualifications should not include years of experience because years of experience is not entry-level. Instead it could list "demonstrated interest in cybersecurity through proactive pursuit of training and skills development." Another way to address this, would be to use the required qualifications as the soft skills or business skills, with the preferred qualifications as years of experience or certifications. When writing job descriptions for junior level positions, the minimum qualifications could show years of professional experience but not requiring a specific industry. Career pivoters come from a variety of backgrounds. Remember the goal is to cast a wide net.

Conversely, do not limit years of experience with a phrase like "no more than 7 years of experience" and don't require that applicants provide the year of graduation on their initial application or resume. When you see a long resume, don't immediately discount it. Consider also the language used. Phrases like "guru," "high-energy" or "digital native" can alienate mature workers, and younger workers as well. Descriptors like "motivated," "focused" or "dedicated" will attract quality professionals of every age.

One of the most common job posting faux pas in this industry is listing the CISSP certification as required experience for entry-level and junior job openings. The CISSP is from (ISC)2 and requires 5 years of experience in the profession in order to obtain the certification. The CISA certification from ISACA is similar. These are not junior level certifications, although (ISC)2 has added an "Associate" qualification for those who pass their CISSP but lack the work experience. This is a positive step, but the cost and time investment required can make it a barrier for many career pivoters.

It is my impression that these types of requirements are related to the FUD (fear, uncertainty, doubt) within cybersecurity. Because operational leaders may not be aware of the various free cybersecurity resources, frameworks and standard operating procedures, these leaders all seek out the most experienced professionals they can find. Employers can use this collection of resources to identify the needs of their organization, but it is still on leadership to identify their biases, invest their cybersecurity teams financially, and overall take steps to prevent those biases from hindering their business.

Remember the goal here is to reduce barriers to entry while recognizing the work that career pivoters have done and are doing. By harnessing various resources, standard practices and frameworks, every organization can be empowered to advance their cybersecurity program. Organizations that hire career pivoters into junior roles are organizations ahead of the rest.

The fact remains that there are not enough experienced cybersecurity professionals to serve every company. But you can create a competitive advantage for your organization by using these recommendations, while also advancing the industry as a whole.

A Note to Job Seekers

Whether you have already started your journey into cybersecurity or you're considering it, please keep going. We need you. If anything, let this article affirm that this industry needs you. A decade ago, cybersecurity was barely a household term and today we have national industry standards for the construction of cybersecurity programs, departments, and careers. When I started years ago, the industry offered nearly no resources to career pivoters but today there are financial scholarships and mentor programs dedicated to adult professionals. This industry is evolving.

Careers in cybersecurity are ideal for people who are perpetually curious and continuous learners. This isn't a career where you arrive and then coast. The threat landscape continues to evolve, even if the foundational infrastructure of data traveling on a network remains the same, the vulnerabilities and threats are ever changing. Adaptability is key to success in this career, regardless of a professional's age. It is your positive attitude and desire to learn that matters most.

When it comes to your path into cybersecurity, professional networking will be your most valuable tool. In many ways, recruiting and human resources departments are still trying to understand this industry and those knowledge gaps affect entry-level and junior professionals the most. Attend the local chapter meetings for professional associations and local meetups. Make it a point to volunteer, whether it's a local event or a larger security conference or both. Make it known that you are interested in a career in cybersecurity and share your progress as a professional. In this age of social media, build your professional brand by sharing what you learn so that others can learn from it too, and in doing so, you are both advertising your capabilities to potential hiring managers, you are also helping to close the skills gap by helping others learn. A rising tide raises all boats.

Additional Professional Resources

www.isc2.org

www.isaca.org

www.issa.org

cloudsecurityalliance.org

www.cisecurity.org

www.nationalisacs.org

owasp.org

iapp.org

www.infragard.org

www.blackcybersecurityassociation.org

www.blacksincyberconf.com

www.ewf-usa.com

www.wicys.org

ABOUT RACHEL HARPLEY

With over a decade in recruiting and staffing, and a recent focus in cybersecurity recruitment and workforce development, Rachel Harpley builds a more secure world one bit at a time by empowering others to advance their cybersecurity careers. While focusing on this industry, Rachel Harpley has given over 3,500 pro bono hours to advancing cybersecurity workforce initiatives collaborating with executives and hiring managers through various public-private initiatives, and while also giving time directly to cybersecurity job seekers.

Professionally Rachel Harpley serves security programs in both small businesses and large enterprises after founding Recruit Bit Security and while also giving through pro-bono service to initiatives as the founder and co-chair of the Cybersecurity Council of Arizona (CCofAZ). Most recently, Rachel launched the first Career Village at CactusCon, Arizona's largest and longest running security conference. They have been a speaker at Women in Cybersecurity (WiCyS) national conference and The Diana Initiative (TDI) as well. Rachel served as chair of the Workforce Readiness initiative of the 2017 RAMPS grant awarded to Arizona by the National Initiative of Cybersecurity Education (NICE), and more recently they were a key contributor to the marketing initiatives of Workforce and Economic Development Sub-group of the Arizona Cybersecurity Team (ACT). Phoenix Chapter.

Conclusion

The stories in this book share a common theme of reinventing ourselves and our approach to security practice. Our hope is that these stories can offer inspiration to others at all stages of their cybersecurity career. The industry has an unlimited potential to change in positive ways, particularly with the collective efforts of many bright, dedicated security practitioners worldwide. The authors of this book are all courageous, bright, and revolutionary practitioners who are leaving a permanent mark on the industry.

Whether you are trying to break into your first cybersecurity role or you have served for many years as a CISO, you have an opportunity to contribute toward a more secure future for everyone. While our organizations face an unprecedented amount of cyber risk, I genuinely believe we can solve the greatest security challenges of today and tomorrow by reinventing our strategies, practices, and ideas.

You can connect with the authors on social media or at an upcoming cybersecurity conference, or at champions@jupiterone.com. We would all love to connect with readers and collaborate to reinvent cybersecurity!

Acknowledgements

I thought writing a book would be easy, but I was wrong. Books are a journey. Thank you to my co-authors, Latha Maripuri, Aubrey Stearn, Carla Sun, Lonye Ford, Dr. Meg Layton, Tracy Bannon, Breanne Boland, Alison Gianotto, Lisa Hall, Rin Oliver, Joyous Huggins, Yvie Djieya, Angela Marafino, Coleen Shane, and Rachel Harpley, for sharing your stories.

Thank you to all the individuals who helped *Reinventing Cybersecurity* cross the finish line. I appreciate the help of Tyler Shields, Tanvi Tapadia, and Kevin Swartz. I am also grateful to Amy Devers, Erkang Zheng, and Sounil Yu for many hours of review.

Editor and layout designer Scott McFarlane spent many weeks making this project a reality. The cover art was produced by a brilliant Ukrainian artist named Lena Semenkova.

Special acknowledgement is due to a small team of smart, hard-working women who collaborated closely on this book. Thank you Ashleigh Lee, Melissa Pereira, Jennie Duong, and Valerie Zargarpur.

Final thanks are owed to you, the reader. Thank you for listening to our cybersecurity stories and sharing our vision. We believe in a world where security is a basic right and security decisions are made by diverse teams. We would love to hear from you, especially if you decide one day to write your own cybersecurity story.

Jasmine Henry

Field Security Director at JupiterOne

Executive Editor, *Reinventing Cybersecurity*

May 2022

Made in the USA
Monee, IL
10 May 2022